Between Camp and Cursi

SUNY series, Genders in the Global South
―――――
Debra A. Castillo and Shelley Feldman, editors

Between Camp and Cursi

Humor and Homosexuality in Contemporary Mexican Narrative

BRANDON P. BISBEY

Cover art from Wikimedia is entitled "El baile de los 41 maricones" (1901); by Jose Guadalupe Posada.

Published by State University of New York Press, Albany

© 2021 State University of New York

All rights reserved

Printed in the United States of America

No part of this book may be used or reproduced in any manner whatsoever without written permission. No part of this book may be stored in a retrieval system or transmitted in any form or by any means including electronic, electrostatic, magnetic tape, mechanical, photocopying, recording, or otherwise without the prior permission in writing of the publisher.

For information, contact State University of New York Press, Albany, NY
www.sunypress.edu

Library of Congress Cataloging-in-Publication Data

Name: Bisbey, Brandon P., author.
Title: Between camp and cursi : humor and homosexuality in contemporary Mexican narrative / Brandon P. Bisbey.
Description: Albany : SUNY Press, [2021] | Series: SUNY series, genders in the global south | Includes bibliographical references and index.
Identifiers: LCCN 2021036724 (print) | LCCN 2021036725 (ebook) | ISBN 9781438486659 (hardcover : alk. paper) | ISBN 9781438486666 (pbk. : alk. paper) | ISBN 9781438486673 (ebook)
Subjects: LCSH: Mexican literature—History and criticism. | Homosexuality in literature. | Queer theory. | Humor in literature. | Gender identity—Mexico. | LCGFT: Literary criticism.
Classification: LCC PQ7122.H66 B57 2021 (print) | LCC PQ7122.H66 (ebook) | DDC 860.9/972353—dc23
LC record available at https://lccn.loc.gov/2021036724
LC ebook record available at https://lccn.loc.gov/2021036725

10 9 8 7 6 5 4 3 2 1

Para Alicia

Contents

List of Illustrations   ix

Acknowledgments   xi

Introduction   1

Chapter 1
The Other Mexican Revolution: Camp and *Cursilería* in the Queer Self-Construction of Salvador Novo   13

Chapter 2
Homosexuales de corazón: Humor, Homophobia, and How to be a Man at the End of the 20th Century   51

Chapter 3
Dressing the Part: Literary Portrayals of *Travestis*, *Locas*, *Vestidas*, and *Jotas*   79

Chapter 4
Having Your Cake and Eating It Too: Bisexual *Bildungsromane* from Dismodern Mexico   117

Chapter 5
Machorra *Camp* and Lesbian *Cursilería*: Sexuality, Gender, and Humor in Narratives by and about Queer Women   157

Conclusions   185

Notes		191
Works Cited		207
Index		223

Illustrations

Figure 1.1	José Guadalupe Posada, "Los 41 maricones"	30
Figure 1.2	José Guadalupe Posada, "El feminismo se impone"	31
Figure 1.3	Masculine and Feminine Scripts	32
Figure 1.4	Modern and Unmodern Scripts	34

Acknowledgments

This book began its long road to publication as my doctoral dissertation at Tulane University. I would like to thank my advisor, Maureen Shea, and the members of my dissertation committee, Idelber Avelar and Fernando Rivera, for their guidance during those years. Claudia de Brito, secretary of the Department of Spanish and Portuguese, cared for me as she does for everyone in that department. I thank Verónica Sánchez of the Latin American Library for her friendship, humor, and assistance with all of my research needs. I would not have survived the doctorate without the love, intellectual exchange, and moral support of my friends and colleagues Shaun Bauer and Caroline Good.

At Northeastern Illinois University, I have benefited greatly from the support and encouragement of my colleagues Paul Schroeder-Rodríguez and Denise Cloonan Cortez de Andersen. Paul's mentorship in the early years of my career was instrumental in my continuation with this project. He moved to another institution several years ago, and I continue to miss him greatly. Denise continues to be the best chair and colleague anyone could wish for. Our office administrator Jeanette Hernández deserves special mention for all that she has done for me over the years. None of my work would be possible without her tireless work behind the scenes. I would also like to recognize the efforts of the staff of the Ronald Williams Library, particularly humanities librarian Mary Thill, who have always helped me acquire the sources I need. This project has been greatly enriched by discussions with my graduate and undergraduate students during my time at NEIU. Their dedication and effort inspire me every day. I am also grateful to the university for a summer research grant and a semester sabbatical leave that allowed me to complete the manuscript.

In addition to this institutional support, a Fulbright García-Robles grant funded by the governments of Mexico and the United States allowed me to teach and work on this project at the Universidad de Guanajuato for one year. I am grateful to the Comexus-Fulbright staff, and in particular to the wonderful Jackal Tanelorn, for their support and guidance during my grant period. I would also like to thank my students and colleagues at Guanajuato, particularly Elba Sánchez Rolón and Lilia Solórzano Esqueda, for the warm collegiality and intellectual exchanges that they provided me while I was there. I must also recognize the indefatigable *doña* Teresa Hernández Ramírez, who runs the Departamento de Letras Españolas, for making me feel at home and for her aid with all things bureaucratic. An earlier version of chapter 4 was published in Spanish in *Revista Valenciana*, the academic journal of the department.

Among the other people who have contributed to this project, I would like to express my gratitude to the following: Anadeli Bencomo for recommending *Púrpura* to me; María Elena Madrigal for her conversation, recommendations, and books; Robert M. Irwin, Héctor Domínguez Ruvalcaba, and Sophie Esch for their advice, recommendations, and comments on the book proposal; Rebecca Colesworthy, my editor at SUNY, for her assistance and encouragement during the submission process; Debra Castillo and Shelly Feldman, editors of the series Genders in the Global South, for their continued support of the project; and the anonymous readers of my manuscript for their excellent and instructive feedback.

Finally, I am most grateful to my family for their love and support over the years. My parents, Becky and Blair Bisbey, instilled in me a love of learning from a young age and supported all of my academic endeavors. My mother, in particular, taught me to love the Spanish language and Latin American people and their culture. Her mother, Charlotte Waitz, has always shown a keen interest in my activities and supported me in everything I do. My dear friend Néstor Villarreal and his family were my first true connection to Mexican culture. They accepted me into the bosom of their family, and I will always be grateful to them for that. My daughter, Alicia Bisbey-Rincón, has been the light of my life since she was born, and I learn from her every day. This book is dedicated to her. Last, but certainly not least, I would like to thank my wife and intellectual and life partner, Catalina Rincón-Bisbey, for believing in me, reading versions of the manuscript, and encouraging me to continue with the project. This book would not have been possible without her love and patience.

Introduction

In 1901, police in Mexico City raided a raucous party in an upscale neighborhood attended solely by men, about half of whom were dressed as women. Forty-one men were arrested, tried, convicted, and sentenced to hard labor off the coast of Yucatán. This event and the ensuing social scandal about it, which was well represented in the media of the time, have been identified as the emergence of homosexuality in Mexico (Monsiváis, "Ortodoxia" 199; Irwin, *Mexican* xi–xii).[1] Indeed, the number "41" has been associated since this event with male homosexuality in Mexican popular culture. A veritable explosion of cultural production related to the scandal, including newspaper and tabloid reporting, *corridos* (folk ballads), cartoons by the legendary José Guadalupe Posada, and even a naturalist novel contributed to the establishment of a particular notion of homosexuality in the Mexican imaginary (Irwin, et al.). Especially important was the association of male homosexuality with gender nonconformity, which contributed to the reification of a stereotype of homosexual men as effeminate. This stereotype has influenced views of male homosexuality in Mexico since that time, or as Carlos Monsiváis puts it: "Desde entonces y hasta fechas recientes en la cultura popular el gay es el travesti y sólo hay una especie de homosexual: el afeminado" ["From that moment until recently in popular culture the gay is the *travesti* and there is only one type of homosexual: the effeminate type"] ("Ortodoxia" 199).[2] Indeed, it is possible to trace the development of this stereotype in Mexican cultural production throughout the 20th and into the 21st centuries, especially in the mass media, where it has been reproduced in its most simplistic forms.[3] In the vast majority of these cases, the homosexual characters are comic figures who are the targets of satire and ridicule. In other words, the use of humor to marginalize and stigmatize LGBTQ people has been a part of Mexican popular culture since at least the beginning of the 20th century.

This stereotype highlights the association of male homosexuality with gender nonconformity and is symptomatic of how homophobia in Mexico, as everywhere, is ultimately related to misogyny. As Raewyn Connell concisely puts it: "Patriarchal culture has a simple interpretation of gay men: they lack masculinity" (143). Monsiváis reaches the same conclusion about the Mexican context but emphasizes how lacking masculinity in Mexico is seen to be one's own fault:

> Según los guardianes de la Norma, un homosexual se degrada voluntariamente al asemejarse a las mujeres, y el registro público y privado de tal envilecimiento justifica la condena machista.
>
> [According to the guardians of the Norm, a homosexual degrades himself voluntarily by becoming like a woman, and the public and private register of that debasement justifies macho condemnation.] (73–74)

On the other side of the binary, female gender nonconformity also became a subject of social anxiety before, during, and after the Mexican Revolution. Similar to the construction of the stereotype of the effeminate homosexual man, there is an association of lesbian sexuality with traditionally masculine behaviors that leads to the reification of stereotypes of lesbian women as "*machorras*" [dykes, tomboys]. These stereotypes have had a less storied, though no less oppressive, history in the mass media, especially television (Ruiz-Alfaro; Muñoz Rubio 58–59; Alfarache 132).

In 2006, more than a century after the 41 were shipped off to a penal colony, the government of the Federal District that encompasses Mexico City passed a law establishing civil unions for same-sex couples. This was followed in 2009 by full equality for same-sex marriages. These events were paralleled by a series of similar laws passed in several Mexican states and a 2015 Supreme Court ruling that mandated the uniform recognition in Mexico of all marriages performed anywhere in the country. Though not without its controversies, marriage equality can generally be considered a sort of barometer of the social acceptance of homosexuality, and in the years mentioned above, Mexico joined other Latin American nations, including Argentina, Brazil, Colombia, and Uruguay, that were moving towards legal recognition of same-sex unions.[4] Around this same time, there was also a greater visibility of queer and homosexual themes and people in the mass media, in popular films like Serio Tovar's *Cuatro lunas* [*Four Moons*] (2014) and Nicolás López's *Hazlo como hombre* [*Do It Like an Hombre*] (2017), *telenovelas* like *La vida en el espejo* ["Life in the Mirror"] (1999), and *El sexo débil* ["The Weaker Sex"] (2011), broadcast on TV Azteca and Canal 3, respectively, and the LGBT-themed sketch comedy show *Desde Gayola* (2002–2013), ["From the Critics' Gallery"] and talk show *Guau* (2000–2015) ["Wow"], which ran on the cable music channel Telehit.[5] Mexican film could also boast the internationally feted art-house work of openly gay directors and producers like Julián Hernández and Roberto Fiesco. In late 2020, the case of the 41 itself made it to the big screen in *El baile de los 41* [*The Dance of the 41*], a dramatic film with high production values directed by the critically acclaimed auteur David Pablos. Literature, on the other hand, now had a tradition of texts portraying queerness dating back to at least the 1930s, as well as a decades-old critical tradition focusing on queer themes and a lively independent and electronic publishing scene.[6]

Many things had obviously changed in Mexican society in the time that elapsed between the 41 and the beginning of the third millennium that contributed to this shift: changes in sexual mores and gender norms during and after the Revolution; the presence of major queer figures like the writers Salvador Novo and Carlos Monsváis and the singers Chavela Vargas and Juan Gabriel; the "sexual revolution" in the 1960s and 70s that intersected with the rise of feminist and homosexual political movements; the AIDS crisis and subsequent political responses to it; the tendency in recent Mexican politics for broad social movements to give way to coalitions of smaller collectives based on subjective identity (Monsiváis, "Introduction"; Carrillo, "How"; Figari; Fiol-Matta).[7] However, these changes do not imply a limitless march towards freedom and equality. For example, in 2016, then-president Enrique Peña Nieto's pinkwashing proposal to obligate every state in the republic to offer same-sex marriage was met by massive protest marches organized by conservative groups, including the hierarchy of the Catholic Church. Recent polls have suggested that a large portion of the Mexican population believes that public displays of homosexuality should be repressed or even punished, and there continue to be relatively high levels of hate crimes based on homophobia perpetrated in the country (Barreda 230–31; "Informe Crímenes de Odio por Homofobia"). Not surprisingly, this takes place in a context in which there is a high level of violence against women.[8] While there are many and complex causes for these social problems, the transmission and reinforcement of heteronormativity through humor in Mexican culture has doubtlessly contributed to the persistence of machismo and homophobia in Mexico. In the interest of challenging these uses of humor that uphold the dominant social structure, the goal of this book is to interrogate how literature uses humor as a queer, decolonizing practice.

The title of this book is *Between Camp and* Cursi, and in it I will be examining the intersection of these two humorous discursive modes (camp and *cursilería*) in Mexican literature. My analysis draws on perspectives from both the United States and Latin America. From the US side, I follow José Esteban Muñoz's reading of camp performance as a strategy of disidentification for queers of color in the United States and Eve Sedgwick's call to read camp texts and practices in a way that balances "paranoid" and "reparative" approaches. From the Latin American side, I draw on Lidia Santos and Carlos Monsiváis's theorizing of *cursilería* in Latin America, which also balances paranoid social critique with a reparative emphasis on the creative, decolonizing possibilities of *lo cursi* as an aesthetic strategy. When combined with theories that explain humor as the portrayal of social contradictions, these perspectives allow me to productively read the intersection of camp and *cursi* humor in the texts below as expressions of queerness that have important implications for questioning the dominant social structure in Mexico and in the wider global context. While humor has long been central to the maintenance of heteronormativity in Mexico, its inherent ambiguity makes it possible to read in ways that question the dominant social structure (Mulkay).

I focus on literature in this study because, as Vinodh Venkatesh argues, Latin American literature is a historical artifact that has played a central role in "shaping national and individual identity from the colonial period to the present" that also facilitates the analysis of gender construction in its intertextual referents, including popular culture (*The Body* 9). Furthermore, literature has long served as one of the most open venues for the expression of sexual dissidence and gender nonconformity in Latin America (Sifuentes-Jáuregui, *Avowal* 239–40n2). Compared with popular culture, I find that Latin American literature generally provides more challenging and profound explorations of queer themes, an observation that seems to be borne out by the number of recent studies examining these themes in literature.[9] My own study owes a particular debt to those critics who have worked towards queering allegorical portrayals of national and regional identities, thus demonstrating how the rejection of the feminine and the queer has been central to the construction of Latin American identities.

For example, in *Modernity and the Nation*, Héctor Domínguez-Ruvalcaba shows how masculinities in Mexican cultural production are shot through with paradoxes resulting from colonial and postcolonial processes that sensualize the masculine body (and the nation it represents) at the same time that they disempower it (3). In *Mexican Masculinities*, Robert Irwin repurposes Doris Sommer's reading of heterosexual romances in 19th-century Latin American novels as nation-building allegories, focusing instead on how male homosocial relations have represented the nation in Mexican literature. Emilio Bejel effects a similar reading in *Gay Cuban Nation*, where he argues that discourses of Cuban national identity are themselves constituted through a rejection of homosexuality, which always threatens to destabilize those national romances described by Sommer (xvi). Moving from a national to a broader hemispheric perspective, Ben. Sifuentes-Jáuregui argues that the construction of dissident identities based on gender nonconformity in Latin America is analogous to the way that national identities in the region (typically allegorized as heterosexual, masculine figures) are constructed through a parodic imitation of constructs from metropolitan areas. When read through a queer lens, these portrayals can undermine the supposed naturalness of both first world constructs and hegemonic masculinities (*Transvestism* 10). More recently, Venkatesh, starting from Raewyn Connell's concept of hegemonic masculinities, has interrogated how the portrayal of both hegemonic and nonhegemonic masculinities in contemporary Latin American fiction allegorizes the economic and social processes of neoliberalism (*The Body* 3–4).

All of these scholars undertake what Domínguez-Ruvalcaba refers to as the translation of queer reading practices and northern theoretical paradigms, a decolonial project that "by deconstructing the gender system questions the foundations of the nation and the state," but that also aims to disrupt the hegemonic flow of theory from North to South (*Translating* 12–13). Their perspectives emphasize the centrality of the experience of colonialism to Latin American subject formation, which is a starting point for many cultural differences with the Global North as well as shared experiences with people of color throughout the world. In this view, heteronormativity is an aspect of colonialism and has profound effects on how genders and sexualities are constructed in Latin America (Domínguez-Ruvalcaba, *Translating* 21, 42, 46; Sifuentes-Jáuregui, *Avowal* 240n4). For Domínguez-Ruvalcaba, queerness emerged in Latin America when European discourse began to translate Indigenous sexual practices into the language of sin, proscribing them with consequences that continue to this day in the form of machismo and homophobia, but also establishing the possibility of queer dissidence in the rejection of such rules (19). Similarly, Sifuentes-Jáuregui defines queerness as "the circuits of desire that disobey any imposed heteronormativity or even homonormativity" (5), and he highlights differences between expressions of sexual dissidence in the Global North and Latin America. For example, rather than the trope of coming out of the closet, in Latin America, "silences and disavowal emerge as central strategies of subject formation of queer Latino America" (16). This is a result, in part, of the centrality of the body in Latin American subject formation, which is another legacy of colonialism, specifically of the way that the domination of racialized bodies was central to the social order established in the colonial period (17).

Another result of this centrality of the body is the primacy of gender crossing as form of identification in Latin American sexualities, an obvious example of which is the figure of the *loca*, or effeminate homosexual man (72–73, 185). This figure, as I noted above, is central to the humorous portrayal of male homosexuality in Mexico, both as a target of ridicule as well as a repurposed figure of resistance. While somewhat similar to effeminate homosexualities from the Anglo-American context, *loca* identities are not exactly the same: "*loca* cannot be translated as gay, or even as queer [. . .]—one cannot translate *locura*, rather one locates queerness, meaning that when we speak across cultures about sexual identifications, we can only approximate those identifications and understand that what we have come across is an ideological template that resonates as something similar, but never the same" (201). Venkatesh expresses a similar view in *New Maricón Cinema* when he rejects the use of the term "queer" as an umbrella term for all LGBT+ identities and instead proposes the notion of "queerying," which entails "the severing of a strictly Anglophone gaze, the acknowledgment or adoption of the local, and the axiomatic addition of the 'Q' to LGBT, and not strictly as an undifferentiated synonym" (214n1).[10] Following these scholars, my goal is to locate queerness, understood broadly as resistance to the norms of gender and sexuality that persist in Latin American societies, in the texts that I analyze below, and to likewise effect a translation of certain theoretical constructs from the Global North to the Latin American context in order to engage in a "queerying" of humorous portrayals of homosexuality. This will allow me to better understand how queerness emerges in the texts in question and how it may be read in a productive, decolonizing manner.

To this end, I argue for the translation of the Anglo-American concept of camp to the Mexican context in order to usefully analyze humorous portrayals of queerness. Like Jonathan Dollimore, I am interested in "that mode of camp which undermines the categories which exclude it, and does so through parody and mimicry" (224). That is, I am interested in a type of camp that is not just a postmodern gay sensibility, but one that is "an invasion and subversion of other sensibilities [that] works via parody, pastiche, and exaggeration" (224–25). Whether this notion can be productively translated to Latin America or not is a subject of debate. For example, Sifuentes-Jáuregui sees camp as a conservative, apolitical sensibility based on consumption and the definition of privilege. He contrasts this with "transvestism," a series of practices based on gender nonconformity from the Latin American context that he sees as much more radical and potentially subversive: "Camp is about placing 'quotation marks' around certain words in order to ironize them; that is, Camp is about defining privilege. Transvestism is about showing that those quotation marks were placed there in the first place by the other and that transvestism works to remove them; transvestism is about exchanging privilege [. . .] Camp is about 'having.' Transvestism is about 'wanting' " (*Transvestism* 63). He has similarly argued that in contrast to the more performative nature of Anglo-American sexualities, Latin American sexualities tend to be more centered on bodily experience as lived through the historical imprint of colonialism (*Avowal* 11). I certainly recognize that camp, as an Anglo-American discourse, cannot simply be transplanted as a concept into Latin America without addressing these problems. I also agree with Sifuentes-Jáuregui's interpretation of Latin American sexualities as less focused on performative aspects of identity such as "coming out." However, I do not believe that camp needs to be eliminated from discussions of Latin American culture.

An alternative approach to translating camp for Latin America is provided by Lidia Santos in her analysis of the novels of Severo Sarduy. In *Tropical Kitsch*, she argues that camp, kitsch, and *cursilería* appear frequently in contemporary Latin American cultural production as part of a rhetoric that allegorizes social conflicts in the region. Her reading of camp, like Sifuentes-Jáuregui's, is informed mainly by Susan Sontag's seminal 1964 essay on the subject. For Santos, however, the use of camp by subjects who attempt to establish a level of privilege as arbiters of taste can itself be subversive with regards to the dominant social structure, especially when the taste in question is ironically posited as an expression of sexual dissidence and postcolonial positionality (95). Sarduy's postneobaroque aesthetic, for example, employs a humor based on transvestic gender parody and the intentional "bad taste" of *cursilería* in order to allegorize the contradictions and conflicts of Cuban history (138–42). His camp, in other words, is *cursi*, and it is that *cursilería*, understood as an allegorical expression of marginality from modernity, that marks his camp as Latin American.

José Esteban Muñoz sees a similar use of camp in the comic theatrical performances of the Cuban American performer Carmelita Tropicana. Muñoz reads her use of camp as a form of disidentification—the appropriation of stereotypes in order to affirm a dissident identity—and locates the particularly Latina difference of her camp in the Cuban practice of *choteo* (popular, humorous insulting discourse): "Her *choteo* style is campy and *choteo* is inflected in her campiness" (138). Although Muñoz is referring to a US Latina subject performing in an English-speaking context in which camp is more of a native concept, so to speak, the notion of camp as a humorous expression of queerness inflected by the low-class "bad taste" of Latin American popular culture is clearly very close to Santos's reading of Sarduy. Additionally, his emphasis on the appropriation and repurposing of negative stereotypes by socially marginal groups makes his reading of camp as disidentification very useful for understanding how humor about homosexuality can function in a subversive manner.

In the texts that I read below, I find that the humor used to signal and talk about queerness includes camp (gender-based humor expressing queerness) that is also always *cursi* (expressing a postcolonial marginality from discourses of modernity). The dialectic of oppression and resistance inherent in these expressions means that they should be read, as Sedgwick suggests for camp in the Anglo-American context, in a way that looks to balance paranoid (critical) and reparative (celebratory) approaches. My goal here is to make this intersection of camp and *cursi* humor the center of an inquiry into how literature has challenged heteronormativity in Mexico, with a particular emphasis on how humor portrays social conflicts related to sexuality, gender, race, class, and modernity in a subversive manner.

In this sense, my study seeks to contribute not only to the work of the scholars cited above but also to the corpus of more specifically Mexicanist literary and cultural studies focusing on homosexualities and/or queerness, such as the work of Luis Mario Schneider, Carlos Monsiváis, Antonio Marquet, David William Foster, Claudia Schaefer, Robert Irwin, María Elena Olivera, and Elena Madrigal, among others. This study aims to highlight, in particular, the relevance of humor to Mexicanist and Latin Americanist literary criticism.

Another goal of this study is to bring attention to many texts that have received scant critical attention. The texts that make up my corpus, all originally published in Mexico, range from canonical works like Luis Zapata's *El vampiro de la colonia Roma* [*Adonis García: A Picaresque Novel*] to "minor" works by major authors like Enrique Serna, out-of-print texts like Calva's *Utopía gay* ["Gay Utopia"], and little-known works by contemporary lesbian writers like Gilda Salinas. All of these texts contain portrayals of gender nonconformity and sexual dissidence with high frequencies of humor that include both the camp and *cursi* discursive modes. They address a range of topics such as sex work, transvestism, bisexuality, same-sex marriage, racism, classism, and homo- and transphobic violence, that are relevant to contemporary discussions of sexuality, gender, race, and human rights Mexico. Rather than a strictly chronological presentation, I have opted for a more thematic organization suggested by the texts themselves. The first two chapters contain what might be called the "foundational" texts of the corpus, in which the use of camp and *cursi* humor is pioneered by authors who portray queerness in ways that challenge hetero- and homonormativity in Mexican society. The following three chapters focus on how later humorous portrayals of queerness through camp and *cursilería* have engaged with particular identities and/or practices, including transvestism, male and female bisexuality, and lesbian sexuality and culture.

Chapter 1 outlines my theoretical approach to camp and *cursilería*, explains how I read these discursive modes as types of humor, and illustrates how they can be combined in the reading of portrayals of queerness that allegorize social conflicts surrounding gender, sexuality, race, class, and modernity. Beginning with a general definition of camp as an expression of queerness, especially through gender parody, I engage with José Esteban Muñoz's reading of camp as disidentification and Eve Sedgwick's call to approach camp in a way that balances paranoid and reparative reading practices. Similarly, I consider Lidia Santos's and Carlos Monsiváis's theorizations of *lo cursi* as a discourse that can creatively express Latin America's postcolonial global position through a parodic recycling of mass culture. In the texts I consider, both camp and *cursilería* tend to appear as humor, that is, a type of discursive mode that expresses social conflict through comic incongruities. Salvador Novo's autobiography *La estatua de sal* [*The Pillar of Salt*] serves as an example of how camp and *cursi* humor combine in the portrayal of a queer subjectivity in modern Mexico, while Monsiváis's reading of this work provides an example of how paranoid and reparative reading practices may be combined in the approach to such texts.

Chapter 2 examines two novels published in the late 1970s and early 1980s that mark a shift in Mexican narrative towards both a more frequent and a more humorous portrayal of queerness. *El vampiro de la colonia Roma* [*Adonis García: A Picaresque Novel*] by Luis Zapata and *Utopía gay* ["Gay Utopia"] by José Rafael Calva both employ camp and *cursi* humor in the portrayal of male protagonists who struggle to reconcile their desire to participate in hegemonic masculinity and northern discourses of modernity with their identities as homosexual men in Mexico. Their anxieties regarding gender and modernity reflect social conflicts in an era of rising movements of sexual dissidence and a growing consumer culture, while their behaviors model reparative uses of camp and *cursi* humor, such as the transcendence of negative affect and the constitution of collectives, that also appear in later texts on the same theme. Both works critically engage the Mexican and Western literary traditions through their parody of key genres and their portrayal of queer subjectivities, as do many of the later texts examined below.

Chapter 3 looks at four texts whose protagonists are *travestis*, *vestidas* or *jotas*, that is, queer subjects who are biologically male but who construct female identities through gender parody, and in particular through the recycling of mass-media tropes of *cursi* femininity. Such individuals tend to face a great deal of oppression in Mexican society, which makes the politics surrounding their representation critical. Engaging with Vek Lewis's critique of the figurative portrayal of cross-dressing subjects in Latin America, I examine how the texts float between more realistic portrayals of subjectivities and engagement with the allegorical tradition. *Brenda Berenice o el diario de una loca* ["Brenda Berenice or the Diary of a Queen"] by Luis Montaño is a little-known text that employs a great deal of camp and *cursi* humor in the portrayal of a *jota* subjectivity that is bent on queering the Mexican literary tradition. *La hermana secreta de Angélica María* ["The Secret Sister of Angélica María"] by Luis Zapata, on the other hand, features an intersex protagonist who functions essentially as a metaphor for gender nonconformity and as a critique of the construction of identities through mass media portrayals of femininity. A similar view is trained on the traditions of Mexican cinematic melodrama in Carlos Velázquez's short story "La jota de Bergerac," while his story

"La marrana negra de la literatura rosa" ["The Black Sow of Romance Literature"] exemplifies how a comic engagement with the conventions of marriage as allegory can provide opportunities for paranoid and reparative readings of portrayals of *jota* identities.

Chapter 4 focuses on three novels whose male protagonists could be described as bisexual. Returning to Octavio Paz's centering of the "penetration paradigm" in *The Labyrinth of Solitude*, I argue that the contradictions inherent in this definition of masculinity can be productively explained with the notion of bisexuality, which appears in these texts as an expression of unresolved social conflicts regarding gender, sexuality, and modernity. In all of these cases, the portrayal of sexuality intersects with a satirical critique of race and class prejudice in Mexico, and in particular with the anxiety surrounding *naquez*, a postcolonial positionality inflected by racism. These novels express such conflicts through their use of camp and *cursi* humor in postmodern parodies of the classic European *Bildgunsroman* genre. In *Mátame y verás* ["Kill Me and You'll See"] by José Joaquín Blanco, the situational bisexuality and humble origins of the protagonist haunt him, imperiling a masculinity he has trouble reconciling with modernity in this allegory of neoliberal Mexico. In *Púrpura* ["Purple"] by Ana García Bergua, the protagonist's undefined sexual orientation and *cursilería* function as part of a larger portrayal of 20th-century Mexican culture as defined by an ambivalent desire for an unreachable modernity. Finally, the semi-autobiographical *Fruta verde* ["Green Fruit"] by Enrique Serna explores the reparative possibilities of camp and *cursi* humor in the processing of unresolved social conflicts while it also offers an incisive critique of racism, classism, and sex and gender norms in contemporary Mexico.

Chapter 5 focuses on several texts that portray women characters who engage in camp gender parody that relates to lesbian identities in Mexico. Camp humor in which women perform (often exaggerated) female masculinities intersects *cursilería* that functions as an indicator of an often-racialized Latin American positionality intersected by sexual dissidence and gender. José Dimayuga's novel *¿Y qué fue de Bonita Malacón?* ["Whatever Happened to Bonita Malacón?"] includes queer female characters as part of a provincial cast whose *cursilería* represents the complex relationship of Mexico to global capitalism. Gilda Salinas's book *Del destete al desempance: Cuentos lésbicos y un colado* ["From Weaning to the Digestif: Lesbian Stories and a Stowaway"] narrates the construction of lesbian subjectivity through reparative uses of humor based on *cursilería* and gender nonconformity, while some of the stories from Elena Madrigal's collection *Contarte en lésbico* ["Tell You in Lesbian"] similarly portray an ironic side of lesbian subjectivity through camp and *cursi* humor. While some of these portrayals have been read as lesbophobic, I propose an alternative reading that recognizes their ambiguous relationship to stereotypes but that ultimately emphasizes their deconstructive and decolonial possibilities.

All of the texts mentioned above invoke camp and *cursilería* in the portrayal of sexual dissidence and gender nonconformity undertaken in a Latin American context informed by the continuing effects of coloniality. That is, they portray the irruption of queerness with specific forms of humor that lay bare the contradictions of (dis)modernity in contemporary Mexico and the struggles of people to live and express their desires and identities there. This book is meant to highlight the ways that they do this and to offer reading strategies that can contribute to the growing current of queer, decolonial approaches to Mexican and Latin American culture.

Chapter 1

The Other Mexican Revolution

Camp and *Cursilería* in the Queer Self-Construction of Salvador Novo

In this chapter, I define camp and *cursilería*, explain my theoretical approach to reading these as humor, and then follow with an examination of the intersection of the two in the persona and work of Salvador Novo. In particular, a close reading of his autobiography, *La estatua de sal* [*Pillar of Salt*], provides an opportunity to analyze the use of camp and *cursi* humor in the portrayal of queer subjectivities in modern Mexico and how we can read them from a perspective that combines paranoid and reparative approaches.

Camp and Queerness

Camp is a postmodern aesthetic sensibility centered on the contradiction between appearance and essence that has its origins in the performance of queerness. Its humorous effects tend to arise from a focus on the incongruity between appearance (performing) and essence (being), and gender nonconformity is one of its main modes of expression (Cleto 1-42). The concept of camp emerges in the Anglo-American context, with some scholars locating its genesis in early modern transvestic practices in 18th-century England, and others citing Oscar Wilde as its ultimate originator (King; Bartlett). While its origins may be in the 18th or 19th century, the first written definition of it dates from the 1950s, when it is defined by a character in Christopher Isherwood's novel *The World in the Evening* (1954) as both a high culture queer reading practice ("high camp") and a pop culture–oriented performance of queerness through gender parody ("low camp"): "a swishy little boy with peroxided hair, dressed in a picture hat and a feather boa, pretending to be Marlene Dietrich" (51). The "low" association with pop culture is what comes to dominate theorizations of camp, which emerges as a major critical category in the 1960s after the publication of Susan Sontag's influential essay "Some Notes on 'Camp'" (1964). Sontag defines camp as an apolitical way of seeing the world that focuses on artifice and stylization (form) instead of beauty (content) (106–7). Although she makes a cursory connection to gay male culture, Sontag's definition tends to elide the homosexual origins of camp and extend its conceptual reach to general pop culture (Meyer). Later theoretical approaches to camp in the 1970s and 1980s attempt essentialist reappropriations of it as a homosexual or gay sensibility,[1] while even later studies from the 1980s and 1990s focused on specific types of camp (gay male, lesbian, heterosexual, etc.) (Cleto 44–48, 88–95, 200–6, 302–7, 365–60).

These last two decades also saw the recuperation of camp by queer theory as a discourse that collapses the opposition between subject and object and, as such, lends itself to theorizations that seek to critique essentialist notions of identity. Judith Butler and others argued for a reconsideration of the liberating possibilities of camp gender parody in opposition to the rejection of camp as apolitical, conservative and/or self-hating by gay and lesbian identity politics of the 1970s and 1980s (Cleto 88–95, 202–6, 356–60).[2] The criticism of camp as apolitical and conservative often hinges on its reproduction of stereotypes, both of queer people (e.g., effeminate men, butch women) and of certain heterosexual gender scripts that it parodies (such as the femininities and masculinities portrayed in the mass media). Arguments for the subversive potential of camp do not ignore this criticism, but instead emphasize the inherent ambiguity of all texts, as well as the particular contradictions of those produced by social minorities that transgressively reinscribe scripts appropriated from mainstream society. As Jonathan Dollimore succinctly puts it, "there is no transgression from the position of the subordinate that is not controversial; it is a virtually inevitable consequence of the disempowered mounting a challenge at all" ("Authenticity" 234). In this view, the subversive possibility of camp lies not in any essentially stable meaning in camp texts but in the way that we choose to read such texts, noting how their ambiguity might be seen to destabilize or subvert the dominant social structure (Cleto 35).

However, as Eve Sedgwick points out, not even such "celebratory" readings are necessarily free of moral ambiguity about the political implications of camp practices. In her influential essay "You're So Paranoid You Probably Think This Essay Is About You," Sedgwick contends that most queer theoretical readings of camp tend to see it as a "mocking exposure of the elements and assumptions of dominant culture [that is also problematically tinged by] self-hating complicity with an oppressive status quo" (149). This is an example of what she calls "paranoid reading," the dominant mode of critical inquiry in our time.[3] Paranoid reading is anticipatory, reflexive, mimetic, focused on exposing what is hidden, tends toward broad application and tautology (i.e., is "strong theory"), and is associated with negative affect (130–43). Sedgwick calls for a greater balance of paranoid approaches with "reparative" reading practices, which might include "weak theory" (that which focuses more closely on specific objects, such as close reading) and, with regards to camp, a focus on the possible functions of community-building and the transcendence of negative affect for the collectives who produce and consume it (150–51). Sedgwick implies that this is a necessary addition to postmodern perspectives that focus more on discovering and tearing down structures but less on constructing alternative epistemologies. However, this does not mean that paranoid reading can simply be done away with. The essay clearly implies a parallel with Kleinian theory: just as the paranoid and depressive ("reparative") positions are connected, and one moves between them, so the reading practices are also connected and readers should move between the two (Love 239).

Christopher Lassen's study of the uses of camp humor in US literature about AIDS provides several examples of how to combine paranoid and reparative reading practices in the study of camp aesthetics. As Lassen argues, camp can be

> deployed to support paranoid as well as reparative reading practices. The former aims at familiar objectives like denaturalization, demystification and exposure. The latter by contrast, aims at equally significant objectives like relief, consolation and healing [. . .] both practices, however far apart in terms of strategy, often converge not only within one and the same community, i.e. on a formative social level, but also within one and the same individual self, i.e. on a formative personal level. Hence each and everyone [sic] may benefit from the utilisation of paranoid *and* reparative camp practices. (34)

Lassen illustrates this approach in his analysis of the short stories in *Monopolies of Loss* by Adam Mars-Jones and the poetry of Rafael Campo (a gay physician), all of which critique the dehumanization of AIDS patients by the medical system while also providing a sort of comic relief for those who are treated and work in this context (34–38). I propose a similar reading of the uses of camp and *cursi* humor in the Mexican texts that I analyze below. Without negating the importance of paranoid reading, which is necessary for any true social critique, I emphasize the reparative enjoyment of camp humor and its possibilities for social regeneration. This most often appears in the ways that the characters model the use of humor to transcend negative affect and in the constitution of imaginary communities, including queer collectives and even the Mexican nation.

Acampando in Mexico

But what does camp have to do with Mexico? As I mentioned above, camp originates in the English-speaking world, and the vast majority of scholarship on the subject focuses on Anglo-American cultural production and practices.[4] The suitability of camp for describing signifying practices and cultural production in Latin America has been a subject of debate since at least the 1960s. One of the earliest Latin American critics to seriously consider it was Carlos Monsiváis, who in 1966 published a chronicle in response to Sontag's essay. In "El hastío es pavo real que se aburre de luz en la tarde (Notas del camp en México)" ["Weariness is a peacock who is bored by light in the afternoon (Notes on camp in Mexico)"], Monsiváis recognizes a certain subversive possibility in camp's lack of seriousness, but he generally considers it too apolitical and decadent to be useful for theorizing Mexican culture (191–92). He does posit, however, an ironic appropriation of older cultural texts, an idea which he will later develop under the rubric of *cursilería* (174). Probably due to the influence of Sontag, there is no explicit connection of camp to homosexuality in this chronicle. Monsiváis does however, connect camp practices to homosexuality in his later work on Salvador Novo. Other critics have also tended to emphasize the association between camp and homosexuality when mentioning it in connection to Latin American culture. For example, Antonio Marquet and José Joaquín Blanco have used the term "camp" to refer to certain cultural practices and aesthetic categories of Mexican queer cultures, such as oblique cultural references, ludism, and self-deprecating humor (Blanco, "Ojos" 189; Marquet 33). José Amícola, writing about the cultural production of the Southern Cone, theorizes that camp functions as a sort of recycling of kitsch that expresses queerness, as in the novels of Manuel Puig.

Other scholars have objected to the use of the term "camp" to describe Latin American cultural practices, arguing that readings of Latin American culture influenced by North American LGBT studies and queer theory often minimize the cultural differences between the two regions. For example, Diana Palaversich has argued for the use of *lo cursi* in place of camp, at least in the reading of certain texts. As I explained in the introduction, Ben. Sifuentes-Jáuregui proposes the notion of "transvestism" as a more subversive alternative to camp, which he sees as apolitical and elitist (*Transvestism* 63). While I certainly recognize the importance of avoiding homogenizing readings of Latin American genders and sexualities from a lens fashioned in the Global North, I do not believe that the notion of camp needs to be discarded. Rather, I believe that it should be qualified and supplemented with concepts that more accurately depict Latin American positionalities.

In the introduction I cited the readings of José Esteban Muñoz and Lidia Santos as examples of how camp can be appropriated in order to talk about Latino and Latin American expressions of queerness. Muñoz's analysis is based on the notion of disidentification, "the third mode of dealing with dominant ideology, one that neither opts to assimilate within such a structure nor strictly opposes it; rather, disidentification is a strategy that works on and against dominant ideology" (11–12). Muñoz sees the performances of the lesbian Cuban American comic and actress Carmelita Tropicana as a form of disidentification with camp itself—in this way, a "predominantly gay white male project" is appropriated in order to give expression to a marginalized Latina life world (25). Carmelita's camp is inflected by her *choteo* (popular Cuban insult humor), while her *choteo* also becomes camp (138). Lidia Santos identifies a similar use of camp from the Latin American context in the novels of the queer Cuban writer Severo Sarduy. In her view, Sarduy's camp gender parody is highly inflected by a particularly Latin American mode of recycling the "bad taste" of mass media that allegorizes the social conflicts of the region. She refers to this as *cursilería* (138–42). Following these two scholars, I center my reading of camp humor in Mexican literature on gender parody, which frequently appears as the potentially subversive recycling of stereotyped gender roles, which themselves also always involve an element of *cursilería*. In other words, this camp is also *cursi*. But what exactly does it mean to be *cursi*?

Cursilería and Modernity

The adjective *cursi*, nominalized as *lo cursi* [that which is *cursi*] or *la cursilería* [*cursi* practices or *cursi*-ness], is often translated into English as corny, cheesy, tacky, or tasteless, none of which fully captures all the resonances of its meanings.[5] The difficulty in finding an exact correspondence is due to the fact that it is a cultural category that belongs, in a very particular way, to the Spanish American context. It first arose in Spain in the mid-19th century as a term used to label and stigmatize attempts by the rising bourgeoisie to imitate the styles and comportment of the aristocracy, broadening in meaning over time to refer to a general sense of belatedness with regards to modernity (Valis). In this last sense, it also became an important part of discourses of national identity in Spain, which often oppose the Iberian Peninsula to Europe (Gómez de la Serna; Valis). Imported to Latin America in the late 19th century, *cursilería* has functioned there to label what are perceived as failed attempts to imitate the cultural codes of higher social strata as well as cultural anachronism in style and discourse marked by sentimentality (Santos 72–81; Monsváis, "La cursilería" 14–15). As in Spain, the uses of the term in Latin America express a sense of marginalization from modernity (Santos 75).

By "modernity," I mean the dominant narrative category that defines the present with relation to the past and the future (Montaldo 153). Currently, this term is generally used to distinguish the era of the rise of global European hegemony from the ancient (Helleno-Roman) and medieval (European) historical periods in the West. The modern expansion of European power is associated with imperialism and chattel slavery, the growth and spread of scientific, technological and economic development, secularism, human rights, democratic forms of government, and the notion that this order of things will continue into the future. However, recent revisionist perspectives on the history of modernity have argued for greater attention to how the colonization of the Americas was an essential part of the development of modernity in the Global North that affected all global social organization in profound ways. For example, Enrique Dussel has argued that modern subjectivity, which is based on the notion of the individual differentiated ego, developed in part through the process by which Europeans distinguished themselves from colonized others during the period of initial contact and colonization of the Americas. Aníbal Quijano, who marks the beginning of modernity with the colonization of the Americas, argues that discourses of modernity tend to reproduce the coloniality of power, that is, the internalization and social transmission of notions of Eurocentrism and white supremacy (533–42). To this notion, which focuses mostly on race and class, we can add the "coloniality of gender" and the "coloniality of sex," or a recognition of the way that colonialism influences genders and sexualities through the imposition of patriarchy and heteronormativity (Lugones 98–99; Domínguez Ruvalcaba, *Translating* 21).[6] Bearing in mind the manner in which modernity is constituted from the exploitative and racist colonization of the region, it is not surprising that Latin America has a very complicated and conflicted relationship with discourses of modernity. Modernization has been an explicit but elusive goal of most political projects in Latin America since independence.[7] According to Quijano, Latin American nations have failed to achieve the articulation of truly modern nation-states (with clearly defined national identity, citizenship and democratic participation) because of the persistence of the coloniality of power in elite governance of the region (564–70).[8] This complex relationship with modernity is likewise reflected in Latin American cultural production.

Latin American cultural engagements with modernity have included the dualistic definition of it as civilization versus barbarism by early 19th-century liberals like Domingo F. Sarmiento, the *fin-de-siècle* cosmopolitanism of *modernistas* like Rubén Darío and José Martí, and the dialogic engagement of European and North American avant-gardes by their Latin American counterparts (including writers ranging from Jorge Luis Borges to Carlos Fuentes and Augusto Roa Bastos, among many others) during most of the 20th century, all of which include themes related to the opposition of tradition and modernity (Montaldo). This opposition finds expression in Latin American literature's attempt to assert a local identity through rhetorical practices that both reject modernity and often "unavoidably [reinforce] the cultural myth of metropolitan superiority" (Alonso 20). The texts that I analyze below display a similar ambivalence towards *lo cursi*, expressing a simultaneous desire for and rejection of participation in modernity.

This expression of ambivalence frequently makes use of themes and rhetorical strategies that might be considered postmodern from the perspective of many of the more influential theories of postmodernism (such as those of Umberto Eco, François Lyotard and Fredric Jameson). The applicability of postmodern theories to the analysis of Latin American culture has been hotly debated, precisely because of the region's peripheral position vis-à-vis metropolitan discourses.[9] One intervention that I find particularly useful for the Mexican context is Roger Bartra's notion of *desmodernidad*, which he defines as "una aniquilación de tensiones por exceso de modernidad" ["an annihilation of tensions due to an excess of modernity"] (240n17). This portmanteau word of *postmodernidad* [postmodernity] and *desmadre*, a Mexican term that employs the oath "madre" to denote disorder, implies that Mexican (post)modernity is different from, and possibly transgressive with regards to, notions of (post)modernity from the Global North. Mexicans are a surplus of modernity, racialized Others that modernity would like to forget, but who are always there, introducing *desmadre* into the system just as the amphibious axolotl of Lake Texcoco (Bartra's main metaphor for Mexican dismodernity) troubles taxonomic discourses with its unpredictable reproductive cycle. One way in which this particular dismodern condition is expressed is through *cursilería*.

En El País De Los Cursis

In *Tropical Kitsch*, Lidia Santos argues that the recycling of mass culture and "bad taste" in recent Latin American literature, art, and popular music functions as an allegory of the social heterogeneity of contemporary Latin America (5). Following the Brazilian social theorist Roberto Schwarz, she argues that kitsch, broadly understood as various elements appropriated from pop culture, functions in Latin American art as an allegory of the notion that Latin American culture is a deficient copy or imitation of the culture of the Global North (7). This notion, while very similar to Homi Bhabha's postcolonial mimicry, actually has a long tradition in Latin American thought going back over a century (51, 59–61, 185n30).[10] Schwarz's argument that "the copy is inevitable, and can be utilized as a theoretical concept as long as ideological prestige is not given to copied models" (60) is developed aesthetically by artists such as the *tropicalistas* in Brazil and the writers Manuel Puig, Luis Rafael Sánchez, and Severo Sarduy. Santos uses the term *cursilería* to encapsulate a variety of terms, such as *huachafo* in Peru, *brega*, *peru* and *cafona* in Brazil, and *picúo* in Cuba, that demarcate social boundaries through judgments about the "bad" taste of others and that in the texts she studies are inseparable from the recycling of kitsch (72–74). While Santos's observations are key for understanding a *cursi* aesthetic, her study does not engage with Mexican culture to any great extent, where the contemporary meaning of *cursi* is highly inflected by notions of sentiment that tend to obfuscate the relation to social class and race. To supplement Santos's analysis in a way that can help make these class and racial elements clearer, we can turn to how Monsiváis has theorized *cursilería* specifically from the Mexican context.

Monsiváis's perspective on *lo cursi* develops over time. In the above-cited chronicle from 1966, he worries that camp might be too closely associated with the US context to really be useful for describing Mexican culture, though he does consider it as a way to ironically recover older texts now considered in bad taste. Almost a decade later, in 1975, his thinking has evolved on this subject, and he now rejects camp for the home-grown concept of *lo cursi*. In a sort of elegy to the late composer and singer Agustín Lara, he defines the sentimental discourse inherent in Lara's songs and public persona as a continuation, through mass culture, of the poetic discourse of 19th-century writers like Amado Nervo. He argues that this type of *cursilería* is not the "fracaso de la elegancia" ["failure of elegance"] famously defined by Ramón Gómez de la Serna but rather "la elegancia históricamente posible en el subdesarrollo" ["the elegance historically possible in underdevelopment"], an expression of the 19th-century Mexican desire to participate in modernity ("Agustín Lara" 64). This connects the "bad taste" of Mexico to a historical marginalization of the region from discourses of modernity, which cannot really be described in terms of camp because this desire forms part of the culture. José Quiroga sums this up quite well: "boleros [the main song form used by Lara] at this point do not seek the return of something that was there before. [. . .] Desire wants sentimentality back, but not the context; it seeks the expression, but wants to pick and choose among the rest" (154). Monsiváis eventually suggests a name for this nostalgia for sentiment—he calls it *cursilería*.

This idea is most fully developed in his later chronicle, "Instituciones: La cursilería" ["Institutions: *La cursilería*"], the title of which implies that *cursilería* is a foundational part of Mexican culture. He begins with a phrase that ironically parodies the same discourse he is analyzing: "Prefiero la muerte a la gloria inútil de vivir sin ti, 'México, País de los cursis,' proclaman desde hace décadas analistas, periodistas y vanguardias culturales" ["I prefer death to the useless glory of living without you, 'Mexico, Land of the *Cursis*,' is the decades-old proclamation of analysts, journalists, and cultural avant-gardes"] ("La cursilería" 13). *Cursilería* is a type of cultural anachronism, the persistence of a discourse characterized by neoclassical, romantic and *modernista* poetic tropes related to sentiment. Its roots are in 19th-century bourgeois culture that saw poetry as the ultimate expression of cultivation and erudition (14–15, 19–20). Such discourses became passé among Mexican elites in the 20th-century with the rise of the avant-garde and the later 1960s counterculture, but they persisted in the melodramatic language of mass culture (film, popular music, television) associated with the tastes of the lower classes and as a sort of problematic substrate in Mexican culture in general (21–31). Monsiváis suggests, then, that Mexicans have a contradictory and problematic relationship to the discursive mode of *lo cursi* since it is something closely connected to the construction of national identity but also disdained by many as lower-class and indicative of the country's perceived lack of modernity.

Monsiváis is not the only critic to make a connection between contemporary Latin American culture and 19th-century expressions of subjectivity. Bartra similarly argues that in the constitution of myths of Mexican national identity, romantic sentiment becomes the basis of ontological universality because it distinguishes Mexicans from other nationalities, especially from the United States (137). Theorizing from the Andean region, Antonio Cornejo Polar argues that a central obstacle to the clear acceptance of the heterogeneity of Latin American culture is the difficulty of overcoming the desire to constitute a type of modern subjectivity proposed by the European colonizers but systematically denied to the colonized and postcolonial subject.[11] The main discourse that transmits this notion of modern subjectivity is romanticism:

> I wonder why it is so difficult for us to accept the hybridity, the ill assortment, and the heterogeneity of a subject thus configured in our space. Just one answer occurs to me: we introject as our only legitimacy the monolithic, strong, and unchangeable image of the modern subject, based on the Romantic "I," and we feel guilty before the world and ourselves, when we discover that we lack a clear and distinct identity. (*Writing in the Air* 9)

This is exactly what Monsiváis argues about *la cursilería*: the exaggerated expression of romantic sentiment is, in part, an expression of a desire for full modern subjecthood: "El feroz sentimentalismo encerrado en el ghetto de la *cursilería* prueba que un Sentimiento Puro es igual a cualquier Sentimiento Puro, si la sinceridad es la norma y no tiene por qué no serlo" ["The ferocious sentimentalism locked in the ghetto of *cursilería* proves that one Pure Sentiment is equal to any Pure Sentiment, if sincerity is the norm and there is no reason for it not to be"] (185).

Returning to Santos's definition of *lo cursi* as a form of social barrier that can be recycled in a productive manner to express social conflict and marginality from modernity, we can describe the persistence of exaggeratedly sentimental romantic/modernista discourse in Mexican culture as a sort of "failed attempt" of the culture of the entire nation to imitate the cultural codes of the Global North. This failure is predetermined—it is only by the exclusion of regions such as Mexico that the North is modern in the first place. However, as Santos and Monsiváis both suggest, this so-called "failure" to produce a perfect copy can actually be productive. In opposition to those who are ashamed of *cursilería*, Monsviáis argues for the acceptance of it as a productive discourse that expresses Mexican (and Latin American) subjectivities that show the effects of the coloniality of power, sex, and gender, thus laying bare the contradictions of modernity that have always been more obvious from peripheral perspectives. For this reason, he rejects the use of the terms "camp" and "kitsch," relating them to the US and European cultural contexts, respectively, and argues that the particular question of taste in Mexico is about *cursilería*, which, to a great extent, is about that problematic relationship with modernity.

If *cursilería* is a kind of parody, copy, or cannibalization of European romantic discourse, or of a Latin American modernismo that itself parodies, copies, or cannibalizes various European discourses, then, as Santos argues, its use in Latin American literature can be read as an allegory of the region's particular participation in modernity as a locus that, through its colonization, permitted the West to define itself as modern. From this necessarily subaltern position, the unresolvable social conflicts engendered by the coloniality of power, sex, and gender persist in all discourse that interpolate modernity and are reflected in the formation of subjectivities. When the subaltern speaks, even in a way that is meant to subvert the hegemonic social order, it must be in the language of hegemony, thus leading to the dialectic between subversion and conservation of the hegemonic order. A similar tension underlies camp humor in the Anglo-American context, where appropriations and reiterations of stereotypes of gender and sexuality can both serve hegemony and undermine it. As is the case with camp, no specific example of intentionally *cursi* humor can ever be called essentially "subversive" or "conservative." What matters most, in these cases, is the way that we choose to read it. As in the case of camp, when we read *cursilería*, we can combine paranoid and reparative reading practices.

Indeed, Monsiváis's analyses of *cursilería* tend to oscillate between these positions. This can be seen in the *crónica* about Lara I cited above, where Monsviáis also signals how the mass diffusion of this type of *cursi* culture can serve to uphold the dominant social order. Specifically, he critiques how Lara's music helps propagate the myth of the "bohemian lifestyle" and the "night life," which normalize the exploitation of women through prostitution and the sublimation of political dissidence through the illusion of self-expression through "rebellious" consumption:

> La Vida Nocturna (mito contemporáneo universal que enmascara una realidad de explotación) al adaptarse en México concilia la divulgación de alegorías occidentales del amor con la realidad del subdesarrollo. Enamorarse de una prostituta es una pasión mortal, una degradación social . . . y una comodidad. Intensificar—así sea muy ensoñadoramente—la vida personal es necesidad íntima . . . y compensación por la falta de vida pública.
>
> [The Night Life (a universal contemporary myth that masks a reality of exploitation), when it is adapted to Mexico, combines the propagation of Western allegories of love with the reality of underdevelopment. Falling in love with a prostitute is a mortal passion, a social degradation . . . and an amenity. To intensify—even day-dreamily—one's personal life is an intimate necessity . . . and a sort of compensation for the lack of a public life.] (81–82)

This critique of the role of mass culture is balanced, however, by Monsiváis's ultimate suggestion that *lo cursi* should be recovered as a specifically Mexican (and Latin American) cultural trait and celebrated as such.

This oscillation between paranoid and reparative reading practices in Monsiváis reflects what Linda Egan describes as his basic style: unfettered social criticism combined with an almost boundless optimism that views popular culture in Mexico as a productive indicator of the country's uneven but inexorable march towards democracy and social equality (24, 37–38). Monsiváis began combining social critique with an optimistic and celebratory view of popular culture in the 1960s, anticipating by three decades Sedgwick's call for this type of balance in feminist and queer cultural criticism. He perhaps most famously and visibly used *cursilería* to this effect in his long-running newspaper column "Por mi madre, bohemios" ["To my mother, bohemians"], which playfully took its title from a line of the famously *cursi* poem "El brindis del bohemio" ["The Bohemian's Toast"] by the19th-century poet Juan de Dios Peza. The basic format was a series of satirical glosses of the unintentionally ironic and *cursi* pronouncements of the rich and powerful in Mexico. At the same time, the title and even the subject matter were also an expression of pride in Mexican culture and an exercise in the creative use of *cursi* humor (Egan 186, 190).

Is *Naco* Beautiful?

It is clear, then, that Monsiváis proposes and even models, in his own work, reparative uses of *cursi* style as an expression of Latin American subjectivity. This becomes more complicated, however, when he engages with the term *naco*. Although Santos does not mention this word in her study, it is one of those epithets, like *huachafo*, *cafona* and others, used in Latin America by the haves to distinguish themselves from the have-nots and that she groups under the rubric of *cursi* (75). In fact, in the Mexican context, *naco* is used much more frequently to mark social class barriers through taste than the term *cursi*, which is usually reserved specifically for expressions of sentimentality (although the two concepts do often overlap). According to the dictionary of the *Academia Mexicana de la Lengua*, the term *naco* is generally used to refer to what the speaker judges to be vulgar or in bad taste or to label a person who seems to lack urbanity or civility and/or appears to be Indigenous and/or poor. The *Diccionario de la Real Academia Española* defines it as a synonym for *indio* ("Indian," itself sometimes used as an insult in Mexico) and notes that it is possibly an apocope of the Indigenous demonym *totonaco*. In other words, *naco* is a term that conflates racial and class identity in order to discriminate against those whom the speaker perceives as socially inferior. In this way, the term plays an important role in expressing racial anxieties.

The dominant discourses of national identity in 20th-century Mexico posit a "raceless" society where nearly everyone is *mestizo* (of mixed Spanish and Indigenous heritage), and the only racialized subjects are those excluded from this imagined community (Indigenous people, immigrants, and people of African, Asian, Middle Eastern, and/or Jewish descent) (Moreno Figueroa 388–89; Navarrete, *México* 67–68, 105–23). The sociologist Mónica Moreno Figueroa argues that in Mexico *mestizaje* actually functions as a "complex form of whiteness" that allows access to racial privilege in a highly relational manner: "while mestizaje offers the possibility of flexible inclusion, it also allows an everyday experience of racism that continues to privilege processes of whitening alongside notions of whiteness and uses the national discourse, such as a 'Mexican' identity, to cover up and render invisible processes of discrimination and social exclusion" (399). In other words, *mestizaje* is a discourse whose true aim is the "whitening" of Mexican national identity through the imposition of Western cultural norms. It provides most people with an opportunity to define themselves relationally in order to occupy a highly unstable position of privilege or ambiguous whiteness (393, 396–97).

The fact that in Mexico defining oneself or another person as a racialized subject is considered controversial, offensive, or even taboo is a symptom of these functions of *mestizaje* (399). By the same token, terms like *naco* function to signal that one, as a presumed *mestizo*, is on "this side" (the whiter side) of the racial hierarchy, in opposition to others (392–93). Although it is sometimes argued in Mexico that the use of the label *naco* has more to do with manners and civility than race (an argument that upholds Moreno's thesis about the normalization of racism), the racial undertone is always present, as clearly illustrated by the way that *nacos* are typically portrayed in Mexican popular culture as ridiculous, brown-skinned, and poor, in contrast to the relative lack of humorous portrayals of light-skinned *güeros* (Navarrete, *Alfabeto* 119–20).[12]

Keenly aware of how racism functions in Mexican society, Monsiváis has struggled with the desire to refashion *naco* into something more reparative. He ends a chronicle written in the 1970s with the slogan "Naco is beautiful," capping off a rather idealized portrayal of young rock musicians and fans in the exurbs of Mexico City and essentializing the figure of the *naco* as the racist rejection of Indigenous heritage. He argues instead for a celebration of that heritage through a repurposing of the originally insulting term (Monsiváis, *Escenas* 237–38; Sánchez Prado 319). However, Monsiváis later seems to abandon this attempt to appropriate *naco* for reparative purposes, focusing instead on critiquing the relational aspect of its application:

Cualquiera, garantizado su aspecto (lo primordial) o su conducta o su nivel educativo, puede ser un naco, y ante el epíteto no cuenta el dinero. Y lo que se afirma es muy sencillo: cualquiera resulta un naco si la idea de Primer Mundo "como que no le funciona." No hay nada que hacer, lo naco es la sujeción eterna al México impresentable.

[Anyone, according to their aspect (most essential), their conduct or their educational level, can be a *naco*, and money does not defend against the epithet. What it affirms is very simple: anyone can be a *naco* if the idea of the First World "doesn't work for them." There is nothing to be done, *naco* is the eternal subjection to unpresentable Mexico.] ("Léperos" 171)

This idea of *naquez* as the expression of a shared sense of racial and cultural inferiority is further developed in an essay by Enrique Serna, who emphasizes how the term arose in the 1960s and 70s with the increased ability of the lower classes to imitate the tastes of higher social strata through consumption of similar goods, thus provoking a reaction of vigilance against the encroachment on the social status of elites (99–101). However, discriminatory practices associated with the label are generalized in Mexican society, a state of affairs that reminds Serna of the racism of the colonial era, when every caste looked down upon the one below it:

El naco pertenece por lo común a la raza de bronce, pero los blancos no tenemos garantizada la aprobación de la casta divina [. . .] La gente acomodada tilda de nacos a los arribistas de clase media, que a su vez miran con desprecio a la chinaca popular, donde también existe la figura del discriminado discriminador [. . .]

[The *naco* generally belongs to the bronze race, but we whites do not have our approval by the divine caste guaranteed [. . .] Wealthy people label middle-class climbers as *nacos*, who in turn look with disdain upon the hoi polloi, where the figure of the discriminating victim of discrimination also exists [. . .]] ("El naco" 97)

What is implicit here is the fact that even the "divine caste," those at the top of the social pyramid in Mexico, can also be considered *nacos* in relation to metropolitan culture. Even Serna, the white grandson of Spanish immigrants, recognizes that not all types of whiteness confer the same level of privilege. His Mexican nationality also makes him subject to being a *naco*, just as the *criollos* of the colonial era had to accept their innate inferiority to *peninsulares*, no matter how wealthy they might be. This illustrates the extent to which Mexican identity itself is racialized despite the workings of *mestizaje* (Moreno), as well as the extent to which racism is internalized by Mexicans and reproduced in their interpersonal relations. In this sense, everyone in Mexico is a potential *naco*, just like everyone in Mexico is somehow *cursi*. In fact, all Mexican *cursilería* is tinged with *naquez*, inasmuch as it is as an expression of the coloniality of power.

While both Monsiváis and Serna argue in favor of and employ in their work what we might call a *cursi* aesthetics based on a special relation with sentiment, neither one seems to see any reparative possibilities for identifying with the notion of being *naco*—the racist overtones of the term would seem to impede any possibility of positive identification. There have been attempts to appropriate the term for reparative purposes, however. For example, the influential 1980s rock band Botellita de Jerez, whose aesthetic might be described as a kind of punk-rock version of working-class Mexican pop culture, titled their 1987 album *Naco es chido* ["Naco Is Cool"] with an obviously subversive intent.[13] Similarly, in the early 2000s the boutique fashion label NaCo of Tijuana produced a line of t-shirts and other apparel with ironic kitsch appropriations of Mexican "bad taste," such as a shirt with the letters NA/CO stylized like the logo of the Australian rock ban AC/DC, and another one with a portrait of the popular Mexican singer Rigo Tovar. Santos, citing the French sociologist Edmond Goblot, argues that in Latin America the lower classes have, in recent decades, used the imitation of the taste of the bourgeois as a way of challenging their exclusion. In fact, she cites this "creative kitsch" as a reaction to precisely the kind of urban exclusion that Serna sees in the rejection of *naquez* in Mexico, a reaction that the bourgeoisie responds to in the urban space with more segregation (78–79). While the work of Botellita de Jerez might be considered an example of this kind of "creative" kitsch, the clothing line would seem to be more of a middle-class appropriation of working-class culture, albeit one that ironically posits the "least favorable" aspects of national identity as a source of pride.

At any rate, I am less interested in the possibility of *naco* as a positive term of identification and more in how *naquez* appears in the texts that I analyze below as an indicator of the intersection of race with other aspects of identity. As I show in the following chapters, the rejection of *lo naco* by several characters in these works serves to highlight the extent to which they have internalized racism and how it informs their interaction with other characters. In general, *cursilería*, as a "cultural anachronism" related to sentiment that expresses a general sense of marginality from modernity, is more directly connected to gender (and therefore to camp and to expressions of queerness) than *naquez*, although the two concepts do tend to overlap since the feeling of marginality from modernity cannot be divorced from the experience of racism. In general, however, I will most often use the term *cursi* to refer to a specific type of relation to sentiment and *naco* to refer to clear expressions of racism. All three of these types of discourse—camp, *cursilería* and *naquez*—tend to appear as humor in the texts below, and a close attention to how this humor functions is essential to a clear analysis of its meanings in its context of production. But what is humor, and how does it work in Mexico?

Defining Humor

The *Oxford English Dictionary* defines humor as "that quality of action, speech, or writing, which excites amusement; oddity, jocularity, facetiousness, comicality, fun;" as well as "the faculty of perceiving what is ludicrous or amusing, or of expressing it in speech, writing, or other composition." Following this common distinction, I also use the term "humor" to refer to both observable phenomena that can elicit humor as well as the experience itself. In this study, I am concerned with textual humor (with fragments of narratives that can be reasonably expected to elicit the experience of humor in an imagined reader), with the manner in which this humorous effect is achieved, and with the possible social functions of this effect. Western civilization has developed four main types of theories to explain the experience of humor: superiority (such as that of Plato); release (such as that of Freud); incongruity (such as that of Kant); and humor as worldview (such as Bakhtin's theory of carnival culture) (Morreal; Kuipers 380–81). It is now generally accepted that humor derives from the perception of incongruity. The other theories more accurately describe psychological and social functions of humor rather than its cause, which in all cases is ultimately the perception of incongruity.

Two main theories of incongruity underlie my analysis of humor in this book, one that focuses more on the analysis of humorous texts and another that focuses more on the social functions of humor. The first is Raskin's Semantic Script Theory of Humor (SSTH), a linguistic theory that defines humor as the resolution of an incongruity that is the result of the simultaneous perception of two opposing semantic scripts. These scripts are a series of semantic association in the receptor's mind that represent general social rules and assumptions that allow for the comprehension of the world and of texts (Attardo, *Linguistic Theories* 196–204).[14] Although the theory was developed to analyze verbal humor, it can be extended to graphic humor as well, such as Posada's caricatures of the 41. These figures incongruously combine what at Posada's time were generally considered masculine and feminine traits. In figure 1.1, from a broadside published in 1901, we can see the essence of the figure of the ridiculous, effeminate homosexual: mustachioed upper-class men in dresses. In figure 1.2, published several years after the scandal, we can see the clear, continuing association of bourgeois homosexuality and effeminacy (here derided as *"feminismo"*).

Figure 1.1. Detail from a 1901 broadside by José Guadalupe Posada titled "Los 41 Maricones," which includes satirical verses about the event. Source: The Metropolitan Museum of Art, https://www.metmuseum.org/art/collection/search/735325.

Tomo V. Epoca II.　　México, Julio 25 de 1907.　　Año V. Número

DEL PUEBLO Y POR EL PUEBLO.
SEMANARIO INDEPENDIENTE DEFENSOR DE LA CLASE OBRERA.

Director Propietario: **FERNANDO P. TORROELLA**

El feminismo se impone

Mientras la mujer asiste	el-hombre barbilampiño
al taller y á la oficina,	queda haciendo el desayuno
y de casimir se viste.	cose, plancha y cuida al niño
y de la casa desiste	y todos con gran cariño (?)
y entra airosa á la cantina,	le llaman **cuarenta y uno.**

Figure 1.2. José Guadalupe Posada, "El feminismo se impone." In English, the text reads: "The Guacamaya / By the people and for the people / Independent weekly that defends the working class / Owner and director: Fernando P. Torroella / Feminism is imposed / While the woman goes / to the workshop and the office / and dresses in cashmere / and avoids the house / and walks jauntily into the cantina / the smooth-faced man / stays making breakfast / sews, irons and takes care of the baby / and everyone, with great affection (?) / calls him 41." In the themes and illustrations of this working-class paper we can clearly see the association of bourgeois masculinities with effeminacy and homosexuality in the popular art of the time. Source: International Center for the Arts of the Americas at the Museum of Fine Arts, Houston, https://icaa.mfah.org/s/es/item/779764#?c=&m=&s=&cv=&xywh=-2001%2C-245%2C6551%2C3666.

Figure 1.3 shows, following Raskin's conventions for illustrating scripts, what very basic scripts related to hegemonic masculinities and femininities in the minds of Posada's intended audience (turn-of-the-century Mexican working-class people) might look like. The incongruous combination of masculine and feminine scripts in a body that is assumed to be ontologically masculine because of its sex is essentially what makes the figures humorous. There is an element of class satire at work here as well since the figures are dressed in upper-class fashions. However, the central incongruity continues to be the masculine/feminine script opposition. This

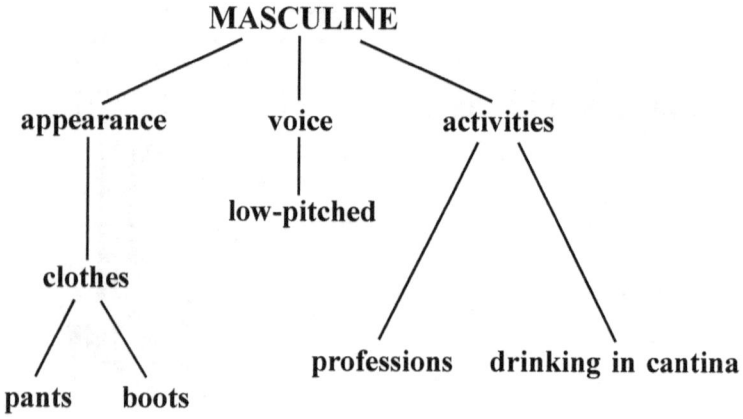

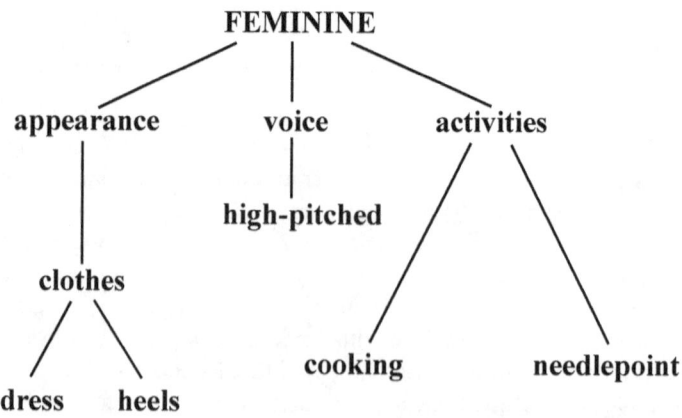

Figure 1.3. Masculine and Feminine Scripts.

is the same basic opposition that underlies much humor based on gender nonconformity, such as that of the effeminate character "La Manigüis" from the sketch comedy show *Desde Gayola*, and that also underlies much of the humor in Salvador Novo's autobiography. While not every humorous aspect of la Manigüis's performances can be explained only by this script opposition, it is the central aspect, I would argue, of the humorousness of that character, which reproduces a stereotyped notion of homosexual men as effeminate. This type of humor, which is based on a gender script opposition, is what I am generally referring to as "camp" humor. Although camp may include many other aspects, gender nonconformity is central to camp signifying as well as to Latin American homosexualities in general (Sifuentes-Jáuregui, *Transvestism*).

A similar opposition is at work in humor based on *lo cursi* and *lo naco*. As we saw above, Santos defines *cursilería* as an expression of marginality with regards to discourses of modernity (74–75), and *naquez* is a similar expression of the coloniality of power that is more explicitly racial. In our analyses, the scripts could be labeled "modern" and "unmodern" since the humor depends on the incongruous juxtaposition of elements associated with a desired modernity (often read as whiteness) and a failed attempt to reach that modernity (associated with a lack of whiteness). In the late 19th century, the modernist writer Manuel Gutiérrez Nájera published a chronicle that made fun of President Porfirio Díaz for drinking from his finger bowl at a ball given for the ministers of Belgium and Portugal (Enrigue 45). Underlying this comic portrayal of Díaz is the opposition of modern and unmodern scripts, based in this case on liberal notions of modernity that equate everything European with modernity and everything autochthonous with backwardness (see figure 1.4). The message is clear: while Díaz may be president of the Republic, he is still an *indio* underneath all that rice powder. He will never be "truly" modern (i.e., white and European). In contemporary terms, he is a *naco*.

While Nájera's chronicle represents a bourgeois perspective, there are examples of working-class humor from the same period that similarly take the upper classes down a notch by reminding them of their own unavoidable Mexican *naquez*. The famous *catrinas* of Posada, which represent elegantly dressed Porfirian-era women as grinning *calaveras*, are one example of this type of humor that sends up the pretensions of wealthy Mexicans who dressed in European fashions by reminding them not only of the democratizing effects of death but also of their unavoidable Indigenous heritage as Mexicans. Posada's caricatures of the 41 also make us aware of this opposition through their association of upper-class

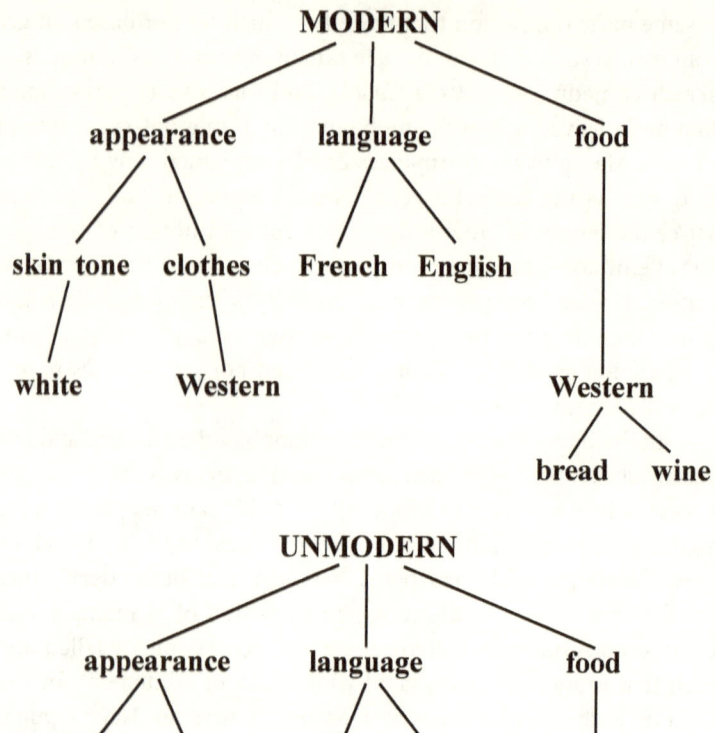

Figure 1.4. Modern and Unmodern Scripts.

fashions (French dresses and hair styles, etc.) with homosexuality and effeminacy. Here we can see the intersection of camp (gender nonconformity) and *cursi* in the ridiculing of these figures. This association of upper-class masculinities with effeminacy was already being made in the penny press before the 41, and it continued after the Revolution as well, notably in public attacks against Salvador Novo and others who were considered effeminate (Buffington 200–12, 220–21). A great deal of the humor in Novo's autobiography relates these notions of class pretension to the performance of gender, as I will demonstrate below. Returning to more recent examples, the plot of one sketch from *Desde Gayola* involves the broke Manigüis being issued a credit card because the bank clerk assumes that all gays have money. Her two friends ask her, respectively, to buy them presents or try to warn her of the consequences of spending money she does not have, thus functioning as foils to her pretension of a consumer lifestyle that is actually out of her reach. This is another example of the intersection of camp and *cursi* humor that can be described with masculine/feminine and modern/unmodern script oppositions.

The second major theory of incongruity that undergirds my analysis is that of sociologist Michael Mulkay, who defines humor as a discursive mode that fulfills the social need to permit interpretative duality and contradiction (35). In this view, humorous discourse opposes, but is ultimately derived from and subordinate to, serious discourse, and both generally serve to help maintain the notion that there is a unitary objective reality in the world (6). A key argument of Mulkay is that incongruities do not need to be resolved in order to result in humor. Rather, they merely need to be accepted (222–23). That means that humor often does not actually resolve anything, but rather allows the simultaneous holding of two or more contradictory perspectives. Although the humorous mode is subordinate to the serious mode, and in most cases serves to uphold rather than undermine the social structure, its focus on the fissures in the worldview bolstered by serious discourse can lead us to question the meanings that happen to be dominant in our society at a particular time and in that sense may be potentially liberating (222).

For example, Posada's caricatures of the 41 may have served, in his time, to help readers accept the incongruities implied by changing gender roles and new discourses on sexuality as well as by Mexico's marginal participation in modernity. Looking at these same works from our perspective, we can read what might seem to us like generally negative portrayals from a positive, celebratory view of the irruption of queerness into Mexican dismodernity at the same time that we critically analyze how they reflect the emerging homophobia of the time. As we saw with queer theory's engagement with camp discourse, the subversive or liberating possibilities of a humorous text depend on how we decide to read it. While Mulkay's theory provides us with a broad understanding of the general social functions of humor, we should also look to theorizations on humorous practices in Mexico to better understand how humor functions in that cultural context.

Humor in Mexico

Some Mexican theorists of humor have focused on the ways that humorous practices in Mexico serve to maintain the dominant social order. This is the general argument about *relajo* (antisolemn, undisciplined and irreverent behavior) put forward by the philosopher Jorge Portilla in his influential essay "Fenomenología del relajo" ["The Suspension of Seriousness"]. Portilla defines *relajo* as a typically Mexican reaction to the proposition of a value to a collective. It consists of a suspension of seriousness that prohibits any real engagement with the value, thereby ultimately contributing to the maintenance of the social status quo. Heavily influenced by existentialism and writing in the 1950s, Portilla seems quite worried that this sort of reaction will prevent serious ethical engagement with the social and political problems of his time.

Writing the late 1980s, Roger Bartra develops Portilla's idea with relation to the mythified figure of the *pelado* (the 20th-century "urban peasant"), for whom *relajo* functions as an escape valve, an "individual revolution" that serves to domesticate potential social subversion and upholds the dominant social structure (182). In both of these perspectives, *relajo*, a humorous practice derived from popular disrespect for corrupt authority in the absence of real political participation, serves to maintain the status quo. In the texts I discuss below, queer characters often practice a sort of *relajo* when they refuse to take themselves or the things around them seriously, an attitude that often intersects with humor based on camp gender nonconformity and *cursilería*. In these cases, we are also faced with the need to consider how *relajo* can be both subversive and conservative with regards to the dominant social order.

Alongside *relajo*, another humorous practice that is frequently associated with Mexican national identity is the *albur*, a type of verbal duel using sexual double-entendres in which the object is to feminize one's opponent by metaphorically penetrating him. Although some women do practice it, the participants are usually men, and the innuendoes are all related to sexual penetration of some kind. The ludic and performative element of the *albur* makes it similar to other types of ritualized comic insult speech, such as the "dozens" in Black US culture, the *peleas por fandangos* (a type of flamenco song) in rural Andalucía, and the act of *chotear* (making fun of someone else) in Cuba and Puerto Rico (Oropesa 49; Muñoz 136). However, *albures* are particularly associated with Mexican culture, and especially with working-class neighborhoods in Mexico City. Armando Jímenez's classic compendium of popular Mexican humor, *Picardía mexicana* ["Mexican Lewdness"], first published in 1958 and re-edited innumerable times, is heavy on *albures* and similar sexual humor, which the author presents as a quintessential part of Mexican culture. This view of *albures* as authentic Mexican expression frequently appears in popular culture and the mass media, with frequent insinuations that they are a sort of anticolonial subversion of standard Spanish.[15] Aside from its origin in Mexico, what really distinguishes the *albur* from other types of ritual insult such as those mentioned above is the preponderance of sexual humor and, especially, of humor related to male homosexuality.

Alongside the more celebratory readings of the *albur* as a source of national pride, it has also been widely criticized for its sexual content, which is generally seen as reinforcing patriarchal values in Mexico. In the first half of the 20th century, the cultural critic Samuel Ramos linked it to the notion of repressed homosexuality in working-class Mexican men (53–54). Octavio Paz, heavily influenced by Ramos, saw the *albur* as an indication of the permissiveness towards the penetrative ("masculine") role in male-male sex in Mexican culture (43). Later, Monsiváis defined the *albur* as a product of the sexual repression operative in Mexican culture that ultimately tends to reinforce male dominance and machismo ("Mexicanerías: el albur"). Recent social scientific studies have also linked the practices to an economy of sexual domination and moral double-standards in low-income communities (González-Block and Liguori) or described it as an expression of homosociality that excludes the feminine and homoerotic in the constitution of hegemonic masculinities (de la Mora 16–17). While other recent readings have explored the ways that the *albur* has been used against dominant social mores about sex and gender (Alzate; Oropeza), it is generally held that the aggressive humor of the *albur*, which has as its aim the denigration of the interlocutor through feminization of that person, upholds both masculine dominance and the rejection of the feminine and male homosexuality. Furthermore, as Enrique Serna has astutely observed, *albures* serve the social function of reducing anxiety about homosexuality within this generally heteronormative framework. They are, he ironically argues, "un pasatiempo inocente que hasta cierto punto minimiza la afrenta de ser penetrado, pues de tanto jugar con esa posibilidad, los albureros llegan a restarle importancia'" ["an innocent pastime that to a certain extent minimizes the affront of being penetrated, since by playing so much with that possibility, the practitioners of *albures* remove all importance from it"] (26).

Relajo, *albures* and other types of humor are analyzed in Rafael Barajas's study of the culture of humor in Mexico, *Sólo me río cuando me duele* ["I Only Laugh When It Hurts"]. Barajas, better known by his pen name, El Fisgón [The Snoop, Busybody, or Gossip], is a cartoonist and author whose darkly satirical work focuses on the various types of violence, corruption, and human rights abuses that are common in Mexico. The title of his book, a reordering of the phrase "sólo me duele cuando me río" [it only hurts when I laugh], uttered by mortally wounded machos in anecdotes portraying the proverbial Mexican indifference toward death,[16] sums up the author's view of the culture of humor in Mexico as an adaptation to an often brutal reality. Starting from Freud's essay "On Humour," which posits that self-referential and gallows humor is a way that the superego allows the ego to overcome negative emotions, Barajas argues that much of Mexico's dark humor ("sick jokes," satirical literature, cartoons like his, etc.) functions as a way of coping with social ills such as corruption, poverty, disenfranchisement, and oppression (16–19, 215–18). While he generally argues for seeing the subversive possibilities of this type of humor, he also recognizes that humor can uphold the dominant social structure, as he argues in his analysis of *machista* humor, such as jokes that denigrate women and homosexual men (103–62).

Notably, however, Barajas goes against mainstream interpretations of both *relajo* and *albures*, preferring to signal what he sees as the subversive potentialities in both, rather than their respective functions as social "escape valve" or expression of machismo and homophobia (170–75, 192–213, 221). While I disagree with his assertion that *albures* are subversive simply because they are obscene, I am more inclined to accept his notion that *relajo* can be a destabilizing practice, and I respect his decision to focus on the subversive possibilities of these Mexican practices of humor. Barajas is, of course, acutely aware of the historical context that has produced the culture of humor in Mexico. He relates all the practices of humor that he describes to the historical experience of Mexico as a postcolonial society situated in the Global South and puts gender inequality (described as *machismo*, or the cultural expression of patriarchy) at the center of his social critique (215–18). In other words, he shows that humorous practices such as dark humor, *machista* humor, *el relajo*, and *albures* are expressions of the social contradictions that arise from Mexico's history and from the continued influence of the coloniality of power, gender, and sex in Mexican society.

In this context, humor can serve the often-overlapping social functions of expressing a sense of superiority, upholding the social structure, transcending negative affect and constructing imagined communities (including the nation itself). I find similar social functions in the camp and *cursi* humor from the texts that I analyze below, and I argue that this humor, like that analyzed by Barajas, also expresses social contradictions that arise in the history of Mexico. By making reference to the script oppositions underlying this humor and by focusing on the destabilizing potential of its inherent ambiguity, I am able to read the humor in these texts reparatively, as a discourse that allows the transcendence of negative affect and the construction of communities, and in a more paranoid fashion as a discourse that illuminates social injustice. I will now examine Salvador Novo's autobiography as an example of the intersection of camp and *cursi* humor, with particular attention to how it has been read by Carlos Monsiváis, whose analysis provides a paradigm for combining paranoid and reparative perspectives of the text.

Salvador Novo: *La estatua de sal*

Salvador Novo was a major literary and cultural figure in 20th-century Mexico. Born in 1904, he was part of the generation that came of age soon after the Mexican Revolution. Novo was a precocious poet as a young man, a member of the Contemporáneos ["Contemporaries"] literary group (named after their eponymous magazine) along with others, including Xavier Villarrutia and Jorge Cuesta. He held many public educational and cultural posts in his youth and later developed a successful career in advertising and journalism that allowed him to subsidize his poetry and dramaturgical work. By the 1940s, he was an established personality in the world of Mexican theater and in the local press, where he contributed greatly to the development of the hybrid journalistic-literary *crónica* genre. His cultural presence was institutionalized in 1965 when he was named official chronicler of Mexico City by President Díaz Ordaz. Novo's proximity to this president apparently led him to express support for the violent oppression of the student movement in 1968. Ostracized by the student movement and the political left, but still a well-known society figure, Novo died in 1974 at the age of 69.

Although Novo's closeness to the Mexican establishment in his later life tarnished his reputation, Carlos Monsiváis spearheaded an effort to recover him as a pioneering figure of sexual dissidence through the editing and publication of his autobiography, which I consider below, and in a book focused on Novo's biographical and literary legacy: *Salvador Novo: Lo marginal en el centro* ["Salvador Novo: The Marginal in the Center"]. For Monsiváis, Novo's dissidence is reflected in his open admission of his homosexuality during most of his life and the way that much of his work reflects this identity. Novo's early life intersected with the emergence of a queer subculture in Mexico City in the first decades of the 20th century, a result, in part, of the crisis of values brought on by the Revolution and the growth of the capital city (Monsiváis, "Introduction" 13–14). At the same time, however, the official culture promoted by the post-Revolutionary government espoused a narrowly-defined hegemonic masculinity associated with war and traditional *machismo* (15). Novo's unapologetic and transgressively public queerness, along with the generally cosmopolitan aesthetic orientation of himself and the other Contemporáneos, were characteristics singled out by his many detractors. The Contemporáneos were the target of many attacks that often conflated judgments of their purported sexual orientation (they were not all homosexual, but all were considered guilty by association) with that of their literary production.[17]

One example of this is the famous literary polemic in 1925 that gave rise to the subgenre of the "novel of the Revolution" by opposing "effeminate" literature (implicitly the modern, experimental and cosmopolitan poetry of the Contemporáneos) to "virile" literature such as Azuela's novel *Los de abajo* [*The Underdogs*] (Monsiváis, *Salvador Novo* 74). The year before that, the group had also been the object of satire in an issue of *El Machete* ["The Machete"], the Mexican Communist Party's magazine, where José Clemente Orozco depicted them in an engraving as a group of effeminate bourgeois men grabbing each other's bottoms (164–69). The title of this little cartoon was "Los anales," which is a pun that can mean both "the annals" and "the anal ones." This caricature demonstrates how the longstanding association of bourgeois masculinities with effeminacy and homosexuality (which we saw above in the earlier works by Posada about the 41) had become part of Revolutionary culture (Buffington 200–12, 220–21). The deviation of the *anales* from hegemonic masculinities and cultural nationalism is expressed humorously in the combination of camp (effeminate) and *cursi* (attempting to be "elegant") aspects of the figures, which center on masculine/feminine and modern/unmodern script oppositions.

Probably the most outspoken member of the Contemporáneos, Novo did not suffer this type of discrimination quietly. He resisted in part by fashioning a queer persona that emphasized an exaggerated gender non-conformity redolent of the stereotypes used against him: "[era] un practicante del 'afeminamiento,' que al subrayarlo satisfac[ía] y casi anula[ba] las expectativas del voyeurismo social" (Monsiváis, "El mundo soslayado" 60) ["he [was] a practitioner of 'effeminacy' and the emphasis he place[d] on this satisfie[d] and nearly annul[ed] the expectations of social voyeurism"]. He also made use of a poison pen: throughout his life, Novo composed many satirical poems (mostly sonnets) in which he attacked friends, foes and himself in the most cruel and erudite manner. A feud with Diego Rivera led to the painter caricaturing him as a decadent ally of the ruling classes in one of his murals, but also to a whole series of poems by Novo, "La Diegada," which were filled with ad hominem attacks on the painter that emphasized how his ex-wife Guadalupe Marín had left him for Jorge Cuesta. In another poem, he satirizes his friend Xavier Villarrutia, whom he calls a *puta* [whore], and in yet another, he makes fun of his own flabby body, sexual proclivities and supposed lack of talent.[19] He composed these poems throughout his life, sharing them with friends and acquaintances, but rarely publishing them in magazines or book form.[20]

For the poet and scholar Luis Felipe Fabre, these bawdy poems "conforman uno de los proyectos más radicales de la poesía hispanoamericana del siglo XX bajo la apariencia de una obra menor y de circunstancia" ["make up one of the most radical projects of 20th-century Spanish American poetry, hidden under the appearance of a minor and circumstantial oeuvre"] (39). Fabre reads Novo's sonnets and autobiography as antiliterature that uses scatological humor to radically disrupt canons of taste that exclude the homosexual. For Monsiváis, this type of self-deprecating and aggressive humor, in combination with his public persona, makes Novo an Oscar Wilde-esque figure who is a precursor of gay culture in Mexico: "En lo internacional y en más de un sentido, como imagen adjudicable, el gay surge de los procesos de Oscar Wilde, que hacen visible al *Otro*. Y en México, con Novo empieza de modo ostensible la sensibilidad gay" ["Internationally and in more than one sense, as an attributable figure, the gay arises from the trials of Oscar Wilde, which make the *Other* visible. And in Mexico, gay sensibility ostensibly begins with Novo"] (*Salvador Novo* 12). Though my own reading of Novo leans more towards a recognition of the transgressive queerness implied by Fabre than the genealogy of gay identity politics traced by Monsiváis, I do recognize that the latter's analysis of Novo's humor balances, in a productive way, paranoid and reparative approaches to it.

This biting sense of humor is very present in Novo's autobiography *La estatua de sal* [*The Pillar of Salt*], which is full of salacious gossip about the queer underworld of Mexico City in the 1920s. The book was written in the 1930s and 40s, published piecemeal in gay-themed magazines in

Mexico and the US in the 1970s and 1980s, and finally published in its entirety by the Mexican state publisher Conaculta (Consejo Nacional para la Cultura y las Artes [National Council for Culture and Arts]) in 1998. The *Advertencia* ["Note"] at the beginning of the book indicates that the long-delayed publication of the text was seen as a crucial and missing part of the complete works of Novo, by then considered an important cultural and literary figure. I have chosen to focus on this text in particular, rather than on the analysis of Novo's sonnets, in order to explore how the author's narrative self-portrayal uses camp and *cursi* humor in the constitution of a persona and subjectivity that are both queer and Mexican. For Monsiváis, Novo represents both the internalization of discrimination based on gender and sexuality as well as the first true representation of sexual dissidence in modern Mexico. As we will see, this ambivalence towards gender norms intersects with an equally ambivalent notion of dismodern, racialized Mexicanness in Novo's strategic use of comic *cursilería*.

This humor is largely satirical, and its targets include Novo himself as well as others. Monsiváis describes this humor as largely based on camp, with a self-deprecating element that betrays the internalization of the discrimination of the dominant social structure ("Introduction" 29–34). Novo repurposes the comic stereotype of the effeminate *joto* [fag] in his portrayal of the queer subculture of 1920s Mexico City, as well as in the elaboration of his own persona. Humor based on *lo cursi*, understood in Monsiváis's terms as cultural anachronism, also forms a part of this portrayal. These two types of humor, based respectively on the opposition of masculine and feminine and modern and un-modern scripts, intersect in Novo's satirical portrayal of himself and other homosexual men. The narrator's obvious ambivalence towards both the feminine as well as *lo cursi* (understood above all as the discourse of open sentiment) leads to a tension in his subjectivity that reflects social conflicts surrounding the emergence of sexual dissidence in 20th-century Mexico.

La estatua de sal is narrated in the first person by Salvador Novo, who presents the reader with the confessional recollections of his childhood, adolescence, and early adulthood, during which time he gradually becomes aware of his sexual orientation, begins to have sexual encounters, and participates in the emerging homosexual subculture of Mexico City. Parallel to his sociosexual development is his discovery of his vocation as a writer, which begins in early childhood and ends with his professionalization as a journalist, educator and published writer interacting with other intellectual figures such as Xavier Villarrutia, Jaime Torres Bodet,

Jorge Cuesta and Pedro Henríquez Ureña. Much of the satirical humor in this book derives from the incongruous superposition of masculine and feminine scripts in one body. Such is Novo's depiction of his friend and initiator into the homosexual subculture of Mexico City, Ricardo Alessio Robles, alias Clarita Vidal, who would suddenly burst into song in the street, singing arias that demonstrated a "gracia operática deliberadamente grotesca que hacía olvidar, que desvanecía por completo la virilidad de su barba cerradísima" ["deliberately grotesque operatic grace that made one forget, that completely dispelled, the virility of his thick beard"] (149).[18] Novo also relates that Clarita would often appear at the office workplaces of his *amigas* ["girlfriends," i.e., male homosexual friends] and get them out of working for an afternoon in order to

> *putear*, lo cual consistía en contonearse con *ellas* por las calles, piropear atrevidamente—y a veces, con inmediata eficacia—a los hombres, en cuya cara soltaba, mirándolos, un cógeme que solía dejarles alelados, y si los hacía volverse a reclamar, él afrontaba con una súbitamente recuperada virilidad, para preguntarles si traían aretes y si se habían creído dignos de semejante invitación.
>
> [go *whoring* with him, which consisted of swishing through the streets with them, brazenly flirting with—sometimes to immediate effect—the men, in whose faces he would blurt out, looking right at them, a "fuck me" that would leave them dazed, and that if it led them to complain, he would confront with a suddenly recovered virility, in order to ask them if they were wearing earrings and if they had thought themselves worthy of such an invitation.] (150)

This caricatured depiction of Clara Vidal's exaggerated, camp gender parody demonstrates how the comic stereotype of the homosexual man as incongruously effeminate could be appropriated as part of a provocative gesture of disidentification with mainstream values. Novo himself exhibits a similar attitude when he relates with pride how Clarita presented him in queer society as his *sobrina* [niece] (150), that he, Xavier Villarrutia, and Gustavo Villa were known as "las chicas de Donceles" [the girls from Donceles Street] (166), and that he was capable of admitting the largest masculine members into his anus, in what Robert Irwin has read as a sort of inversion of traditional machismo (Novo 170; Irwin, "La Pedo Embotellado").

Clarita Vidal, who gave him/herself this nickname, is particularly talented with regards to the bestowing of humorous and somewhat cruel monikers, such as *la Nalga que Aprieta* [The Clenching Ass Cheek, a humorous substitution of the common expression "la mano que aprieta" (the grasping hand)], *la Madre Meza* [Mother Meza], *Sor Demonio* [Sister Devil], *La Golondrina* [The Swallow] and *La Virgen de Estambul* [The Virgin of Istanbul] (151, 162–63). Monsiváis considers such feminizing names to be an example of the type of self-deprecating humor that Novo blandished as a response to discrimination and that shows not only resistance, but also a certain level of internalization of the notion of one's own inferiority:

> En la mecánica del ghetto, común a todas las minorías acosadas, el vituperio de sí y el ultraje a los semejantes mediatiza el filo de exterminio de los epítetos machistas "Lo que me digan yo ya me lo dije pero con la elegancia, la ironía y la malicia que ustedes desconocen."
>
> [In the mechanism of the ghetto, common to all oppressed minorities, offending oneself and insulting one's fellows mitigates the exterminating edge of homophobic epithets: "Whatever you may say to me I've already said to myself, but with the elegance, the irony and the malice of which you are ignorant."]
> ("Manos" 25–26)

Here, Monsiváis signals the unresolvable tension in the disidentification with social norms that Novo's camp humor uses as its raw material while also suggesting possible paranoid and reparative readings of the text: while this humor does reflect internalized heteronormativity and machismo, it is also a way of personally transcending the pain of discrimination and constituting a community based on similar experiences, as fragmented and riven by individualism as that community might be. Part of this negative individualism that Monsiváis describes is Novo's apparent rejection of the possibility of love, which is manifested in the text in an almost total rejection of sentiment.

Novo's disdain for sentiment is apparent in his satirical, caricatured depiction of his first lover in Mexico City, Enrique Tovar Ávalos, who is portrayed as *cursi* in his recycling of romanticized discourses of sentimentality and in his pathetic attempts to emulate European elegance. An effete dandy in the street, Tovar Ávalos (later nicknamed *la Perra Collie* [The Collie Bitch] by Clara) is actually an impoverished, mediocre dramatist who lives off of young women with illusions of becoming actresses. Novo describes his morning routine, which includes a meticulous *toilette* during which he sings arias from *La Bohème*:

> *Chi son? Sono un poeta—che cosa facio—scrivo—e come vivo—VIVO—*, y al pronunciar este *vivo*, encogía los hombres y cargaba el vocablo con toda la sincera amargura de quien verdaderamente no sabe cómo va pasando los días, entre el vencimiento del alquiler de su cuarto y el abono a las comidas de la fonda a que después de acicalarse yo le acompañaba a tomar un tardío y frugal desayuno que cancelaba la necesidad de gastar en almuerzo.
>
> [*Chi son? Sono un poeta—che cosa facio—scrivo—e come vivo— VIVO—*, and as he pronounced that final *vivo*, he would shrug his shoulders and load the word with all the sincere bitterness of one who really does not know how he survives from day to day, between the rent coming due for his room and the tab for his meals in the cheap restaurant where after getting dressed up I would accompany him for a late and frugal breakfast that would eliminate the need to spend any money on lunch.] (145)

Novo, seduced by the promise of starring in a film he soon realizes will never be made, eventually abandons Tovar. The latter takes revenge by informing young Salvador's uncle (the patriarch of the family) that his nephew is a homosexual. Novo resolves to murder Tovar before an arranged personal confrontation of the three can take place, but upon arriving at his ex-lover's dwelling, he finds him broken down and pathetically apologetic: "Se echó a mis pies [. . . y] sollozaba, pálido, suplicante, miserable, transfigurado. Frente a su lamentable figura, mis absurdos propósitos asesinos se diluyeron en el más indiferente desprecio" ["He threw himself at my feet [. . . and] sobbed, pale, supplicant, miserable, transfigured. Faced with his lamentable figure, my absurd plans of murder dissolved into the most indifferent contempt"] (154–55).

These descriptions paint Tovar as *cursi*, in the sense that he aspires to be what he is not (a wealthy dandy, a successful dramatist, actor, and film director) and openly displays sentiment in a melodramatic fashion. Although Novo does not explicitly mention the notion of modernity as related to his satirical portrayal of Tovar, his behaviors clearly set up a script opposition in which we can read an incongruous combination of notions associated with bourgeois modernity (purchasing power, Europe, cynicism) with the unmodern (poverty, Mexico, sentimentality). However, even more than with nonmodernity, there would seem to be an association of sentimentality with effeminacy, a characteristic that Novo both rejects and embraces at the same time.

Just as Novo's humorous portrayals of self and others demonstrate a generally negative evaluation of the feminine, his text also betrays an ambivalent relationship to *cursilería* understood as a sort of effeminate, poetic expression of sentiment. This is clear in his use of somewhat trite poetic language to describe some of his early erotic experiences, such as a kiss from another boy:

> Se inició quizá en un choque, tan repentino y sin embargo tan maduro como la eclosión de una rosa que ha sido largamente un botón [. . .] lo único que ha quedado indeleblemente grabado en mi recuerdo, es el furtivo instante en que Jorge me llamó al camerino en que se maquillaba de anciano para recitar sus "Recuerdos de un veterano," y sujetando mi cabeza entre sus manos, oprimió sus labios húmedos contra los míos [. . .] sólo ahora veía los ojos oblicuos y negros, la piel blanca y tersa, la boca roja dueña de mi dulce secreto.
>
> [It began perhaps with a shock, as sudden and yet as mature as the blossoming of a rose that has long been a bud [. . .] the only thing that has remained indelibly engraved in my memory is the furtive moment when Jorge called me to the dressing room in which he was making himself up as an old man in order to recite the "Memories of a veteran" and, grasping my head in his hands, pressed his moist lips to mine [. . .] only now did I see the black, slanted eyes, the white and smooth skin, the red mouth that owned my sweet secret.] (105)

Monsiváis has argued that the wellspring of *cursi*, melodramatic language in contemporary Mexican culture is the 19th-century bourgeois practice of reading and reciting neoclassical, romantic, and modernist poetry, of which

Juan de Dios Peza, author of "Recuerdos de un veterano," ["Recollections of a Veteran"] is one of the most important figures ("La cursilería" 15). This type of *cursi* discourse was the foundation of the sentimental education of the young Novo, who, in his autobiography, parodically reinscribes this language in order to evoke nostalgic memories of his youth. Given Novo's ironically self-deprecating tone in the entire autobiography, this use of *cursi* language should also be read as ironic or tongue-in-cheek. In this sense, *cursilería* forms a part of the camp persona that Novo creates in his texts and public appearances, contributing to his gender nonconformity.

In this way, Novo's appropriation of *cursi* discourse prefigures the recycling of melodramatic *cursilería* gleaned from the mass media that Lidia Santos reads in the works of late 20th-century writers like Severo Sarduy and Manuel Puig and that I also find in the works of Mexican authors such as Luis Zapata, José Joaquín Blanco, and Gilda Salinas. These later texts portray an ambivalent orientation towards *cursilería*, parodying and exposing its contradictions while at the same time celebrating it, sometimes with fondness and nostalgia. Similarly, Novo's use of *cursi* language to describe his youth is ambiguous—he both pokes fun at this sort of discourse through a parody that forms part of his cynical, nonserious, camp persona, at the same time that he imbues it with a certain nostalgia. Thus, his attitude towards *cursi* language is similar to that expressed by the Spanish poet Ramón Gómez de la Serna in his seminal essay on the topic, in which he distinguishes between *cursi malo* [bad *cursi*] (the kitschy imitation of refined style) and *cursi bueno* [good *cursi*] (fond nostalgia for naïve sentimentality). Such ambiguity reflects the importance of *cursi* rhetoric to Mexican and Latin American identity which, in the case of Novo, intersects with his sexual dissidence.

It also intersects with his racial identity, another point where Novo's self-deprecating descriptions of himself mine a humor based on a modern/unmodern script opposition that reflects the coloniality of power in Mexico. The racism endemic to Mexican society, while not openly discussed by Novo, is evident in various passages. For example, among the cruel nicknames Clara Vidal bestows on the homosexuals of Mexico City is that of "Emma Moreno," whom Novo describes as indeed being "excessively" *moreno* [brown or dark-skinned] (149). Salvador also tends to remark on the skin tone of the people he describes in physical terms, usually as either *moreno*, *blanco* [white], or *pálido* [pale], which clearly reflects the racial hierarchy in Mexican society (156, 158, 163, 164, 167, 168, 169, 174, 176, 177, 179, 183). Novo himself was the son of a Spanish immigrant and a mestiza Mexican woman and appeared phenotypically more European than Indigenous, a fact that most certainly contributed to his relative social privilege. He folds references to this heritage into his self-presentation by opposing the decadent and sickly aspects of his physique, inherited from his father, to the healthy and vigorous corporality of his mother. In contrast to her middle-aged son, she still has all her teeth, which are "admirablemente blancos, parejos y firmes" ["admirably white, straight and strong"] and maintains "abundante y negro un cabello que se solaza desafiante en cepillar con vigor frente a mi calvicie; sin arrugas su piel morena" ["abundant and black a head of hair that she insolently takes pleasure in vigorously brushing in the face of my baldness; her brown skin free of wrinkles"] (112). In comparison to this vigor, his father, who died from tuberculosis at a relatively young age "fue siempre pálido, delgado" ["was always pale, thin"] (112).

This is not a rejection of his European heritage by any means, but rather a proud appropriation of it through an ironic privileging of decadence similar to the exaltation of his own homosexuality, promiscuity, and effeminacy. Here Novo effects something similar to what Sylvia Molloy has described as the *modernista* appropriation of European decadence as a mode of regenerating regional aesthetics (191). As Molloy notes, this translation of decadence is "patchy and uneven." For example, the influence of Latin American heteronormativity explains why writers like Martí and Darío seem to be horrified by Oscar Wilde's camp persona and his homosexuality (187–92). In contrast, Novo looks to writers like Wilde and Gide as models precisely because of their decadent queerness. His own queer identity, of course, also reflects the coloniality of power and sex. For example, while enjoying the privileges of whiteness, he fetishizes brown skin and his favorite sexual partners are working-class bus and taxi drivers with whom he never forms any sort of sentimental attachment. In a typical anecdote, he describes the penis of the first driver he ever has sex with, his uncle's chauffeur, as being "de un hermoso color moreno" ["of a beautiful brown color"] (135). While Novo takes pains to mention that this encounter leads him to develop a paraphelia focused on the smell of gasoline, his almost offhand description of the brown phallus clearly points to his conflicted notions about racial identity.

This uncomfortable recognition of *mestizo* heritage also finds expression in Novo's parody of the cultural nationalism that was in vogue in the 1920s. He describes how he and his friends decorated the studio apartment that they used for their sexual encounters: "Un idolillo nalgón, a quien llamábamos San Polencho, colgaba a la cabecera del *couch* o 'piedra de los sacrificios' a presidir las escenas. Y un nacionalismo extremado me indujo a emplear una jícara pequeña como el depósito más a tono de la vaselina necesaria para los ritos" ["A big-assed idol, whom we called San Polencho, hung from the headboard of the couch or 'sacrifical altar' to preside over the scenes. And an extreme nationalism induced me to employ a gourd as a more appropriate container for the vaseline that was needed for the rites"] (166). Novo and his friends' humorous appropriation of contemporary Mexican kitsch actually renders these nationalist clichés camp, as they become expressions of queerness.

There is a similar queering of Mexican kitsch in Cristina Rivera Garza's 1999 novel *Nadie me verá llorar* [*No One Will See Me Cry*]. At one point before the Revolution, the protagonist Matilda Burgos comes to work in the high-class bordello "La Modernidad," run by the cross-dressing Madame Porfiria. The décor features the work of Eurocentric decadentist Mexican painters like Julio Ruelas and Ángel Zárraga alongside kitschy local details such as "estatuillas de sospechosa ascendencia maya y bajor-relieves con la figura de Cuauhtémoc" ["little statues of dubious Mayan provenance and bas-reliefs with the figure of Cuauhtémoc"] (180). Like Novo and his friends, here the Mexican elite comes to imagine itself in a sort of Orientalist paradise:

> Al terminar la función, saludaban a Porfiria y luego, con unas copas de champaña entre los dedos, se dedicaban a lucir tan modernos como sus cuerpos y el color de su piel se los permitían. Las conversaciones en francés eran comunes y también lo eran los cigarrillos de hachís, las lengüetas de opio y los narguiles para fumar marihuana.
>
> [After the show, they would greet Porfiria and then, with glasses of champagne between their fingers, they would be as modern as their bodies and the color of their skin would allow them to be. Conversations in French were common, as were hashish cigarettes, opium pipes and hookahs for smoking marijuana.] (181)

The humor at work in both Novo and Rivera Garza's works can be described as a modern/unmodern script opposition since sexual dissidence is here associated with European whiteness and cosmopolitanism at the same time that there is an ironic acknowledgment of the Latin American positionality of those participating in the transgression of social norms. In the case of Novo, this tongue-in-cheek reference to nationalism goes hand in hand with his literary *cursilería* as part of the expression of his dismodern, *mestizo* Mexican queerness.

In *La estatua de sal*, the use of humor based on a masculine/feminine script opposition (camp), and on a modern/unmodern script opposition (*lo cursi*) allows us to approach the text's conflicted attitudes towards gender, race and modernity from both paranoid and reparative perspectives. While Novo's camp gender parody undoubtedly betrays the internalization and reiteration of machismo, it also provides the possibility for a transcendence of discrimination through self-effacing humor and the constitution of dissident communities. The tension between these two positions cannot be resolved, inasmuch as it reflects the necessary use of the language of heteronormativity in order to express queerness. Similarly, Novo's ambiguous portrayal of *cursilería* can be seen as both ironically satirizing its pretensions and anachronisms and constituting it, through nostalgia, as a central part of his identity. Another part of this identity is a conflicted racial consciousness that finds expression in Novo's self-deprecating descriptions of his own *mestizo* body, sexual proclivities, and kitschy decorating style. Novo's entire self-presentation, then, can be understood as a disidentification with the dominant cultural nationalism, infused with *machismo*, of his time. As we will see in the following chapters, the use of camp and *cursi* humor to disidentify with dominant social structures becomes an increasingly common theme in Mexican literature on queer themes as the 20th century ends and the 21st begins.

Chapter 2

Homosexuales de Corazón

Humor, Homophobia, and How to be a Man at the End of the 20th Century

Novo's autobiography, the most explicit literary portrayal of his sexuality, was not published widely and completely until decades after his death. This delay reflects, in part, the difficulty in publishing portrayals of queer sexualities in Mexican literature during most of the 20th century. I do not mean to suggest that this never occured. For example, Novo's collection of poetry *Nuevo amor* ["New Love"] (1933) and Villarrutia's *Nocturnos* ["Nocturns"] (1936) both contain obvious metaphorical allusions to homoeroticism, and Novo did publish, in magazines, books, or personal editions, many of his obviously homoerotic poems (Balderston and Quiroga 45, 58; Monsiváis, *Salvador Novo* 112–15). However, these portrayals of homoerotic themes used metaphorical, poetic language that may have been more acceptable to publishers and the general public at the time. This does not mean that the more "realistic" representations characteristic of much narrative are somehow more authentic than more figurative poetic expressions. For example, Quiroga argues convincingly that Villarrutia's poetry of the 1930s is just as queer as anything published in more recent decades, if not more so (19, 52). I agree with Quiroga's insistence on reading the queer aspects of this poetry that tend to undermine the very notion of stable identity as this perspective can illuminate not only the context in which the poetry was produced but also our own contemporary society. In the works that I analyze below, I will similarly focus on the ways that clearly-defined, more "modern" notions of sexual identity tend to slip away from the protagonists as they embody contemporary social conflicts. The narrative texts that portray this process are not inherently "better" than poetry or narrative from earlier decades, but they do portray a different time period in which social conflicts are expressed in different terms, notably through narratives that depict sexuality more openly and with a high frequency of humor.

Speaking of narrative, it would seem that for most of the 20th century, homosexuality is an acceptable theme for the genre in Mexico as long as the portrayal is negative. Homosexuality begins to appear as a theme right after the case of the 41 (in naturalist novels condemning it), and by the 1950s, it appears in canonical literature as a typical (if unsavory) part of Mexican life, notably in Carlos Fuentes's seminal novel *La región más transparente* [*Where the Air Is Clear*], which offers a panoramic critique of contemporary Mexican society (Irwin, *Mexican* 200). It is not until the 1960s that narrative texts with relatively sympathetic portrayals of homosexual protagonists begin to appear. According to Luis Mario Schneider, *El diario de José Toledo* ["The Diary of José Toledo"] (1964), by Miguel Barbachano Ponce, was the first such text, soon followed by other works such as *41 o el muchacho que soñaba en fantasmas* ["41, Or the Boy Who Dreamed of Ghosts"] by Paolo Po (1964); *Después de todo* ["After All"] by José Ceballos Maldonado (1969); *Cielo tormentoso* ["Stormy Sky"] by Carlos Valdemar (1972); and *Mocambo* by Alberto Dallal (1976).[1]

It is at this point that Luis Zapata's novel *Las aventuras, desventuras y sueños de Adonis García, el vampiro de la colonia Roma* (1979) [*Adonis García: A Picaresque Novel*] appears. *Vampiro* achieved a notoriety and popularity unmatched by any previous Mexican novel dealing with themes of sexual dissidence. In 1979 it was awarded the Juan Grijalbo literary prize and became, due to its subject matter, a source of polemics in academic circles and the press. Blanco has argued that this controversy derived from an initial rejection of the text's dignified treatment of homosexuality but that the critical and commercial success that it garnered ultimately allowed queer-themed literature to transcend the gay "ghetto" of Mexico and become part of the wider national literary tradition (Blanco, *Crónica* 547–49).[2] The commercial and critical success of the novel is evidenced by its continuous reprintings, the relatively large critical bibliography that focuses on it (only part of which is cited here), and official public recognition of its importance (such as a series of conferences held to commemorate the 30th and 40th anniversaries of its publication in 2009 and 2019, respectively).

Vampiro was a watershed not only because of its popularity but also due to the relatively unproblematic way that the main character narrated his sexuality, which contrasted with the existential pessimism of many earlier works on homosexual themes. This aspect of the novel has been compared to the parallel trend of the deproblematizing of homosexuality in North American gay fiction of the 1970s and would seem to indicate a cultural shift in Mexico regarding perceptions of sexuality (Westmoreland 45). For Schneider, the main indicator of this change in *Vampiro* is the high frequency of self-referential humor, which he considers to be the expression of a mature homosexual culture coming to terms with itself (87–88). José Joaquín Blanco reacts to the novel in a similar way, noting how the negative elements of the narration (which portray the alienation of the protagonist) do not negate the positive aspects of the text: "La novela—hecha de miseria, carnalidad desesperada, enfermedades, hambres, persecuciones, desamparos, aspectos de nota roja, etc.—resulta, como por arte de magia, una de las más alegres y *positivas* que recuerdo" ["The novel—made of poverty, desperate carnality, sickness, hunger, persecution, helplessness, sensationalistic details, etc.—turns out to be, as if by magic, one of the most cheerful and *positive* ones that I can remember"] (*Crónica* 544). Both Blanco and Schneider, in other words, focus on the reparative possibilities that *Vampiro* holds for readers, and especially readers who identify with the protagonist because of their sexual orientation.

I agree with Schneider's suggestion that the key to reading the novel reparatively is to focus on its use of humor. Although Zapata's work portrays the depression, substance use, and marginalization of the main character and includes an ambiguous ending that could be interpreted as tragic, the frequency of humor is nonetheless striking in comparison with earlier Mexican novels featuring homosexual protagonists, such as *El diario de José Toledo*. As Schneider suggests, after *Vampiro*, humor does indeed begin to appear in Mexican literature on queer themes with more frequency. But this does not mean that after this point all portrayals of homosexuality in Mexican literature have been humorous. For example, Blanco's best-known novel, *Las púberes canéforas* ["The Pubescent Canephores"] (1983), has an overall dark and tragic tone, although it does contain many examples of humor. Nevertheless, there is a greater frequency of humor in sympathetic treatments of male homosexuality after *Vampiro* in works such as José Rafael Calva's *Utopía gay* ["Gay Utopia"] (1985), which Schneider cites as another example of a work that employs humor in a reparative fashion as part of a positive, sympathetic portrayal of homosexual characters.

In this chapter I will consider Zapata's *Vampiro* alongside *Utopía gay*. Though much less well known than the former work, Calva's novel is an important expression of queer subjectivity from the same period that, like *Vampiro*, deals with themes of sexual dissidence, gender, and modernity through camp and *cursi* humor. Both of these novels contain portrayals of sexual dissidence and gender nonconformity that dialogue with anxieties about modernity, consumerism, and the relation of gender roles and norms to sexual dissidence in Mexico in the late 1970s.[3] Generally speaking, they show characters whose rejection of camp and *cursilería* in the constitution of their own subjectivities belies a very conflicted relationship with their positionalities as homosexual men in Latin America. These aspects point us inexorably towards paranoid readings that reflect on how these characters embody social conflicts and contradictions. At the same time, their use of humor can lead readers to a reparative identification with the characters and their situations that focuses on the uses of humor in order to constitute empathy and collectives in the Mexican context.

There is a relatively large critical corpus that focuses on *Vampiro*, and I do not intend to engage with all of that criticism here.[4] Instead, I will take as a starting point some readings that point out certain ideological similarities between *Vampiro* and *Utopía gay*. For Schneider, these two texts represent a paradigm shift in literature on homosexual themes, away from pessimism and towards a more positive homosexual or gay identity expressed through humor (87–88). Undoubtedly, this perspective is influenced by contemporary political organization around sexual dissidence as an identity category and the concurrent liberalization of Mexican society. Claudia Schaefer's reading of these novels in her book *Danger Zones* complements Schneider's broad view with a more detailed look at the socioeconomic context in which the texts were produced. Schaefer reads the books side-by-side as postmodern "critical utopias" that satirize the rising consumer society of late-1970s Mexico and suggest oppositional strategies of social organization based on homoerotic bodily pleasure (37–58). Generally speaking, this perspective situates these novels as literature that expresses anxieties about how the rise of consumer culture in Mexico interacts with emerging movements of sexual dissidence. Schneider's comments focus overwhelmingly on the reparative possibilities of these texts, while Schaefer tends towards a more paranoid reading that focuses on social critique (although she does mention bodily pleasure in a reparative manner as a starting point for social organization).

Another critical text that can help contextualize these two works, and that also includes paranoid and reparative readings of expressions of sexual dissidence in 1970s Mexico, is Blanco's 1979 chronicle "Ojos que da pánico soñar" ["Eyes I Dare Not Meet in Dreams"].[5] The eyes to which he refers are those of male homoerotic desire, personified by the young men searching for sexual partners in the streets and plazas of the city, the space where same-sex encounters have been relegated by the discrimination of mainstream society. Shifting from this symptom of marginalization to the burgeoning acceptance of gay men in Mexico City, the text expresses Blanco's anxiety about what he sees as the imminent cooptation of sexual dissidence in Mexico by the market. He argues that the historic persecution of homosexuality has made its very practice an act of rebellion and has led to the development of a rich subculture shared by those who have suffered that persecution (185–90). Part of this subculture includes the reparative uses of humor similar to Novo's arch use of satire and self-deprecating humor: "al reírnos de la sociedad y también de nosotros mismos pudimos muchas veces habitar días y años inhabitables" ["by laughing at society and also at ourselves many times we were able to inhabit uninhabitable days and years"] ("Ojos" 189). In other words, the male homosexual subculture in Mexico has long used camp self-deprecation as a way of disidentifying with heteronormative, mainstream society.

The danger that Blanco sees is that middle-class gay men—the sexual dissidents with the most social privilege in terms of class and race—may be lulled into passivity by a tolerance based on their participation in the consumer economy: "Es predecible que nuestra 'marginalidad' deje de serlo, como en Estados Unidos, y se vuelva una modalidad del conformismo imperante. Nos habrán de privilegiar porque tolerarnos será un acceso a nuestros bolsillos" ["It's predictable that our 'marginality' will cease to be such, like in the United States, and will become a modality of the dominant conformism. We will be privileged because tolerating us will allow access to our pockets"] (188). In other words, male homosexuality will be tolerated (but not truly accepted) as an alternative "lifestyle" available to those who can afford it, while the oppression of poor queers continues unabated. In opposition to this, he proposes a politics of dissidence that rejects the commodifying of sex in favor of a politically engaged polymorphous perversity that eschews labels of sexual orientation (190).

Although Blanco is writing specifically about the Mexican context, in which emerging political movements of sexual dissidence are closely linked to revolutionary Marxism (Domínguez-Ruvalcaba, *Translating* 93–132; Figari; Fiol-Matta), he gives voice to concerns that by the 1980s and 1990s would be widely recognized in the Anglo-American world as well (Altman, Bell and Binnie, Bersani) and even prefigures, through an insistence on the liberating potential of polymorphous perversity, the anti-essentialist view of queer politics that would arise around that time. In this way, he also anticipates contemporary queer critiques of assimilationist politics in Latin America, such as the legalization of same-sex marriage (Domínguez-Ruvalcaba, *Translating* 93–132; Figari; Fiol-Matta; Vargas, "Defendamos"). Zapata and Calva belong to the same generation as Blanco, and their literary texts from this period engage with many of these same themes. They focus on the anxieties surrounding the interaction of sexual dissidence with the market, but also emphasize how certain assumptions about gender underlie the somewhat essentialist notions of identity espoused by their protagonists. In the end, their texts employ camp and *cursi* humor to portray these characters in ways that invite readers to uncover problems and conflicts in society but also to identify with the characters through their reparative uses of humor. This includes the connection of camp humor to homosexual subjectivities and collectives as well as the generalized Mexican anxiety about being *cursi* or ambiguously situated with regards to discourses of modernity. Both novels portray protagonists who disidentify with hetero- and homonormativity in ways that reflect the persistence of the coloniality of power, sex, and gender in Mexican society.

El vampiro de la colonia Roma

Zapata's novel narrates the life of Adonis García, a 25-year-old *chichifo* [male prostitute] who plies his trade on the streets of Mexico City's Roma and Cuauhtémoc neighborhoods.[6] Adonis recounts his life story to an unnamed and silent interlocutor who is presumably tape-recording the conversation. The book is presented as the transcription of his oral autobiographical narrative, divided into seven *cintas* [tape reels], each of which is preceded by an epigraph from a novel connected to the picaresque tradition.[7] The orthography of the text, explained in a note from the author at the beginning, avoids capitalization and regular punctuation, instead using blank spaces of varying length between the words on the page to represent the pauses of the narrator's natural speech.[8] Each *cinta* begins with an epigraph, a quote from a novel, and a description by the protagonist of one of his dreams. He then narrates a portion of his life story. In chronological order, Adonis's life narrative can be summarized as follows: he is born in Mexico City to a Spanish father and a Mexican mother; his mother dies when he is young; his father dies some years later, and he goes to live with an older half-brother in León, Guanajuato; he leaves Guanajuato and returns to Mexico City to live with his older brother; he has his first sexual experience with another young man and then discovers that he can earn money by prostituting himself. The rest of the narrative is a description of Adonis's relationships and experiences of the next few years, which include incarceration, addiction, and venereal disease. Most of the story takes place in Mexico City, more specifically in the Roma and Cuauhtémoc neighborhoods, although Adonis does mention his travels to other Mexican cities such as León, Acapulco, Cuernavaca, and Veracruz. He begins with his early experiences, but it soon becomes apparent that he considers the most important part of his life to be his years of sexual activity, that is, approximately the last eight years leading up to the moment of enunciation.

The comic stereotype of the effeminate homosexual man has a central role in *Vampiro*. The humor of this figure derives from the perception of the incongruous combination of "masculine" and "feminine" semantic scripts in one body, and this humor may have several functions in society. On the one hand, it can help maintain the social order through the discrimination of queer subjects and the neutralization of anxiety surrounding gender and sex taboos. On the other hand, particularly when it is part of intentional camp gender parody, it can serve as a form of disidentification that helps dissident communities based on shared experiences transcend the psychological pain caused by discrimination.

Humor based on gender plays an important role in the narration of Adonis, who evinces a very ambivalent relationship to gender norms and their role in the homosexual culture in which he participates. While he rejects the *joto* stereotype and attempts to distance himself from people whom he sees as upholding it through their effeminate gender performance, he also has close relationships with many of those very same people and even engages in camp gender parody himself, most often as a way of transcending negative affect. This ambiguity betrays an unstable sense of self illustrative of the effects of homophobia in Mexican society (Ruiz, "Prostitución" 333; Domínguez-Ruvalcaba, *Modernity* 138–39) as well as the complex coexistence of gender-based and object choice-based categories of sexual identity in late 20th-century Mexico.[9]

Adonis displays a similarly conflicted rejection of *lo cursi*, which he identifies as cultural backwardness evidenced by the open expression of sentiment and the performance of traditional gender roles. Nevertheless, he demonstrates a deep familiarity with *cursi* discourse and a propensity to reproduce traditional gender roles and sentimentality in spite of himself. This reflects Adonis's complex notion of Mexican identity, which includes both pride and shame regarding the ambiguous modernity of Mexico and the possibility of living a sexually liberated life there. Ultimately, these contradictions in Adonis's personality are indicative of his disidentification with mainstream values and a constitutive aspect of his subjectivity. As such, they can also be read as an allegory of social conflicts of 1970s Mexico. His conflicted view of *cursilería* and the desire to be modern, in particular, situate this novel in that Latin American literary tradition that engages critically with the problem of the region's marginalization from modernity.

Early in his narrative, Adonis distinguishes himself from effeminate gay men, or *locas*, with a caricature that draws a direct connection between the performance of gender and the expression of sexual identity: "las locas son las que nos desprestigian a los homosexuales//de corazón/a los homosexuales serios/je//a los que no tenemos que andar gritando a los cuatro vien-//tos que somos putos" (48) "it's the queens who drag down/ the reputation of us dedicated homosexuals//us serious homosexuals/ha// those of us who don't have to go//around letting it all hang out and letting the whole world know that we're fags" (46).[10] The "serious" homosexual, who performs a hegemonic masculinity, can pass as straight. The *loca*, who performs a nonhegemonic masculinity, or even a type of femininity, cannot, because s/he incongruously combines masculine and feminine scripts in the same body. Adonis frequently uses this script opposition to describe his lover René, as when he interprets René's sexual jealousy as the result of the stereotypically *loca* fantasy of seducing a masculine straight man: "ya ves la mentalidad de las//locas/ bueno/de algunas locas/o sea//piensan que pueden encontrar un tipo que/no//gustándole los hombres/se acueste con ellos ¿ves?//por eso te digo que algunas locas están de atar" (62) "y'see that's//the way a queen's mind works//well// some queens//i mean/they think they can find a guy who//even though he doesn't like men/who will make love to them/y'understand?/that's why i tell ya some//queens belong in a nuthouse" (59). This comment illustrates how Adonis's concept of himself as a masculine-identified homosexual man clashes with René's expectations that both men should conform to gender-based categories of sexual identity (i.e., if Adonis's comportment is close to hegemonic masculinities, he must "really" be heterosexual).

Adonis's joking suggestion that some *locas* are "de atar" both invalidates their discourse and underlines his rejection of gender-based sexual identity categories as not fitting reality.[11] Ironically, he upholds these very same categories through his caricatured depiction of René as the quintessential *loca*, so effeminate that his body is even similar to a woman's and can fool a blind beggar who gropes him on a bus, initially mistaking him for a girl (when the beggar finally reaches René's penis, he begins to scream in a sudden fit of homosexual panic) (84–85).

Adonis also uses a masculine/feminine script opposition in the portrayal of his lover Zabaleta, a wealthy older man with whom he lives for several months. Adonis characterizes him as "tan loca que/cuando hablaba/en lugar de//decir 'yo'/decía 'ya'" (114) "such a queen that/when the talked/instead of saying//'i'/he'd say 'shi'" (108). This joke, an exaggerated parody of the ostentatiously effeminate language used by *locas*, forms part of a caricature of Zabaleta as an effete dandy whose behaviors, such as gossiping on the phone, recall those of a stereotyped rich woman: "se//ponía a hablar por teléfono/como buena loca//durante horas/con el secretario de no sé qué y con la//primera dama/y con la segunda dama y la señora de la//casa chica del presidente y con las putas de los embajado-//res" (122) "he'd start talking over the//telephone/just like a proper queen/for hours and hours//to the secretary of god knows what and to the first lady//and to the second lady and the president's mistress and the//ambassadors' whores" (114).

Significantly, Adonis qualifies this behavior as being permitted by Zabaleta's wealth. In other words, his social standing allows him to transgress gender norms that Adonis cannot because of his precarious economic situation. Ironically, this social inequality often puts Adonis in a position of inferiority with relation to Zabaleta that recalls the subordinate position of women in the dominant social structure of Mexico. For example, he complains that Zabaleta did not want him to work as a prostitute anymore and obliged him to stay in the house: "así es que//áhi me tienes instalado como rey en la mansión [. . .] entonces me//pasaba las tardes como virgen provinciana/encerrado//y poco me faltó para que empezara a bordar de tan aburrido que me sentía" (124) "so there i was living//like a king in the palace [. . .] anyhow so i spent my afternoons like a small-//town spinster/shut in the house/i was so bored i almost took up embroidery" (117). Notably, Adonis begins by comparing himself to a masculine figure (a king), but then he jokingly describes himself as a stereotypical female figure (a spinster) and suggests that he would begin to undertake a traditionally feminine activity (embroidery) out of boredom. Here Adonis sets up a masculine/feminine script opposition in his own body through an appropriation of camp gender parody that highlights the connection that he makes between his precarious economic position and the feminine, as well as the conflicting feelings about being subordinate to Zabaleta. This is illustrative of a trend in which Adonis uses camp gender parody to refer to himself in socially degraded situations, which I read as a reparative coping mechanism in which self-referential humor serves to achieve cognitive distance from the distress caused by his social precariousness.

This use of humor can be seen in several instances when Adonis parodically compares himself to female pop culture icons in a camp fashion. When he faints due to a sudden drop in blood pressure caused by his drug use, he likens his situation to that of teen pop idol Angélica María, who supposedly went into labor from the shock she experienced when she saw the movie *Jaws* (167). Later, he recalls that a friend once joked that his sexual promiscuity deserved to be commemorated in a statue and describes how such as monument would look: "como la tigresa/¿tú has visto la estatua de la//tigresa que está en su teatro encuerada?/¿una madre//dorada/así/de tamaño natural/pero con los//ojos verdes y la boca roja roja?/pues así iba a//estar yo en el cine de las américas/pero con la verga bien//parada" (112) "like la tigresa//y've seen that statue of la tigresa that's there in her//theatre?/naked/all covered with gold paint/like//so/life-size/but with green green eyes and a red red//mouth?//well that's the way i'd be at the las américas//theatre/but with a big hard on" (105) The statue he imagines combines a phallic masculinity and an exaggerated, sexualized femininity (embodied by the famously transgressive singer and actress Irma Serrano, "La Tigresa" [The Tigress]) in a single figure. It is notable, however, that the reason that his friend makes this joke is because Adonis spends so much time at the "magic corner" of Baja California and Insurgentes trying to pick up clients. In other words, it is directly related to his constant work as a prostitute, which he claims to enjoy, but which is also a very marginal and dangerous occupation.

In other situations, Adonis compares himself to female prostitutes, betraying his internal conflicts regarding this occupation, most frequently undertaken by women. For example, recounting how Zabaleta had tried to frighten him into abandoning sex work, he compares himself to the character Santa from one of the film adaptations of the classic novel by Federico Gamboa:

me la había pintado tan gacha que ya hasta me imagi-//naba que iba a terminar como santa/¿sí viste la pelícu-//la?/que acababa en una como casucha/en una//como cabaña/cayéndose de vieja/ la cabaña//y ella también/pues/y enfermísima de//tuberculosis/ no es cierto/de sífilis/flaca//flaca y sin poder hablar (123)

he had//painted things so black that i even thought i was gonna end up//like *santa*/you saw the movie/didn't you?/who//ended up in a kinda hovel/a kinda hut/falling apart with//age/the hut i mean/and her too/well//and//real sick with tb//that's not true/ with//syphilis/thin as a rail and not even able to speak (116)

These self-deprecating comments contrast with Adonis's satirical targeting of *loca* characters such as René and Zabaleta in order to distance himself from them. This ambivalent attitude towards the feminine and towards the use of camp gender parody in gay culture reflects Adonis's fragile sense of self, which personifies conflicts about categories of sexual identity in 1970s Mexico. However, it also models the use of self-deprecating humor in order to transcend negative affect. These camp elements of Adonis's self-presentation intersect, as they must in this context, with *cursilería*.

The self-comparison that Adonis makes with Santa is somewhat melodramatic and, in that sense, somewhat *cursi*. Adonis's familiarity with this type of discourse, illustrated above, is another contradictory aspect of his personality since he generally expresses disdain for the open expression of sentiment. For example, he shuts down a friend who said that he missed his absent lover so much that he began smelling his shirts: "y le dije /'mira//yo entiendo estas cosas//y yo sé que pasan//yo sé que existen todavía//pero pues a mí no me las vengas a contar//no me interesan//es más// me parecen demasiado cursis'" (26) "and i told him/'look/i understand those//things/i know that they happen/i know that they still//exist/ but i mean don't come telling me about them/they don't interest me/and what's more/i think they're just//too sentimental and ridiculous'" (25). Adonis sees this behavior as distasteful and implicitly contrasts it with his idea of how relationships should be (cynical and open), setting up a modern/unmodern script opposition.

He sets up a similar opposition in his own body when he describes his actions in a dream in which he is on the beach picking up shells "como vieja cursi" (163) "like any sentimental old dame" (151). This observation evidences the association that the narrator makes between *cursilería* and the feminine. Adonis, who considers himself both masculine and modern, perceives an incongruity in his dream action of collecting shells on the beach, which for him is the sort of romantic cliché that a woman would undertake. Like the young Salvador Novo in *La estatua de sal*, he sees no place for love or sentiment in his sexual relationships, which should either be business transactions or free associations based solely on pleasure, and he likewise associates certain *cursi* attitudes with a devalued femininity.

While Adonis's rejection of love, like Novo's, may be understood in part as a result of his social marginalization, it is also due to currents that arose in Mexican culture during the 1960s and that saw the open expression of sentiment as démodé and shamefully unmodern (Monsiváis, "Manos" 25–26, 31–33; "La cursilería" 25–29). Such views typically opposed notions of "the modern" to aspects of traditional Mexican culture. It becomes clear that Adonis holds such attitudes when he discusses the conflicts in his relationship with René, such as their inability to maintain an open relationship because neither one can overcome his jealousy: "no/ si te digo//que era una onda muy enferma/ muy tercermundista//¿no?/ a veces con escenas de celos y toda la cosa" (97) "no/i tell you/that was a real sick scene/real un-//sophisiticated/real old fashioned/right?/with jea-// lous fights sometimes and the whole shebang" (92).

This jocular and somewhat self-deprecating description of their conflict sets up an opposition between modern and unmodern scripts. Adonis attributes the incongruously traditional behavior of the supposedly modern couple (melodramatic expression of sentiment and attachment to traditional relationship norms) to the cultural backwardness of their social context. He associates *lo cursi* with a benighted expression of sentimentality, traditional gender roles, and monogamy, which he links to old-fashioned Mexican and Latin American culture. However, his self-presentation also contains an element of proud identification with the Mexican nation that oscillates with a sort of shame about the country's perceived underdevelopment. He proudly refers to Mexico City as "la ciudad más cachonda del mundo" ["the horniest city in the world"], where a gay man could have all the sex he wants, no strings attached, but he also laments the "tercermundista" ["Third-World"] details of his love relationships and financial situation (200, 97, 165). This is yet another aspect of what is often read as an unstable subjectivity, one that I would add is marked by a highly contradictory process of disidentification with mainstream Mexican culture.

The ambiguity and instability in Adonis's sense of self with regards to his attitudes towards effeminate gay men have been read as a symptom of

the internalization of homophobia and an attempt to transcend the active/
passive binary inherent in gender-based sexual identity categories (Ruiz,
"Prostitución" 333; Domínguez-Ruvalcaba, *Modernity* 138–39). Ironically,
the object-based sexual identity category that Adonis imagines for himself
(the masculine "homosexual de corazón") is also based on gender norms
since it requires the exclusion of an effeminate "other" that constantly
threatens masculinity. Such a macho posture actually brings him much
closer to the traditional gender norms that he sees as *cursi* and as an
impediment to his achievement of a modern lifestyle. Adonis attempts to
neutralize the threat of the feminine and *lo cursi* through humor, which
serves both to subordinate *locas* and women and to relieve anxiety about
his own conflicted sense of self.

However, the novel also shows how this humor can function as a
positive mode of self-expression that gives Adonis a way to cope with
the negative affect he experiences as a result of his sexual orientation
and occupation as a sex worker. This makes his humor very similar to
that used by Novo in his poems and his autobiography, a humor that, as
Monsiváis points out, reiterates internalized machismo and homophobia
at the same time that it allows its practitioner to survive and to carve out
a space in Mexican society as part of a collective ("Manos" 25–26). The
intersection of this kind of camp humor with *cursilería* is indicative of
the position of the queer subject in Mexico, where all aspects of culture
are affected by the region's marginalization from discourses of modernity.

This marginality is reflected in particular through the novel's parodic
engagement with the literary tradition, especially the naturalist, picaresque,
and essay genres. *Vampiro*'s attention to bodily urges that transgress social
norms and the bodily and social consequences of those transgressions, such
as physical and mental illness and social marginalization, insert the novel
in the tradition of naturalism, wherein the writer portrays the social ills of
the body politic while exploring the tension between genetic and environ-
mental determinism (Domínguez-Ruvalcaba, *Modernity* 139; Salmerón 75).
The most famous example of literary naturalism from Mexico is Federico
Gamboa's novel *Santa* (1908), about a young girl who becomes a prostitute
and eventually dies of syphilis. Adapted four times for the silver screen
and once for television, the story of Santa has entered Mexican popular
culture as a paradigmatic cautionary tale about the negative effects of
the transgression of sex and gender norms by women. The positive spin
that Adonis puts on his own sexual agency as a prostitute subverts the
negative and more deterministic portrayal of prostitution in works like

Santa (Balderston and Maristany 209–10). However, his struggles with the health effects of social marginalization, including addiction, can also be read as expressions of unresolved social conflicts due to the persistence of the coloniality of power, gender, and sex in Mexico.

The picaresque is an even older genre that is even more central to Spanish American cultural expression. *Vampiro* has in common with other picaresque works the first-person narrative voice, the marginal social position of the protagonist, the critical portrayal of different patrons (here lovers and/or customers), the emphasis on the lower body stratum and corporeal desires, and, of course, the satirical use of humor. The choice of this format is particularly significant because the picaresque has been considered not only an important precursor of the modern novel but also the foundational genre of Latin American literature (González-Echevarría). It is also the form taken by what is generally considered the first Mexican (and Latin American) novel: José Joaquín Fernández de Lizardi's *El Periquillo Sarniento* [*The Mangy Parrot*], which makes it even more significant to the critique of Mexican national identity.[12] Significantly, it is the critical perspective of the socially marginal *pícaro*, rather than the narcissism of the romantic hero, that represents the first great portrayal of modern subjectivity in Spanish and Spanish American literature.

While the protagonists of most of the "classic" picaresque narratives, including *El Periquillo Sarniento*, are not usually described as racially different (though the works sometimes hint at the Jewish ancestry that was a common source of discrimination in early modern Spain), the racial element is represented in *Vampiro*, albeit in a somewhat oblique manner. Though he rarely mentions race explicitly, the emphasis that Adonis places on the life history of his Spanish exile father can be understood as a strategy to appropriate white racial privilege in order to have the authority to tell his own story (Sifuentes-Jáuregui, *Avowal* 79). Furthermore, as I suggested in the previous chapter, Mexican anxieties about modernity, expressed here through Adonis's rejection of *cursilería*, generally contain a racial element as well, however latent it may be. The symbolic weight of Adonis's mixed-race parentage also connects his life story to (racialized) allegorical interpretations of the Mexican national character, such as Paz's famous reading of the Mexican (man) as tormented by the unresolved trauma of the symbolic rape of the Indigenous mother by the Spanish conquistador father in the historical foundation of the nation (*Laberinto*).

Vampiro's parody of naturalist conventions, along with its renovation of the picaresque genre and its dialogue with philosophical discourses of

Mexican identity, makes the novel an allegory of contemporary Mexico that reinscribes the nation as a queer hustler, thus challenging the reader to accept sexual dissidence as a part of Mexican culture and society. Furthermore, this hustler's entire attitude towards life seems to be one of *relajo*, the very Mexican attitude of refusing to take anything, especially oneself, seriously. The text thus lends itself to an approach combining paranoid and reparative readings, in which the conflicted, humorous assertions of the narrator portray, both allegorically and realistically (through the character's psychological development), the emergence of sexual dissidence and the relationship of Mexico to metropolitan notions of modernity in the late 20th century. The main source of the positive, optimistic perspective that Blanco finds in the novel is Adonis's humorous worldview, a disidentification with both hetero- and homonormativity that relies on a connection with camp and *cursi* Mexican queer culture in order to transcend the negative affect associated with suffering discrimination and marginalization, but that is far from free of the effects of homophobia, colonialism, and sexism.

Utopía gay

We find a similar exploration of subjectivity and engagement with allegorical tradition in José Rafael Calva's *Utopía gay*. This novel tells the story of a male couple in a long-term monogamous relationship, one member of which inexplicably becomes pregnant.[13] This absurd proposition gives the pair—who are also the protagonists—a basis to contemplate the utopian possibilities of their relationship. The book is structured as a series of interior monologues that are intermittently interrupted by dialogue and, about three-fourths of the way through the novel, by a metanarrative "prologue" inserted by the author. The pregnant man is named Adrián, and his stream of consciousness is represented by a Joycean text with no punctuation, capitalization, or any other division, an orthographic convention that seems to reflect the ludic and undisciplined nature of his thinking. The stream of consciousness of his partner, Carlos, by contrast, follows standard punctuation and capitalization rules that reflect his more disciplined and rigid manner of thinking, obviously influenced by his occupation (as his name suggests, he is a Marxist professor of philosophy at the National University of Mexico). In these monologues, both Carlos and Adrián tend to focus on their relationship—in which their love appears as a unifying cosmic force—and a particular utopian vision that they imagine for themselves: they fantasize about moving to Baja California to raise their unborn child on a secluded beach, establishing a new society free from homophobia. The novel includes both a positive portrayal of a same-sex relationship as well as a critique of how the coloniality of sex and gender can influence the relationships of even the most progressively-minded homosexual men. It employs camp and *cursi* humor in an ironic but sympathetic characterization of the two protagonists as well-intentioned but unaware of the conservative aspects of their own behaviors. In this way, it includes both a social critique that lends itself to paranoid analysis and a positive use of camp and *cursi* humor that is ripe for reparative reading.

The plot begins with Adrián's first interior monologue, in which he sets out the novel's basic premise and its implications. This is interrupted by a phone call from his mother, whom he has been avoiding so that she will not learn about his now physically obvious pregnancy. She browbeats him into agreeing to bring Carlos to her house for dinner that night. He returns to his thoughts but is soon interrupted by a visit from his friends Olga and Gisela, two *travestis* that Carlos hates for their cross-dressing and exaggeratedly feminine personae.[14] The first stream of consciousness of Carlos appears after this—he is in his car on his way home from the university, thinking about his relationship with Adrián and how they are different from (and in some sense superior to) heterosexual people and other gay men, particularly effeminate ones. Much to his chagrin, Carlos is obliged to accompany Adrián to dinner with his meddling and overbearing mother, Ana, who is in denial about the fact that the two are a couple. During the course of the visit, however, she discovers that Adrián is pregnant, a fact that dismays her not because of its uncanniness but because she reads it as irrefutable evidence that her son has been the receptive partner in anal sex with Carlos. After much melodramatic arguing and posturing, mother and son finally reach a détente of sorts, and the two men return home.

On the way home, Adrián, who has drunk almost an entire bottle of wine by himself, regales Carlos with a ludic, humorous parody of philosophical discourse, something that both attracts and frustrates Carlos, whose own manner of thinking and speaking is always informed by rigorous Marxist discipline and the logic of grammar. Upon arriving, they discover Carlos's friend Guillermo drunk on their doorstep, lamenting an unrequited passion. Adrián hates Guillermo, a professor and poet, because of his sexual promiscuity, heavy drinking, and literary pretensions. Guillermo has a discussion with the couple and recites a poem of his own composition whose subject matter is a recuperation of the biblical Sodom as a sort of utopia. Carlos celebrates the poem, while Adrián trashes it, along with Guillermo's entire worldview. After their guest leaves, Carlos and Adrián make love and fall asleep.

At this point, the author inserts his prologue, which explains the genesis of the book as well as his reasons for writing a utopia featuring a gay couple. On the one hand, his portrayal of the pair—while it should not be taken as any sort of realistic or typical representation—offers an alternative to the model of the relationship between Oscar Wilde and Lord Alfred Douglas.[15] On the other hand, he also claims that he wanted to write about a utopia that would be relevant to his personal experience as a gay man. The prologue also states that humor is used in the novel in order to treat serious ideas and make the text more amenable. Calva celebrates the use of humor in literary and philosophical texts, considering texts with humor more alive and indelible in many cases than those that only make use of serious discourse.

The prologue is followed by a stream of consciousness from a recently awakened Carlos, who is heading for work. A stream of consciousness from Adrián follows as he wakes up, hung over, and prepares coffee. His mother phones, and they argue about her inability to accept her son's homosexuality. After he hangs up with her, Carlos calls to tell him that Guillermo has committed suicide. Carlos blames Adrián for this—he says it is due to the way that Adrián spoke to him the night before, destroying all of Guillermo's illusions. Adrián hangs up, angrily, and the novel ends with one final stream of consciousness from Adrián, an escape to the utopia where he imagines himself dying at the end of his days in a sort of phantasmagoric sexual climax in the arms of Carlos.

One of the most remarkable characteristics of this novel is the way that it engages with the theme of same-sex marriage several decades before this was even a political possibility in Mexico. Notably, the theme of same-sex cohabitation was also explored in this era, at least tangentially, in the films of Jaime Humberto Hermosillo. The portrayal of two ostensibly heterosexual female roommates in his 1979 film *Amor libre* ["Free Love"] can arguably be read as containing a lesbian subtext (Venkatesh, *New* 54), and *Doña Herlinda y su hijo* [*Doña Herlinda and Her Son*] (1985), released the same year that *Utopía gay* was published, focuses on the manner in which the mother of the protagonist organizes a ménage-à-trois, so that her son can marry a woman but continue to have a sexual-affective relationship with his male partner. These films, with their sympathetic and somewhat humorous view of nonnormative sexualities, explore how traditional gender norms influence and are challenged by same-sex cohabitation and relationships, thus reflecting preoccupations similar to those of contemporary writers like Calva and Zapata. However, neither of these films directly addresses the issue of a same-sex union based on the marriage model in as much detail as *Utopía gay*, which makes the novel a critical intertext for any discussion of Mexican cultural production on this theme in the 1970s and 1980s.

In more recent years, and particularly since the partial legalization of marriage equality in Mexico, there have been more works that have also focused on this theme. For example, the plot of Luis Zapata's novel *La historia de siempre* ["The Same Old Story"] (2007) hinges on the fantasies of infidelity of its gay male protagonist, who is involved in a monogamous relationship based on the marriage model. *Telenovelas* such as *El sexo débil* ["The Weaker Sex"] (2011) and *La casa de las flores* [*The House of Flowers*] (2018–20) have also portrayed the theme of same-sex unions and marriage. The films *La otra familia* [*The Other Family*] (Gustavo Loza, 2011) and *Pink* (Francisco del Toro, 2016) have engaged with the theme of same-sex marriage and parenthood from diametrically opposed viewpoints. In the former, a wealthy, married gay male couple adopt the child of a narco in what Venkatesh describes as a didactic portrayal of a conservative version of gayness as part of the culture of neoliberal modernity (Venkatesh, *New* 186–87). The latter is essentially a propaganda film against marriage equality and same-sex parenthood made from an evangelical Christian perspective. In contrast to the couple in *La otra familia*, here the men fail completely at properly raising their adopted child because they do not adhere to traditional gender roles. Unsurprisingly, neither of these films treats its theme with anything close to the depth and complexity of Calva's novel, which makes his work, though marginal and several decades old, an important touchstone for serious discussions about same-sex unions in Mexican culture.

In particular, *Utopía gay* includes a positive, if somewhat ambivalent, portrayal of a couple in a marriage-like relationship that anticipates both the humanizing arguments in favor of such relationships as well as queer critiques of them. One such critique is advanced by the British legal scholar Nicola Barker, who argues that same-sex marriage is structurally identical to heterosexual marriage, tends to result in the reproduction of traditional gender roles, and does not address issues of economic inequality intersected by gender, such as the privatization of domestic labor within the family (130, 156–57). A key point in Barker's argument is that since there are very few clear legal definitions of marriage in the world, discussion of the issue should not focus on a stable definition of "marriage" but rather on the broader notion of a "marriage model" or "marriage framework," by which she means the values (such as monogamy) that influence legal definitions of marriage and the various types of cohabitation (such as civil unions) that are obviously modeled on legal definitions of marriage (4–5).[16] For example, Barker observes that in the United Kingdom, procreation has not historically been part of the ideology of marriage (the collection of legal definitions and court decisions that define marriage) (35–37).

To understand this novel, however, it is important to take into account the influence of the coloniality of sex and gender on the ideology of marriage in Mexico. In Mexico City's Federal District, for example, the legal definition of marriage did indeed include the intent to procreate until it was recently amended in order to permit same-sex marriage (Salinas, *Matrimonio*). This is a result of the imposition of heteronormativity during the colonial period, when native nonprocreative sexualities were labeled as sinful and punishable by the authorities (Domínguez-Ruvalcaba, *Translating* 19–23). The Catholic Church's definition of marriage as a holy sacrament oriented towards procreation heavily influenced the ideology of marriage in Mexico, even in the secular postrevolutionary state. *Utopía gay* develops the possibility of a transcendent same-sex union starting with a conceit that satirizes this imposed morality: a gay man in a monogamous relationship becomes pregnant, in an obvious parody of the Immaculate Conception of Mary and the Virgin Birth of Jesus.[17]

However, while Adrián and Carlos hope that their relationship will transcend the limits of heteronormativity, their performance of traditional gender roles actually makes their union very similar to heterosexual marriage. Adrián's pregnancy, which undermines one of the chief objections to homosexuality (and same-sex marriage) of a mainstream morality heavily influenced by Catholicism, ironically serves to install the two men in a relationship based on the marriage model. Their exaltation of masculinity as a supreme value, which is based on an exclusion and denigration of the feminine, makes them blind to the role of gender in their own relationship (Ruiz, "*Utopía gay*" 305–6). This is apparent most often in their humorous stereotyping of effeminate homosexual men, whose camp and *cursi* practices they consider a counterexample to their own behaviors, but it is also apparent in their attitudes toward Adrián's mother and in their own unconscious reiteration of traditional gender roles.

As I mentioned above, Carlos's interior monologues are much more rational and logically organized than Adrián's, even to the point of following standard rules of punctuation and capitalization. While he argues in favor of the intellectual and spiritual superiority of homosexual men over heterosexuals, he always does so from a position that also reiterates the superiority of logic and masculine privilege. In other words, his gay utopia is one inhabited by men who are equals, and equally masculine, and this is the ideal that he believes that his relationship with Adrián follows. Because of this, he expresses that he is glad that Adrián has not become more effeminate with his pregnancy:

> en realidad esperaba que se afeminara de veras, que se ajotara en todos sus ademanes al punto de temer que se transformara en una de esas locas trasvestistas que cantan y bailan en los bares *gay* porque no hubiera soportado verlo destruirse sin que yo también quedara hecho pedazos para siempre.
>
> [I actually expected him to become really effeminate, to become so faggy in all of his behaviors to the point of being afraid that he would turn into one of those cross-dressing queens who sing and dance in gay bars, because I would not be able to bear seeing him destroy himself without also going to pieces forever.] (66)

The masculinist and homophobic ideas that underlie Carlos's prejudices against *locas* are evident here in his use of sarcasm, stereotype, and caricature to ridicule a figure in which masculine and feminine scripts are present in the same body.

This figure is personified in the text by Adrián's friends Olga and Gisela, two *travestis* whose behavior Adrián himself satirizes thus:

> Olga y Gisela no consiguen marido y me envidian si se portan peor que mujeres si por eso los hombres las aguantan nomás un ratito porque no dejan de jotear un minuto las pendejas si por eso Carlos no quiere nunca salir a la calle con ellas [. . .] tiene razón si queman gratuitamente a quienes las acompañen [. . .]
>
> Olga and Gisela can't find a husband and they're jealous of me but they behave worse than women that's why men can only stand them for a little bit because they don't stop camping for

even a minute the stupid bitches that's why Carlos never wants to go out with them [. . .] he's right since they gratuitously out anyone who's with them [. . .] (43–44)

Just like Carlos, Adrián focuses on the incongruous performance of femininity in masculine bodies. He complains that his friends behave worse than women, who are obviously not highly valued in his perspective. Adrián's comments reduce his friends to pathetic figures who are fooling themselves about their ability to be feminine and who believe, ironically, that the rest of the world sees them as they see themselves. The importance of passing as heterosexual to Adrián is evident here: he is afraid of being outed by association. He does not want to be seen as gay if being gay is associated with effeminacy.

Carlos and Adrián's rejection of camp is based, in part, on a view of it as unmodern and retrograde. Carlos criticizes camp gender parody as pure performance that inhibits the development of an authentic dissident identity and that reinforces negative stereotypes about gay people in mainstream society: "son el esperpento de sí mismos ante la impotencia de afrontarse [. . .] porque [lo *camp*] no es otra cosa que representación constante [. . .] Y eso me da tanto coraje porque es precisamente lo que ha elaborado nuestra leyenda negra" ["they are a grotesque parody of themselves facing their inability to confront their own problems [. . .] because [camp] is nothing more than a constant representation [. . .] And that makes me so angry because that is precisely what has been the basis of our black legend"] (71–72). This perspective, which is similar to criticisms leveled at camp by gay rights discourses in the United States in the 1970s and 1980s,[18] is here closely connected to discourses of modernity, such as Marxism, that the protagonists see as the necessary way to overcome discrimination and oppression.

Despite his ostensible rejection of effeminacy, however, Adrián also engages in camp gender parody. While he levels his criticisms at Olga and Gisela above, he is also knitting clothes for his unborn child, an activity, like cooking, that he learned from his two *travesti* friends. In fact, during the majority of the narration, Adrián is at home knitting and undertaking other domestic activities traditionally associated with women. Although Carlos argues that Adrián does so without losing any masculinity, the overall effect of these repeated references to domesticity, combined with the pregnancy, is to create a masculine/feminine script opposition in the body of Adrián, the humor of which is enhanced by his and Carlos's ironic negation that he is becoming effeminate. This contradiction is further illustrated by Adrián's ambivalent use of camp humor when in the presence of other characters.

For example, when Olga and Gisela come to visit him, Adrián immediately switches to a mode of gender nonconformity reflected by the use of feminine pronouns in his stream of consciousness:

> —hermanas queridas—si besarnos en las mejillas es deliciosamente relajante que si no seríamos como víboras entre nosotras mismas que eso también tenemos de las mujeres esa falta de solidaridad y camaradería producto de considerar a todas rivales en potencia
>
> [—my dear sisters—kissing each other on the cheek is deliciously relaxing otherwise we'd be like vipers among ourselves since we're also like women in that way we have that lack of solidarity and camaraderie a result of considering everyone a potential rival] (61)

Adrián also lets slip certain elements of camp gender parody at other times, as when they go to his mother's house and she confronts them about his bulging stomach (he pretends to faint), and on the way home when Carlos argues with him about his refusal to have a serious discussion:

> —¡Ya!, nomás enredas.
>
> –me dicen la culebrosa
>
> —Que no loquees en las escaleras. Vas a acabar siendo el escándalo del edificio
>
> [—Enough! you just confuse everything.
>
> —they call me the snake-lady
>
> —Don't camp on the stairs. You're going to be the scandal of the building] (119)[19]

In all of these situations, Adrián is using camp, *loca* humor for reparative purposes. In the first case, when he relates to Olga and Gisela, camp serves as a way of identifying with others who also form part of a collective.

In the second case, he obviously uses camp humor as a sort of psychic self-defense and to cope with his anxiety before, during, and after the confrontation with his mother. In this way, Adrián models reparative uses of humor that are based on gender nonconformity at the same time that he and Carlos claim that he is not at all effeminate. Notably, Carlos finds Adrián's incessant campy *loquera* both aggravating and endearing, thus illustrating how his own rejection of camp humor is not definitive (119–20).

The couple have a similarly ambivalent and complicated relationship with *cursilería*, which they understand as a cultural anachronism associated with effeminacy and which they claim to reject in the name of achieving modernity. Their views in this regard, heavily influenced by Marxism, are reflected most often in their satirical critique of the behavior of others. As is the case with their critique of camp, however, their rejection of *cursilería* belies the *cursi* aspects of their own behavior and relationship, which is much more traditional than they assume. Humor about *lo cursi* is based on a modern/unmodern script opposition that highlights the notion of cultural backwardness or belatedness with respect to discourses of modernity. Carlos and Adrián associate *cursilería* with traditional Mexican society, which they view as anachronistic and as an obstacle to be overcome in a dialectical march towards progress that they believe can only be achieved through their utopian relationship. This attitude is neatly summarized in one of Adrián's interior monologues where he expresses his belief that Mexico is too underdeveloped to experience a true socialist revolution:

> la revolución marxista con todo y Cuba es un lujo que sólo se puede dar una nación superindustrializada si recuerdas en *El salmo rojo* que lo dijeron Marx y Engels [. . .] acá estamos bien lejos de dar ese paso de adulto cuando al caminar nos pesan los pañales llenos de mierda y embutes y robos

> [the Marxist revolution with Cuba and everything else is a luxury that only a super-industrialized country can give itself if you recall in the *Communist Manifesto* Marx and Engels said so [. . .] here we're really far from taking that adult step since when we walk we're weighed down by our diapers full of shit and corruption and scams] (109–10)

There is a modern/unmodern script opposition underlying this self-deprecating caricature of Mexico as a dirty-diapered baby for whom the Marxist discourse of modernity is out of reach. This perspective situates

Mexico as a newcomer on the world stage attempting, and failing, to imitate the modernity of industrialized socialist countries.

In this novel, as in *Vampiro*, *lo cursi* is heavily gendered and associated not only with unmodernity, but also with effeminacy. This is apparent in the characterization of Adrián's mother Ana, whom he describes as someone with one foot in modernity and one in tradition, attributing her success as a real estate agent more to luck than to her intuitive knowledge of market forces and how to manipulate them to her advantage:

> cree en la buena suerte como pocas gentes y es natural porque desconoce las fuerzas que le dan el triunfo al grado que si le hablara de la mano invisible de Adam Smith sería capaz de buscar hasta el cansancio una novena para resarle [*sic*] a Smith o algo por el estilo porque no irá a misa y en la práctica es más atea que Voltaire pero a la hora de lo desconocido es más fervorosa que Juan Diego

> [she believes in good luck more than most and it's natural because she doesn't know about the forces that give her success if they told her about the invisible hand of Adam Smith she'd be likely to look everywhere for a novena to pray to Smith or something like that because she may not go to mass and in her practices she might be more of an atheist than Voltaire but when confronted with the unknown she's more devout than Juan Diego] (58)

This humorous depiction of his mother is based on a modern/unmodern script opposition in which modern aspects of her personality and life (she is a widow with an active sex life and a successful career) coexist with traditional cultural beliefs (folk Catholicism). Furthermore, despite having achieved a level of liberation from traditional gender norms, she rejects homosexuality and is perturbed by her son's pregnancy not because it is a freak of nature but because she takes it as evidence that he has been anally penetrated by Carlos and therefore lost his masculinity. Her insistence on traditional gender roles, like her superstition, is associated in the text with traditional Mexican cultural values, considered unmodern by the protagonists.

Cursilería understood as cultural anachronism can refer to the attachment to traditional religious values and gender roles, as in the case of Ana, but also to the persistence of the discourse of romantic sentiment in Mexican culture (Monsiváis, "La cursilería"). This notion of *lo cursi* takes center stage in the argument between Adrián and Carlos's friend Guillermo, who appears drunk on their doorstep, lamenting a failed love affair. After he recites his new poem in which he postulates the biblical Sodom as a sort of ideal community that rejects Christian morality, Adrián makes fun of him, insinuating that his display of emotion is as *cursi* as *ranchera* music. His Mexican sentiment, in other words, spoils his attempt at being modern. We should note, however, that Guillermo levels the same criticism at his hosts. When Adrián calls Guillermo "un engendro el Averno" ["a hell spawn"], Guillermo responds: "—Lástima. Tan bien que ibas. Sólo que salir con esa frasecita de solterona provinciana te jodió la noche" ["Too bad. You were doing so well. It's just that that little country-spinster phrase of yours ruined your night"] (133). In other words, Adrián has fallen into *cursilería*, the reiteration of traditional discourse associated with religion and the provinces, considered the *locus* par excellence of *lo cursi* because of its supposed opposition to the modernity of the city (Monsivaís, "La cursilería" 29).

This rejoinder also includes a feminizing aspect: Adrián is compared to a stereotype of women in an insult that highlights the intersection of camp gender parody and *lo cursi*. This can also be seen in Guillermo's teasing remark to Carlos when he first arrives: "No sabes la falta que me haces desde que te casaste con esta mujer y cometes la tontería de serle fiel. ¿No que tan moderno?" ["You don't know how much I miss you since you married this woman and continue to make the mistake of being faithful to her. Weren't you supposed to be modern?"] (122) Here camp discourse based on gender parody intersects with an explicit argument that Carlos and Adrian's relationship, so clearly based on the heteronormative marriage model, is not really very modern at all, which is actually quite accurate. If anything, their relationship is *desmoderna*. Adrián and Carlos believe that their own behaviors transcend the traditional values of Mexican society and that their family unit can be the beginning of a utopian society free from homophobia. They do not realize, however, that their very notions of liberation and social progress are heavily influenced by discourses that reiterate the coloniality of gender and sex. In other words, in spite of their intention, their relationship itself is rather camp and *cursi*, and they actually seem to like it that way.

In order to grasp the full social critique of the novel, it is necessary to approach it from a paranoid reading position. However, the work also includes uses of humor that suggest reparative approaches. As I mentioned above, in a manner similar to both Salvador Novo and Adonis García, Adrián models the use of camp gender parody as a way of constituting a collective and transcending negative affect. Furthermore, the prologue frames the rest of the narrative as an argument about the positive social utility of humor and an optimistic portrayal of the possibilities for same-sex relationships. This makes the novel's satire less Juvenalian than Horatian. By that, I mean that it is a satire in which the author situates himself not above, but on the same moral level as the targets of the humor, and sympathetically chides them for the kinds of mistakes into which all human beings can fall (this is reinforced by the author's mention that he himself is in a relationship much like that of his characters). Because of this combination of perspective, *Utopía gay* is a work that is best approached with a reading strategy that looks to balance paranoid understanding of critique with reparative enjoyment and positive identification.

The plot is, of course, a parody of utopian literature as well as the Virgin Birth. However, the characters do not end up on a secluded beach in Baja California but continue to live in their own social context. Escapism, then, is obviously not the answer. However, the portrayal of the characters suggests that perhaps empathy and love are. Adrián, Carlos, and the author, through their first-person interventions, center their own subjectivities in the narrative. The two protagonists both look to disidentify with hetero- and homonormativity and in doing so fall into many contradictions. Carlos represents masculine, modern discourse, embodied by Marxism in this particular case. He is *macho* and serious, but he is also best friends with the melodramatically *cursi* Guillermo and, of course, he also loves the rather camp Adrián. The entire presence of the latter can be read as an irruption of queer *relajo*. Both queerness, with its challenge to heteronormativity, and *relajo*, with its rejection of modernity's seriousness, find expression in Adrián's irrepressible self-expression. The author, despite his ironic view, does not judge the characters too harshly. Furthermore, his view does not offer a resolution of conflicts but an optimistic recognition and acceptance of them through humor. In this way, the text's answer to what a gay utopia would be like is not in the wholesale rejection of the feminine and the cultural anachronisms of Mexico but rather in the acceptance of those aspects of Mexican queerness that make it a unique source of pride for those who, like the author, disidentify with the dominant social structure. This includes a recognition of the possibilities and limits of the marriage model. As Héctor Domínguez-Ruvalcaba argues, same-sex marriage reinforces heteronormativity and homonormativity, but it also queers the state by normalizing the queer and deprivileging the heteronormative (*Translating* 132). This is precisely what *Utopía gay* does with the marriage model.

In this chapter I have attempted to show how both *Utopía gay* and *Vampiro* use camp and *cursi* humor in the portrayal of protagonists whose contradictory notions about gender, sexuality, and modernity reflect social conflicts about these same themes in 1970s Mexico. Notably, the protagonists of these narratives are very focused on conforming to hegemonic masculinities, something that leads them to uphold stereotypes and prejudices that are part of the dominant social structure. In particular, they position themselves as against the association of gender nonconformity with homosexuality and as desirous of a modernity that is opposed to traditional Mexican culture. However, they also engage in camp gender nonconformity and have a close affective relationship to *cursilería*, demonstrating the importance of the reparative social functions of humor for queer subjects in Mexico. The narratives reflect, ironically, the positionality of Mexican subjects who desire modernity and try to achieve it through different models (consumerism, Marxism) that are incapable of resolving the social contradictions of Mexican society. Both paranoid and reparative approaches can be combined in the reading of these texts, which model how camp and *cursi* humor can serve as practices of disidentification enacted by queer subjects in Mexico, as well as how humor can expose social contradictions that must be addressed in order to further the objectives of creating a more just society.

Chapter 3

Dressing the Part

Literary Portrayals of *Travestis, Locas, Vestidas,* and *Jotas*

At the beginning of this book, I cited Carlos Monsiváis's assertion that the case of the 41 in 1901 established a connection between male homosexuality and effeminacy that was reified in Mexican culture through stereotypes ("Ortodoxia" 199), and I cited numerous examples from the mass media as well as literature that support that argument. This stereotyping and marginalization of men who have sex with men, in Mexico and elsewhere, has its roots in the devaluation of the feminine. In this view, homosexual men lack masculinity and choose, perversely, to be like the supposedly inferior female of the species ("Ortodoxia" 73–74; Connell 143). As the literary works analyzed in chapters 1 and 2 attest, misogyny and homophobia can sometimes be internalized by queer subjects to the point of becoming a major component of their identities. This is evident in Novo's ambivalent use of a camp and *cursi* feminine persona and his satirical portrayals of others as effeminate, as well as in the way that the protagonists of *El vampiro de la colonia Roma* and *Utopía gay* reject effeminacy as part of their attempts to construct an "authentic" homosexual or gay identity. In these last two novels in particular, the main characters define themselves against a stereotyped version of the effeminate homosexual man, often labeled as a *loca, jota* or *travesti*. In this chapter, by contrast, I will examine some texts in which *locas, jotas* or *travestis*, that is, queer male subjects who perform femininities, are the protagonists.

In contemporary Mexico, *travesti* and the related terms *loca*, *jota* and *vestida* are frequently used as markers of identity by men who identify as homosexual and feminine but not as women (Lewis 6–7; Vargas, "Travestis y vestidas").[1] In the English-speaking context, the terms "transvestite" and "transgender" are used to refer to cross-gender dressing and identification, respectively, but are generally considered to be independent of sexual orientation. However, Latin American *travesti*-type identities, while they involve biological men dressing in women's clothing and/or performing femininity, are also usually considered part of a "homosexual continuum" (Lewis 6–7). That is, subjects who identify as *travesti* or with related terms usually identify as both feminine (or at least effeminate) *and* homosexual (as biological men who are attracted to men). Such identities are indicative of the complex ways that cross-gender identification functions as queerness in Latin America.

Paul Julian Smith's analysis of four recent Mexican films on this theme illustrates quite well the diversity of experiences and identities that relate to cross-gender identification in Mexico. In the documentary *Morir de pie* ["To Die Standing Up"] (Jacaranda Correa, 2011), the main subject, Irina Layevska (born male and assigned masculine gender at birth), says that she became a woman when she first began to dress in women's clothing, an attitude similar to Anglo-American notions of transgender (82). In Roberto Fiesco's 2013 documentary *Quebranto* ["Disrupted"], which focuses on a former child star and her mother, the central subject Coral Bonelli identifies as *gay* or *joto* and is labeled a *travesti* by the film's synopsis, usages that are more in line with traditional Mexican notions of gender and sexuality (82). In Flavio Florencio's 2015 documentary *Made in Bangkok*, which focuses on the international odyssey of male-to-female transsexual opera singer Morganna Love, the international subjects use a vocabulary that includes terms such as *transgender* and *transsexual*. Finally, Rigoberto Perezcano's *Carmín tropical* [*Tropical Lipstick*] (2014), described by the director himself as a noir thriller with documentary elements, has as its central character a *muxe'*, a member of a traditional Zapotec Indigenous third sex that is "irreducible to international models of homosexuality and integrated into traditional society" (102).[2]

All of the examples cited above illustrate the complex ways that cross-gender identification appears in Mexico. In this chapter, however, I will be focusing particularly on *travesti, jota, loca,* and *vestida* identities. Individuals who identify this way in Mexico tend to belong to low-income sectors of society and to experience discrimination and violence related not only to their gender identity and sexual orientation but also to their social class and race (Vargas, "Travestis y vestidas"; Domínguez-Ruvalcaba, *Translating* 135–36). Due in part to this discrimination, *travestis* have a high level of participation in socially marginal and sometimes dangerous occupations such as sex work (ibid.). This makes those who identify as *travestis, vestidas, jotas,* and/or *locas* some of the most vulnerable members of Mexican society. For these reasons, the politics surrounding their representation is critical. As Susana Vargas's book *Mujercitos* amply illustrates, the *nota roja* (sensationalistic crime reporting) in Mexico has long depicted *travestis* as abject, grotesque figures of public scorn and ridicule. In many popular *fichera* [cabaret dancer/prostitute] sex comedy films of the 1970s and 80s, such as Rafael Portillo's *Noches de cabaret* ["Cabaret Nights"] (1978) and *Muñecas de medianoche* ["Midnight Dolls"] (1979), *travesti* characters serve as abject, one-dimensional figures of comic relief whose main purpose seems to be to reinforce the hegemonic, heterosexual masculinity of the male protagonists (de la Mora 116–18). A notable exception to this tendency is Arturo Ripstein's 1978 film *El lugar sin límites* [*The Place without Limits*], which "tells the tale of a rural transvestite's tragic affair with a Mexican macho" (Smith 5). Although this film contains a transgressive deconstruction of violent masculinity (de la Mora 133), it still exhibits certain tendencies towards the objectification and stereotyping of the cross-dressing character as a grotesque victim (Lewis 77; Venkatesh, *New* 6).

A more recent example of the continued marginalization of cross-dressing characters in Mexican culture can be seen in the Netflix dark comedy *La casa de las flores* [*The House of Flowers*] (2018–2020), which is a pastiche of the *telenovela*. In defiance of traditional Mexican values, this show's protagonists include a gay man, a bisexual man, a bisexual woman and a trans woman. However, in line with traditional *telenovela* conventions, these characters are all upper-class and relatively white (the trans woman is played by a cisgender male Spanish actor). The *travesti* or *vestida* characters, who are all portrayed as working-class subjects by dark-skinned actors, are a group of performers who imitate famous divas in a cabaret. Though their portrayals are slightly less one-dimensional and stereotyped than those in *fichera* films, they continue to serve essentially as foils for the whiter and wealthier protagonists whose sexual and gender identities are more in line with those that are acceptable in the Global North.

This sort of marginalization of *travesti* subjects is also common in Mexican literature, where they tend to serve not as protagonists but as secondary characters who are foils to cisgender characters in allegorical narratives. This is the case in Cristina Rivera Garza's *Nadie me verá llorar*, where the brief appearance of Madame Porifria, "un aristócrata venido a menos cuya única debilidad consistía en vestirse de mujer" ["a down-and-out aristocrat whose only weakness was dressing like a woman"] (179), serves as an ironic comment on the sexual politics of the Porfiriato. Other examples can be seen in Enrique Serna's novels *El miedo a los animales* [*Fear of Animals*] and *La doble vida de Jesús* ["The Double Life of Jesús"]. In the former, the brief comic appearance of a *travesti* serves essentially to illustrate the contradictions inherent to the exaggerated machismo of a minor character.[3] In the second case, the *travesti* character plays a much more central role as the love interest of the main character, a small-time politician whose vertiginous and short-lived rise to power as the mayor of Cuernavaca, Morelos, coincides with a midlife crisis in which he explores his sexuality. Nevertheless, the *travesti* here is essentially a foil for the exploration of the protagonist's bisexuality, which allegorically represents shifts in Mexican sex and gender norms (Venkatesh, "*La doble vida*" 268–69). A similar plot device is employed in Carlos Reyes Ávila's novel *Travesti*, where a heterosexual cisgender male protagonist falls in love with a *travesti* sex worker who is unable to requite him.

While these works may have aesthetic and social value beyond their portrayals of *travesti* characters, particularly through their incisive exploration of masculinities, it is also important to bear in mind the manner in which they can reinforce the social marginalization of cross-dressing subjects through these portrayals. In particular, they would seem to be incurring in what Vek Lewis terms *travestizaje*, or the tendency to portray and read cross-dressing subjects as a metaphor for national and regional identity construction, a practice that can lead to the erasure of trans subjectivity (32). According to Lewis, this happens not only in texts where the cross-dressing subjects are minor characters, but also in those where they are central figures, such as Luis Zapata's novel *La hermana secreta de Angélica María* ["The Secret Sister of Angélica María"]. For Lewis, the intersex protagonist of this novel does not constitute an authentic portrayal of trans or intersex subjectivity but rather a metaphorical use of this condition to portray social conflicts about gender and sexuality that reinscribes marginalizing discourses about intersex individuals (155–56). While I agree that this novel's portrayal is more figurative than realistic and that it includes some problematic representations of the intersex protagonist, I digress from Lewis's tendency to establish a clear opposition between texts with portrayals that are believable and those that are too allegorical to be useful for a politics of trans or cross-dressing identity.[4] In my view, this argument does not give enough attention to the centrality of allegorical representation in the history of Latin American culture. While this tendency towards figurative portrayals has undoubtedly served to oppress and silence marginal groups, it has also been a site of queer resistance, particularly through disidentification with this very tradition.

I do not find a sharp dichotomy between figurative and authentic portrayals in most of the texts I analyze. Rather, most of these works combine figurative and realistic portrayals through their parodic use of camp and *cursi* humor. This combination can be seen in Novo's autobiography, in *Vampiro*, and in *Utopía gay*, all texts where a plot based on a first-person narrative that expresses subjectivity in a realistic manner is combined with a self-conscious, ironic intertextuality with one or more allegorical literary traditions. However, even some texts in which figurative portrayals overshadow more realistic representation offer possibilities for paranoid and reparative readings undertaken from a perspective critical of dominant social norms and the Latin American literary tradition. While figurative writing and reading have definitely been tools of social oppression, they have also been sites of resistance. Allegorical portrayals may reiterate, in various ways, the coloniality of sex and gender, but they also provide a language with which to undermine and transform that order. This is especially true due to the centrality of the body to the construction of national and individual identities in Latin America, a legacy of the colonial history of the region (Figari 231; Sifuentes-Jáuregui, *Avowal* 10–11). Although the domination of bodies is central to the colonial project, the resistance of those bodies to domination is also central to the construction of queer Latin American subjectivities and narratives of resistance.

Below, I will reconsider *La hermana secreta de Angélica María* as a text that posits a disidentification with Mexican gender norms through an ironic reiteration of the recycling of mass-media tropes in the construction of a queer identity. The other texts that I consider in this chapter also contain portrayals in which the centrality of gender parody to the construction of *travesti* or similar identities are illustrated through the lives of the protagonists, who also figuratively portray social conflicts. In Luis Montaño's novel *Brenda Berenice*, the main character attempts to write her *jota* subjectivity into the Mexican literary tradition through an intentional use of parody and an incongruous combination of high and popular culture that reflects the social contradictions lived by a queer subject in late 20th-century Mexico. In the short stories "La jota de Bergerac" and "La marrana negra de la literatura rosa" ["The Black Sow of Romance Literature"] by Carlos Velázquez, a highly ironic parody of the ideology of gender transmitted through pop culture posits a carnivalesque, *relajiento* rejection of social norms. All four of these texts portray *travesti*, *vestida*, *loca* or *jota* characters through the use of camp and *cursi* humor that lends itself to both paranoid and reparative reading approaches.

La hermana secreta de Angélica María

This novel tells the story of a single protagonist who appears in three different incarnations: first as Álvaro,[5] an intersex child with indeterminate genitalia who has been assigned the masculine gender; then as the mediocre balladeer Alba María, with the same body now identified as feminine; finally, as Alexina, a postoperative transsexual female cabaret performer. Abandoned by his parents, Álvaro lives in a small town with his grandmother. Like Toto in Manuel Puig's *La traición de Rita Hayworth*, he finds solace in the cinema, the source of not only his sentimental education but also his entire worldview. Álvaro adores the teen pop star Angélica María,[6] obsessively follows her career, and writes her fan letters. Shunned by most of the other boys in town, he befriends Toño, a recent arrival from Mexico City. However, when Toño discovers Álvaro's intersex condition, he reacts violently and attempts to rape him. Álvaro kills Toño in self-defense and flees to Mexico City, where he begins to dress as a girl and call him/herself Alba María.

Convinced that she is the long-lost sister of Angélica María, the protagonist unsuccessfully attempts to gain entrance to the former's house, resulting in her arrest and interment in a (female) psychiatric ward. There, she hones her modest talent for singing and later escapes by assaulting a nurse and donning her uniform. Alba María then works as a café singer, records an unsuccessful single, and joins a group of mediocre entertainers on a tour of provincial Mexican cities. She is pursued sexually by Betto, the leader of a rock band, whom she presumably kills after he discovers the secret of her sex. Back in Mexico City, Alba María lives with her friend Amanda Murillo, a has-been film actress, and becomes romantically involved with a tabloid newspaper reporter, Alberto Muñiz. His discovery of Alba María's intersex condition while attempting to drug and rape her leads to his violent death at her hands, just as it did for Toño and Betto. The fallout from this murder pushes Alba María to move to Tijuana, where she undergoes sex reassignment surgery to become Alexina, a cabaret performer. While her new female body initially seems to be the answer to all her prayers, it soon begins to show signs of wear from her medical use of hormones, extreme work regimen, and abuse of drugs and alcohol. By the end of the story, a disillusioned and delusional Alexina comes to blame her "secret sister" for usurping her deserved position. An altercation with the real Angélica María leads to Alexina's internment in a psychiatric ward, where she believes that she is participating in the filming of a picture titled *La hermana secreta*.

From textual clues, it is evident that the story takes place from about 1964 to 1970 in various parts of Mexico, including the capital, Acapulco, Guadalajara, and Tijuana. The plot is divided into three "episodes" composed of alternating fragments that narrate three plotlines corresponding to the incarnations of the main character. Over the course of the novel, it becomes evident that these represent the trajectory of a single protagonist. The stories intersect in the second episode, where there is a backshift in the Alba María storyline, and the book ends with an episode that chronologically precedes the opening scene. The plot is narrated in free indirect style by an omniscient third-person narrator who focalizes through the protagonist, sometimes addressing her in the second-person singular or third-person plural. The narrator always maintains a critical distance from the protagonist and an ironic and sarcastic attitude towards all the characters and their actions.

This distance makes the portrayal of an indeterminate body less a representation of trans or intersex subjectivity than a metaphorical portrayal of the constructed nature of gender (Lewis 155–56). The intersex body of the protagonist likewise problematizes all readings of camp gender parody based on the masculine/feminine script opposition since both his/her performed and supposedly ontological gender are highlighted as social constructs. Humorous uses of *cursilería*, which are based on a modern/unmodern script opposition, appear in this novel in the form of the failed attempts of the characters to imitate higher social strata, the main character's cultural anachronism, as well as in the related parody of melodramatic discourse associated with the mass-media repetition of romantic sentimentality. The constant reiteration of the modern/unmodern script opposition in the frustrated expectations and incongruous behaviors of the protagonist and other characters is the main source of humor. This repetition points to the mass media, and especially cinema, as a key source of discourses of modernity that are divorced from the characters' lived experiences. This emphasis on frustrated expectations allows us to abstract the reading of humorous situations from the modern/unmodern script opposition to one of unreal/real, wherein the "unreal" refers precisely to the illusive world created by the mass-media discourses of modernity. These discourses include contradictory notions of femininity that lead to the protagonist's failure to implement them in a meaningful way in his/her life. Despite the reiteration of the unreal/real script opposition the novel is not a realistic portrayal of queer life or queer subjectivity, but rather a metaphorical critique of the parodic recycling of mass-media portrayals of modernity and femininity in the construction of queer Mexican identities.

The humor based on camp gender parody in this novel is best understood as the parodic reinscription of performances of idealized femininity. Chronologically, this first appears associated with Álvaro, who learns the basics of gender performance from the cinema:

> Sabe cómo demostrar enojo con una simple mirada, indiferencia dando bruscamente la espalda a quien no merece una respuesta, altivez elevando al barbilla, languidez entrecerrando los ojos, sorpresa enarcando una ceja, displicencia mirando hacia un lado y frunciendo apenas la boca.
>
> [He knows how to show anger with a simple look, indifference by quickly turning his back on someone who doesn't deserve a response, arrogance by lifting his chin, languor by lowering his eyelids, surprise by lifting an eyebrow, disdain by looking to the side and slightly pursing his lips.] (24)

Though intersex, Álvaro is considered male by the people of his town and the performance of gestures he has learned from film actresses is read as humorously incongruous by those around him, that is, as a masculine/feminine script opposition. Álvaro's obsession with Angélica María in particular leads him to a methodical imitation of her film acting and public persona that will form the basis of the identity of Alba María who, more than anything, is a sort of watered-down imitation of the star situated in sordid surroundings. This situation of Alba María in marginal contexts can be read as a metacritique of Mexican popular culture as an imitation of US culture, represented here by the images of urban modernity portrayed in the films of the real Angélica María. For example, Alba María develops her persona while interned in a mental hospital in Mexico City:

> Estimulada por los aplausos y las sonrisas de la otras internas, canta para ellas como lo haría su hermana secreta, aunque, a falta de orquesta, se ve obligada a silbar el principio de una melodía; luego, canta mientras camina, colocando un pie en seguida del otro, como si pisara una línea imaginaria: "Paso a pasito llegaré donde vive tu corazón."

> [Stimulated by the smiles and applause of the other patients, she sings for them the way her secret sister would, although, without an orchestra, she's obliged to whistle the beginning of a melody; then, she sings as she walks, putting one foot in front of the other as if she were walking an imaginary line: "Step by step I'll arrive at the place where your heart lives."] (135)

In contrast to Álvaro, the body of Alba María is considered female, so the audience of her performance (the other patients in the hospital) presumably would not read this as a humorous opposition of the masculine and feminine scripts. As readers, however, we know this body as intersex, which allows us to interpret it as an opposition of indeterminate gender/feminine, thus emphasizing the constructed nature of Alba María's feminine performance. The opposition of unreal/real scripts is also operative in this scene, inasmuch as the association of success and glamor with the imitation of Angélica María takes place in the mental hospital rather than on a stage or a similar space associated with the entertainment industry.

A similarly parodic performance of femininity occurs in the construction of Alexina, who rejects the virginal purity of Angélica María's mediatic persona in favor of the hypersexualized femininity of a *cabaretera* [cabaret dancer], such as the characters portrayed by actresses like Ninón Sevilla and Yolanda "Tongolele" Montes in numerous films:

> Alexina, mujer de lava y fuego, energía indómita, diosa de las profundidades de la tierra, nacida al otro lado del mar, en las islas lejanas y misteriosas. Un tímido aplauso la saluda al hacer su entrada. Ella agradece con una sonrisa de Alba María que cambia de inmediato en un gesto despreciativo: nada tiene

que agradecer, los hombres están ahí para rendir pleitesía a su belleza, para admirar su talento.

[Alexina, woman of fire and lava, untamed energy, goddess of the depths of the earth, born on the other side of the sea, in the distant and mysterious islands. A timid applause greets her as she makes her entrance. She thanks the audience with an Alba María smile that immediately changes to a gesture of disdain: she has nothing to be grateful for, the men are then to show respect for her beauty, to admire her talent.] (133)

The audience in this case (the men in the cabaret) would not interpret this performance as an example of an incongruous combination of masculine and feminine scripts in one body. The reader, however, knows that Alexina's body, though possessing a feminine form, continues to exhibit intersex characteristics. For example, in order to maintain her development of female secondary sex characteristics, she must take hormones that cause uncomfortable side effects. Even more important, we know that this is the third time that the protagonist has (re)made him/herself in the image of celluloid and that this performance is based on a similarly uncritical reproduction of portrayals of femininity. It is in this sense that we can read this performance as an example of gender-based humor, in which a problematically ontological "feminine" script is opposed to a feminine script derived from movies. And once again, the protagonist's desire for success contrasts with her reality: she is not in a glamorous cabaret in 1940s Mexico City (as in *cabaretera* films), but in a third-rate club in Tijuana in the late 1960s. The opposition of unreal and real scripts is apparent here again, just as it is in the use of *cursi* humor, which, in this novel, frequently intersects with humor based on camp gender parody.

Lo cursi appears in this text most frequently as cultural anachronism or failed attempts by the characters to imitate higher social strata or be "modern," the knowledge of which they derive from the mass media. We can see this in the contrast between Álvaro's dusty village and the images of urban sophistication projected on the silver screen. It is precisely his attempt to imitate the "crueldad refinada" ["refined cruelty"] and "cinismo elegante" ["elegant cynicism"] of the women who populate this imaginary world that make him a ridiculous figure in the eyes of his classmates. While he attempts to imitate this image of modernity, of bourgeois consumerism in the big city with attendant melodramatic cynicism, he is still just a poor boy in a village in rural Mexico. This desire to take part in a consumerist modernity is also evident in Álvaro's dreams about Angélica María, where she whisks him from his village to the capital and they throw parties attended by other teen idols, "comen sandwiches en triangulitos, beben refrescos con popote y bailan un twist interpretado por las Hermanas Jiménez" ["eat sandwiches cut into triangles, drink sodas with straws and dance a twist sung by the Jiménez Sisters"] (68). This description, in particular, parodies the *comedia juvenil* [youth comedy] film genre, a part of the sentimental education of the 1960s that recycled traditional national myths in terms of a "modern" young, urban middle class (Bencomo, "*La hermana*" 77). In the example above, the modern/unmodern script opposition resides in Álvaro's attempt to participate in such myths despite his marginal, impoverished, rural (unmodern) social condition.

This contradiction continues with the travails of Alba María, whose dreams of success and romance (also based on the myths cited above) are frustrated by her lived experiences. The contrast is notable in the series of letters that she writes to her deceased grandmother, which interpret everything in terms of what *should* be happening, what no doubt *will* eventually happen, rather than what actually *is* happening. She describes her participation in the regional tour thus:

> "Empiezo esta carta en Cuernavaca, a la que le dicen la Ciudad de la Eterna Primavera por su clima tan Bonito aunque ahorita hace bastante calor, sobre todo yo creo que porque estamos encerrados todos en un mismo camerino." Tacha "estamos encerrados todos en un mismo camerino" y escribe (ni modo, tendrá que pasarla en limpio): "el teatro está lleno a reventar."
>
> ["I begin this letter in Cuernavaca, called the City of Eternal Spring because of its Pretty climate although right now it's very hot, I think especially because all of us are shut in the same dressing room." She crosses out "all of us are shut in the same dressing room" and writes (oh well, she'll have to rewrite the whole thing): "the theater is full to bursting."] (18)

The modernity that she aspires to, based on her understanding of a successful show business career, is contrasted with her sordid surroundings, producing a humorous passage that can be read both as an opposition of modern/unmodern and unreal/real scripts. This opposition is highlighted in her interactions during the tour with the rock singer Betto, who writes his name with two t's because he thinks it gives it "un toque exótico" ["an exotic touch"] and wears buttons with English-language slogans to associate himself with the US counterculture (19–20). Both he and Alba María are portrayed as attempting, and humorously failing, to imitate higher social strata that they identify with discourses of modernity: middle-class US hippies and teen pop idols.

Betto, whose interest in Alba María is purely sexual, and who ends up dead as a result, exemplifies how the protagonist's ideas about love and gender relations, also learned from the mass media, clash with her lived experience. In another example, Alberto Muñiz, the reporter she dates (whose beat is entertainment and *nota roja* ["red news," violent crimes and sensational accidents]), is described as "corrientito" ["common"] and "prietito" ["dark-skinned"] (75). That is, he does not conform to the image of the handsome, bourgeois, white boyfriend, portrayed by an actor like Enrique Guzmán, that Angélica María would have in one of her films. Alberto's presence in Alba María's life is narrated in a series of scenes that can be read humorously as modern/unmodern and unreal/real script oppositions, in which the aspirational mate exemplified by a relatively wealthy, white, and chivalrous character is replaced by a dark-skinned, economically marginal, and lecherous subject whose courtship does not involve chaste, saliva-free kisses but the aggressive pursuit of sex. This relationship represents a node of internal conflict for Alba María because while she insists on preserving her virginity, she suspects (rightly) that Alberto will not interview her for his newspaper if she does not accede to his demands. Her friend and roommate, Amanda Murillo, the has-been film actress, argues that she should give in in order to further her career. Her ironic references to Alba María's decency highlights another aspect of her *cursilería*: that of cultural anachronism.

Cursilería can be understood as a cultural anachronism inasmuch as it reiterates cultural tropes and values that are considered, from the perspective of certain discourses of modernity, as passé. Such is the case with romantic sentiment (Monsiváis, "La cursilería"). For Alba María, this anachronism centers not only on sentiment but also on values related to gender, such as that of female virginity. For example, when Betto takes her hand while they are walking on the street, she worries what this will mean for her sense of decency: "No le preocupa lo que [Betto] pueda pensar de ella (con seguridad trata a otro tipo de mujeres, a quienes la moral las tiene sin cuidado), sino lo que ella misma pueda pensar de ella—barroca Alba María" ["She is not worried about what Betto might think of her (surely he's used to dealing with other kinds of women, who don't care about morals), but what she might think about herself—she's baroque, this Alba María"] (22). This passage, which illustrates the narrator's constant sarcastic and ironic orientation towards the protagonist, also exemplifies her exaggerated sense of feminine decency, which she has learned mainly from the films of Angélica María.

The actress is particularly relevant to this, since her 1960s film roles projected a persona that was both very feminine and also asexual, in a sort of Mexican recycling of the characters played by North American actresses like Mary Pickford in the first decades of the 20th century (Bencomo, "*La hermana*" 75). The incongruity inherent in this figure is summarized in Alba María's contradictory assertion that both she and her idol are "modernas pero decentes" ["modern but decent"] (95). That is, Angélica María represents a notion of modernity defined by the possibility of participating in bourgeois consumerism while maintaining traditional Catholic values that include a tight social control of female sexuality. She incarnates, in this sense, an opposition of modern and unmodern scripts, and thus she represents conflicts in Mexican society related to the desire to participate in modernity and to simultaneously maintain traditional values. In the novel, however, the humor of this script opposition does not center on the figure of Angélica María herself but rather on her imitator, Alba María, who repeatedly encounters frustrated expectations since her lived experience differs radically from the idealized modernity of the films she has seen.

Eventually, Alba María comes to reject this model of femininity in favor of that which she incarnates as Alexina. This change, however, does not overcome the conflicts inherent in Alba María's desire to be modern and decent. Rather, it represents the exchange of the virginal figure of Angélica María, from 1960s cinema, for the equally cinematic figure of the *cabaretera*, which had its heyday in the 1940s. While the aggressive sexuality of such figures might be read as a challenge to traditional morality, it is also inscribed in the economy of male desire and may also be considered a reiteration of the virgin/whore dichotomy operative in traditional Mexican culture. In the end, neither the "good" nor the "bad" girl characterizations of the protagonist allow her to achieve her desired social ascent which, as always, is enunciated in melodramatically *cursi* terms associated with love stories: "¿Volverá a tocar el amor a las puertas de su debilitado corazón? Ojalá" ["Will love once again knock on the door of her weakened heart? Hopefully"] (105).

This last quotation, which illustrates the longing of Alexina to participate in love as she understands it, shows both the ironic stance of the narrator with regard to the main character and the manner in which the formal parody of *cursi* melodramatic language is used in the construction of the plot. This use is evident in the division of the novel into three "episodes," each of which carries the title of a film starring Angélica María: *Mi vida es una canción* ["My Life Is a Song"]; *Vivir de sueños* ["Living on Dreams"]; and *El cielo y la tierra* ["Heaven and Earth"]. The first pages of the second of these includes a series of subtitles that parody the melodramatic narrative conventions of genres such as the *fotonovela* [photo-novels, a type of magazine with stories illustrated with photographs]: "Hay una intervención favorable del azar en la vida dolorosa de Alba María. El azar interviene favorablemente y hace olvidar a Alvaro sus dolores" ["There is a favorable intervention of fate in the painful life of Alba María. Fate intervenes favorably and makes Álvaro forget his pains"] (69). Such organization reinforces the modern/unmodern and unreal/real script oppositions in the events of the protagonist's life by highlighting the difference between the conventions of melodramatic narrative that she expects to order her experiences and what actually happens. Similarly, the narrator uses epithets, which may be read as a parody of the conventions of *radionovelas* [radio soap operas] (Bencomo, "*La hermana*" 74), or of entertainment journalism, in a manner that highlights the modern/unmodern script opposition inherent in the characters' attempts to imitate higher social strata. For example, Alba María's friend and roommate Amanda Murillo, the has-been film actress, is known as "la otrora" ["the erstwhile"] (45, 57, etc.) and "la célebre ex-estrella" ["the celebrated ex-star"] (26), while Betto is known as "el cantante del pronto internacionalmente famoso grupo Amok" ["the singer of the soon-to-be internationally famous group Amok"] (28), or "el Inminente" ["the Soon-to-Be"] (40), and Alba María is referred to as "la Futura" ["the Future"] (32), "la Inevitablemente Destinada a la Notoriedad" ["the Unavoidably Destined for Fame"] (65), "la Muchacha de los Ojos Esperanzados" ["the Girl with the Hopeful Eyes"] (72), "la Nacida Para Cantar" ["the Born to Sing"] (144), and "la Muchacha de la Mirada Límpida y la Sonrisa Benévola" ["the Girl with the Clear Gaze and the Benevolent Smile"] (146).

There is also a great deal of *cursi* language used by the characters themselves, as when Amanda tells Alba María the story of how she had a daughter with a married man who would not leave his wife because she was a paraplegic and how the child died while she was filming in Central America but no one notified her until well after the fact, so that her performance would not be affected. While Alba María is thinking that the story is suspiciously similar to the plot of a film, Amanda interrupts her thoughts: "Sí, la vida es como una película, chula, sólo que más larga y, por lo mismo, más dolorosa" ["Yes, life is like a movie, honey, only longer, and because of that, more painful"] (59). In the context of the novel, the sheer melodrama of this passage is humorous, inasmuch as it can be read as a parody that highlights the modern/unmodern script opposition that opposes the epic, modern, economically successful reality of cinema to Amanda and Alba María's current circumstances (living in poverty in Mexico City). Whether these events actually took place in the life of Amanda Murillo is beside the point, since their real importance has to do with the contrast between imagined and actual experience and the parodic critique of melodrama.

Despite the importance of the real/unreal script opposition to the humor of this novel, its organization around the formal parody of melodramatic clichés distances it from a truly realistic style (Bencomo, "La hermana" 73). Furthermore, the narrator's ironic, unsympathetic portrayal of the protagonist inhibits the reader's identification with him/her and the novel presents his/her intersex condition more than anything as a theoretical construct, factors that make it difficult to read this novel as a portrayal of trans or intersex subjectivity (Lewis 155–58). Indeed, it has been suggested that in the context of the novel's camp humor the main character's intersex condition might simply be a metaphor for male homosexuality (Westmoreland 45n2). This is a critical point since there are very few portrayals of intersex individuals in Latin American cultural production, far fewer, indeed than of *travestis*. Significantly, there have been two films, both from Argentina, that have included intersex protagonists in recent years: Lucía Puenzo's *XXY* (2007) and Julia Solomonoff's *El último verano de la Boyita* [*The Last Summer of La Boyita*, 2009]. As Venkatesh argues, both of these works exemplify a shift from a specular portrayal of queerness in Latin American cinema to one in which the establishment of viewer empathy with main characters is central to the ideological content.[7] Their sympathetic and profound portrayal of intersex characters contrasts sharply with the ironic distancing of *La hermana secreta*, which tends to inhibit readerly identification with the protagonist.

This begs the question of whether it is even possible to truly approach Zapata's novel from a reparative perspective (its aptness for paranoid interpretation is amply illustrated above). For Bencomo, this possibility seems to lie in the way that the text portrays aspects of the author's own subjectivity. Reading the novel alongside Zapata's autobiography, she notes how Álvaro's childhood obsession with the cinema (and with Angélica María in particular) as an escape from his dreary, rural existence is very similar to Zapata's own lived childhood experiences and his own early idealization of the actress ("La hermana" 78). For these reasons, she argues, the text is something of an ambivalent tribute to the sentimental education provided by the Mexican mass media in the 1960s, during the childhood of Zapata, that includes a sort of self-referential irony in which the author pokes fun at his own earlier internalization of that ideology. In other words, the novel, above all else, can be understood as an expression of disidentification with gender norms and contemporary Mexican consumer culture.

As I suggested above, Álvaro/Alba María/Alexina is portrayed as the copy of a copy, a figure who imitates figures who themselves imitate notions of femininity and modernity with origins in the Global North. In this way, a great deal of the humor of the novel ironically critiques the ideology of Latin American culture as a copy (Santos 7, 51, 59–61, 185n30). Of course, this also means that this is a text in which a cisgender gay male author (Zapata) has appropriated an intersex figure in order to figuratively portray his own ideas about the discourses of gender and modernity, which brings us back to Lewis's critique of the marginalization of trans and intersex subjectivities. However, I would argue that the novel's queer humor offers possibilities for readerly identification that transcend Zapata's own gay male identity to the point of being relevant to any reader whose sentimental education and gender identity have been influenced by the Latin American mass media. To the extent that readers are able to identify with the novel's self-referential critique, as Bencomo (a cisgender, heterosexual woman from Venezuela) does in her reading, a reparative approach to the text is certainly possible. As I argued above, most of the portrayals of *travesti* and similar protagonists that employ a high frequency of camp and *cursi* humor tend to include highly figurative portrayals that allegorize certain social processes and conflicts. In the case of *La hermana secreta*, that portrayal is almost completely metaphorical, while in the other texts that I analyze below, there is often a greater emphasis on the construction of subjectivities that does not preclude, however, a self-conscious engagement with the highly allegorical Mexican literary tradition.

Brenda Berenice o el diario de una loca

Brenda Berenice o el diario de una loca (1985) is the only novel published by the Sonoran author Luis Montaño (1954–1985). As the title suggests, it takes the form of a diary in which the protagonist, Brenda Berenice, narrates a series of experiences that encompass most of her life story. In part a parody of *Vampiro*, which is mentioned as an ironic intertextuality, this novel gives voice not to the conflicted "homosexual de corazón" but to his opposite, a screaming *loca*. Addressing the diary in the second person, the narrator intersperses autobiographical anecdotes with reflections on love and culture in an attempt to constitute a dissident identity in opposition to mainstream Mexican society. Through this narration, we learn that Brenda was baptized Gerardo Urbiñón Campos in a small town in an unnamed state in northern Mexico. Conscious of his effeminacy and homosexuality at an early age, Gerardo clashes with the conservative values of his family and the surrounding society. His incipient queer consciousness is bolstered by childhood friends with the same inclinations and by his first lover, with whom he elopes to Mexico City. The end of this relationship marks an important point in the protagonist's development, for it is at this moment that he first dresses as a woman and assumes the identity of Brenda Berenice.

Brenda identifies alternately as a *loca*, a *jota*, and a *mujir*, three terms that denote an identity based on an attraction to men, an identification with effeminacy, and self-expression through gender parody and cross-dressing (19, 36, 67). Brenda identifies closely with the gay male culture of her time and place, and the diary entries portray several aspects of this culture, including drag performance and the experience of police harassment. The protagonist also makes forays into the world of the university, the fashion industry, and the gay club scene of Los Angeles, California. A common thread in almost all of these stories, which are presented in nonchronological order as if by association, is Brenda's failure in her attempt to find true and lasting love. This desire, which is couched in *cursi* terms gleaned from the mass media, can be read as a metaphor of the search for social acceptance.

Brenda's embrace of camp gender nonconformity and attendant *cursilería* constitutes a disidentification with dominant social norms expressed through a privileging of the feminine over the masculine and unmodern, *cursi* sentimentality over modern rationality. Her uncritical reiteration of prejudices related to gender, class, and race, along with the book's somewhat truncated plot, makes the unresolved conflicts in her character and the society she inhabits stand out. These are the aspects that are most apt for paranoid interpretation. However, her uses of camp and *cursi* humor to transcend negative affect, foster collective identification, and queer the Mexican literary tradition also provide opportunities for reparative reading. This text also combines, albeit somewhat clumsily, a portrayal of subjectivity with an ironic engagement with the allegorical tradition. In fact, the desire to subvert the traditional ways that people like her have been represented by that tradition forms a central part of Brenda's narrative, thus illustrating how more "realistic" portrayals of subjectivity can be combined with figurative portrayals.

The theme of this novel is Brenda's construction of her dissident identity, and camp gender nonconformity plays a large part in this. She defines herself as "Hija de reina y nieta de general; hasta la fecha mujir de cuatro maridos y aventuras varias. Brenda Berenice me llamo por decisión propia, aunque alguna vez mis padres me pusieron Gerardo Urbiñón Campos" ["A queen's daughter and a general's granddaughter; to date a woman of four husbands and many adventures. My name is Brenda Berenice by my own choice, though my parents once named me Gerando Urbiñón Campos"] (37). Here she makes an explicit contrast between her given name and assigned gender and her self-chosen name and gender, setting up a script opposition in her own (biologically male) body that performs an exaggerated femininity narrated through mock-heroic and melodramatic exploits. We can also observe the use of Mexican *loca* argot in the use of the word *mujir* (a distortion of *mujer*, woman), a characteristic that is evident in all of Brenda's discourse.

While her self-definition is clearly individualistic, she also understands herself as part of a collective of individuals with similar experiences. In this sense, camp and *cursi* humor intersect in the constitution of a collective of *jotas* who serve as moral support for each other, a clearly reparative use of humor. A considerable portion of her diary is given to the description of her best friends, whom she refers to as the *Batichicas* ["Bat-girls"]. The leader of this group is "La mamá grande" ["Big Mama"]: "deja frío a todo el mundo pues la gente espera que hable como David Reynoso, y ella sale con la vocecita de la chilindrina, ni más ni menos. Se presenta como mujer del norte, ancha de cadera y muy paridora" ["she shocks everyone since they expect her to talk like David Reynoso, but she has the voice of la chilindrina, exactly. She introduces herself as a northern woman, with wide hips and capable of bearing many children"] (52).[8]

This character incarnates the masculine/feminine script opposition, while Brenda's humorous description of her includes the sort of deprecatory ribbing that Monsiváis identifies in the homosexual culture that Novo formed a part of in the 1920s and 30s ("Manos" 25–26). Although such humor reflects the internalization of homophobia and machismo, it also functions as a type of self-defense, and may also be used aggressively to this end, as in Salvador Novo's satirical attacks on Diego Rivera in his poem "La Diegada." Similarly, Brenda's self-defense sometimes includes the humorous feminizing of masculine figures who have used violence against her. For example, Brenda/Gerardo's father, when he learns of his son's homosexuality, comes to beat him "convertido en una perra, en una loba que echaba espuma por la boca" ["transformed into a bitch, into a she-wolf foaming at the mouth"] (111). At another point, Brenda refers to a police officer as "Mrs. Changa" ["Mrs. Monkey"], in a feminization of her original characterization of the officer as gorilla (111, 34).

"Mrs. Changa" appears in an episode (very similar to one in *Vampiro*) in which Brenda and several friends are arrested and held by the police until they are able to produce money for bribes, an abuse perpetuated against them since they are dressed as women and therefore (presumably) homosexual. Brenda narrates this entire traumatic experience through her habitual lens of camp humor, thus illustrating the importance in her worldview of humor as a method of overcoming the negative affect associated with suffering violence and discrimination. When she is finally released, Brenda meets up with a young man she had met on the inside (referred to as "Bambi" because of his doe-eyed look), and with whom she enters into a romantic relationship soon after:

Decidimos esperar a Bambi en la esquina. No tardó en salir. Entonces, sin reprimir mi alegría le grité al tiempo que corría hacia el [*sic*] con los brazos extendidos "¡Bambi Bambi!" Y él, al descubrirme hizo lo mismo: "¡Brenda Brenda!" Y yo otra vez "¡Bambi Bambi!" Querido diario, la distancia que nos separaba parecía eterna, infinita. ¡Qué Descartiana me ví! [*sic*] Te juro que aquella escena nos salió mejor que la de "Amigos."

[We decided to wait for Bambi on the corner. He didn't take long to come out. Then, without repressing my happiness, I yelled, at the same time that I ran to him with open arms, "Bambi Bambi!" And he, upon seeing me, did the same: "Brenda Brenda!" And again "Bambi Bambi!" Dear diary, the distance that separated us seemed eternal, infinite. How Cartesian! I swear that that scene came out better than the one in "Amigos."] (35)

Reading this scene from a perspective informed by Cartesian dualism, as Brenda's own comment suggests, we can see that the narration here sets up a masculine/feminine script opposition both in Brenda's body (masculine sex, feminine performance) as well as in her mind—she references both Descartes and a *telenovela* (*Amigos*) in order to describe the scene. This incongruous combination of sources can be read as a masculine/feminine script opposition if we take into account the longstanding cultural association of high culture and rationalism with the masculine and the contrasting association of emotion and "frivolous" popular texts with the feminine (Gundermann 37).

Brenda Berenice's juxtaposition of elite and vulgar allusions effects a carnivalization of "serious," "masculine" high culture and an elevation of "frivolous," "feminine" mass culture, thus creating humor based on a masculine/feminine script opposition. This incongruous combination of high- and low-culture elements is a central part of Brenda's self-expression, and she frequently makes ambivalent references to her erudition that also include self-deprecating camp humor, describing herself as "descartiana" ["Cartesian"] (14), "hegeliana" ["Hegelian"] (45), "marxiana" ["Marxian"] (113), or insisting that after she studied philosophy and literature at the National University she felt like "la ramera más culta de latinoamérica" ["the most cultured whore in Latin America"] (14). While this humor is used by the character for reparative coping purposes and in order to construct her identity, it also reflects internalized homophobia and conflicts related to social class and modernity.

These internal contradictions are intimately related to Brenda's experience of modernity as a Mexican, which she expresses most frequently through humor related to *cursilería* and *naquez*. While her humorous parodic reinscription of high- and low-culture elements might be read as postmodern, they are more properly described by Bartra's term *dismodern*. That is, they reflect how discourses of modernity have largely been imposed through colonization and the projects of political elites that have reiterated the coloniality of power, gender, and sex. Humor related to *lo cursi*, which is based on the simultaneous perception of modern and unmodern scripts, is one expression of the ambivalence felt towards these discourses in Mexico. This script opposition is evident in Brenda's simultaneous evocation of Descartes and a *telenovela* in melodramatic terms that echo the *cursi* clichés of that genre. The philosopher is not only associated with rational masculinity, but his works are a cornerstone of modernity as defined from the Eurocentric perspective. The other side of the coin is the *telenovela*, here unmodern (despite being a product of contemporary industry) because of its melodramatic, feminine sentimentality and peripheral (Latin American) production and reception. Brenda's disidentification with dominant Western masculinist culture includes a constant juxtaposition of *cursi* mass-media and erudite references that rests on both the celebration and denigration of the feminine and the simultaneous celebration and rejection of Eurocentric notions of modernity.

For example, at the beginning of one diary entry, writing about another of her failed attempts to find love, she references the song "Señora" by the popular singer Rocío Jurado:

> Voy a aumentar los mares con mi llanto, voy a llorar, y llorar y llorar; siempre llorar. Él me dijo que era libre, querido diario, y yo lo creí. Ahora es tarde señora, ahora es tarde . . . ¡Qué bueno que hay tantas canciones populares para expresar los sentimientos, si no, me volvería loca!

> [I'm going to overflow the seas with my tears, I'm going to cry, and cry and cry; cry forever. He told me that he was free, dear diary, and I believed him. Now it's late, madame, now it's late . . . Thankfully there are so many popular songs to express our feelings, otherwise, I'd go mad!] (68)

Immediately following this, to underline how great her loss is, she notes that the man in question had complimented her bottom with a recherché cultural reference that she would not have understood had she not gone to university.[9] With one foot in the feminine world of sentiment and one in the masculine world of history, Brenda signals both the importance of *cursilería* as her main source of sentimental education and her desire to distinguish herself as cultured in a modern, Eurocentric sense. There is also an element of class consciousness underlying these declarations that becomes clearer when she uses humor related to *cursilería* and *naquez* to signal social boundaries.

Although she has experienced poverty in the city, Brenda implies that she is from an upper-middle-class background and has had corresponding privileges and experiences (such as studying humanities in the university).[10] One of the ways that she signals this is through the contrast with other characters, especially her two friends "La Sulfurosa" and "La Nacarada" (whose name evokes the class- and race-based insult *naco/a*), *travestis* who are streetwalking sex workers. She comments on the appearance of one of them in the dress shop that she owns with a friend thus:

> No es que yo sea mala pero ella nunca podrá descollar en sociedad. ¡Es tan pobre y tan ilutsa! [. . .] Llegó con una falda estampada con manchitas de tigre y una blusa color naranja ¡qué desfiguros! para verguenza [*sic*] no gana una. Violeta estaba fúrica y casi me tragaba con la mirada por tener ese tipo de amistades.
>
> Not to be malicious, but she could never stand out in society. She's so poor and so naïve! [. . .] She showed up with a tiger-striped skirt and an orange blouse, how unsightly! she couldn't be more embarrassing. Violeta was furious, staring daggers at me for having that sort of friend. (127)

This description clearly uses humor based on a modern/unmodern script opposition to signal what Brenda sees as la Sulfurosa's failed attempt to imitate a higher social stratum (represented by Brenda and her friend Violet, who own a boutique that sells what they consider tasteful clothes).

Brenda's class prejudice also has racial undertones that are indicated by certain details in her comments. For example, she says that wearing tennis shoes and exercise clothes outside of athletic competition, in imitation of US fashions, "resulta más insoportable que comer chilaquiles con champagne, como acostumbran los nuevo ricos" ["is more unbearable than eating chilaquiles with champagne, like the nouveaux riches do"] (77). This hyperbolic critique juxtaposes the modern, European luxury product with traditional Mexican cooking (derived from Indigenous tradition) in a script opposition that communicates, once again, the notion of a failed attempt to imitate higher social strata. Her critique of dilettante athletes with large guts who rush to imitate US fashions in their desire to be modern is a pointed critique of the Mexican bourgeoisie. It also contains an element of internalized racism, since it insinuates that Mexicans are both culturally and physically inferior to North Americans and, therefore, incapable of achieving the same sort of physical fitness, an index of modernity.

The notion of being *cursi* or *naco* that underlies these comments delimiting class boundary actually reflect a generalized anxiety regarding modernity—the fear that no matter how high on the social pyramid one might be, one will never be as modern as those in the Global North (Monsiváis, "Léperos"; Serna, "El naco"). Brenda expresses this anxiety when she relates how her boyfriend in Los Angeles took her to a bath house where men had anonymous sexual encounters.

> De inmediato, esa sangre latina de la que tanto alardeo, roja y celosa hizo ebullición. Después recapacité que ya no era una mocita para comportarme así [. . .] me había ocurrido que Michael sería sólo para mí. ¡Ilutsa, pobre ilutsa romántica emperranida de mí!
>
> Immediately, that Latin blood that I'm so proud of boiled, red and jealous. Later I reconsidered that I wasn't a little girl and shouldn't be acting like that [. . .] I had thought that Michael would only be for me. Naïve, poor naïve romantic foolish me! (117)

Here she explicitly links her desire for monogamy to unmodern sentimentality and is ashamed of it, thus establishing a modern/unmodern script opposition in her own persona. This attitude is notably similar to the shame Adonis García feels in *Vampiro* about the "third-world" sentiment in his relationships and reflects the contradictory desire to construct an identity that can be Mexican and modern at the same time. For Brenda this ambivalence is particularly poignant since her entire self-image is one of a femininity that takes *cursilería* not only as its sentimental education but also as its very basis of expression. Notably, she still appeals to humor as a coping mechanism for making sense of the conflicting aspects of her identity.

I have shown that Brenda uses camp and *cursi* humor, most specifically gender parody, to construct her identity by disidentifying with mainstream culture and values through the transcendence of negative affect and the constitution of collectives. It is also important to note how she insists, through the parodic reinscription of dominant discourses, on the writing of her dissident life story into the history of Mexico and Mexican literature. This is evident in the self-definition cited above that not only invokes Revolutionary history ("nieta de general") but also places her heritage as daughter of a beauty queen ("hija de reina") on the same level as that of granddaughter of a general. In this way she subverts the traditional masculinist bent of official Mexican history in order to include an equivalent valuation of the feminine as well as her own queer subjectivity. A parallel subversive gesture can be found in her proposed addition to the dictionary of alternative definitions for the term "jota." From the letter j, or a dance, or a type of soup, we pass through increasingly queer definitions in order to arrive at a basic definition of herself: "Dícese del joto que ya perdió toda concepción de los límites. Hombre de grandes vuelos" ["Said of the *joto* who has lost all concept of limits. Man of great flights"] (19).

However, at the end of this diary entry, she laments that she will never, ever become part of the Royal Academy of the Spanish Language, which seems to signal a rather fatalistic sense of marginality. This fatalism is reinforced by Brenda's failure to ever satisfy her desire to find true love, and the novel ends with her lament: "Ahí tienes a Sor Juana quejándose amargamente que ella quiere a Favio, y Favio ve tu [*sic*] a saber a quien [*sic*] diablos, menos a ella [. . .] Si a Sor Juana no le hicieron caso, ¿qué esperanzas tengo yo? Dime: ¿qué esperanzas?" ["There you have Sor Juana complaining bitterly that she loves Favio, and who the hell knows who he loves, but not her [. . .] If they didn't pay attention to Sor Juana, what hope do I have? Tell me: what hope?"] (147) If we read her search for love as a metaphor for her search for social acceptance, this seems like a very pessimistic ending for the book, one that does not posit any sort of resolution of the social conflicts lived by the protagonist. In this way, the ending is somewhat similar to the existentially pessimistic tone of Mexican novels with homosexual characters that were published before *Vampiro*, such as *El diario de José Toledo*.[11]

However, *Brenda Berenice* contains something that *El diario* does not: a clear project of disidentification through the reparative uses of camp and *cursi* humor and the queering of the Mexican literary canon. Montaño's novel leaves much to be desired in terms of its narrative structure, literary style, and even editing (the text is full of typographical errors, as evidenced in the quotes above), but it also connects a portrayal of *jota* subjectivity to the allegorical literary tradition in Mexico and offers many examples of how camp and *cursi* humor can serve to transcend negative affect and constitute collectives. One of the few academic studies of this text criticizes it for recycling gender tropes in a way that does not problematize the norms that underlie mass media texts (Gordus 289–90). I do not completely agree with this assessment. While the *character* Brenda Berenice does indeed have a blind spot regarding gender norms, the *novel* as a whole can be read as a critique of how gender and class norms are internalized by the protagonist. The unresolved nature of Brenda's conflicts, both internal and social, might be clumsily portrayed, but they do reflect real social conflicts that do not have any easy dialectical resolution.

Chronologically speaking, *Brenda Berenice*, which was published in 1985, belongs to the same time period (late 1970s-early 1980s) as *Vampiro* and *Utopía gay*. Not surprisingly, it also portrays some of the same social issues, including police harassment and the intersection of consumerist modernity with sexual dissidence. Like these other novels, *Brenda Berenice* also portrays Mexico City as the locus of contemporary homosexual culture in Mexico, in opposition to the provinces where it is much more difficult to live as a gay man or *jota*. The next two texts that I will consider also offer portrayals of *jota* or *vestida* protagonists, but they refer to a different context—not Mexico City in the late 70s-early 80s but northern Mexico in the early 2000s. These narratives also use camp and *cursi* humor in ways that combine the portrayal of subjectivities and ironic engagement with the allegorical tradition. Like *Brenda Berenice*, they are also best approached from a perspective that takes this combination into account through both paranoid and reparative reading practices.

La marrana negra de la literatura rosa

Carlos Velázquez's short story collection *La marrana negra de la literatura rosa* ["The Black Sow of Romance Literature"] focuses on socially marginal characters from a perspective characterized by the use of grotesque, sarcastic humor and the irreverent, parodic reinscription of mass-media tropes and northern Mexican cultural references. It includes two stories, "La jota de Bergerac" and "La marrana negra de la literatura rosa," that can be read as portrayals of subjectivities where male homoeroticism and identification with female gender intersect. The first of these stories presents a highly ironic, but ultimately positive, portrayal of *vestida* subjectivity that uses satirical humor to question traditional sex and gender norms and their transmission through allegorical film narratives. The second story is an even more ironic portrayal of the construction of a queer identity that parodies the typical narratives of romance literature. Both stories use camp and *cursi* humor along with a stylistic parody of traditional, figurative writing in a way that creates a tension between the construction of dissident subjectivities and discourses that uphold basic values of the dominant social structure. For these reasons, an approach combining both paranoid and reparative reading practices is well suited to exploring all the signifying possibilities in these texts.

The title of "La jota de Bergerac" refers to Alexia, a *jota*, *loca*, *travesti*, or *vestida* (as she prefers to be called), whose nickname references her enormous nose, the only physical aspect that mars an otherwise perfect beauty and, as such, is the only obstacle standing between her and the crown of Miss Gay in her native city of Torreón, Coahuila.[12] Though she has worked for several years as a prostitute, Alexia, who is of low socioeconomic status, has never been able to save enough money for the operation. This situation changes with the arrival of Wilmar, the new Cuban pitcher for the local baseball team, who becomes a regular customer and promises, among other things, to pay for her plastic surgery. When Wilmar perceives that Alexia brings him good luck when seated in the stands, he begins to court her formally, eventually proposing marriage. As her value as a totem increases, however, Wilmar loses interest in her sexually and begins an affair with a younger *travesti*. He maintains his control over Alexia by keeping her in the role of wife, refusing to allow her to return to the street while constantly postponing his promise to pay for her surgery. Though she has fallen in love with Wilmar, Alexia recognizes that he is stringing her along and decides to leave him, resolving to compete in the Miss Gay pageant and participate in the local gay pride march despite not having replaced her nose. After she is kidnapped, beaten, and raped by men hired by Wilmar to intimidate her, the Cuban arrives, apologetic, and insists that she accompany him to the baseball stadium for a championship game. Alexia begins to fellate him and, as he reaches the point of climax, amputates his member with a pocket knife. Bruised, beaten, and with her dress in tatters, Alexia returns to the street, phallus in hand, to take her place at the front of the pride march.

Much of the humor in this story derives from the third-person narrator's depiction of how Alexia constructs her identity with camp and *cursi* humor, particularly through the parody of mass-media portrayals of femininity. Alexia and Wilmar's desire to achieve and represent a level of economic success that they perceive as modern can also be read as a type of *cursilería* that intersects with their respective performances of gender. "La jota" ends with a parodic subversion of the traditional melodramatic plot of Mexican Golden-Age cinema in which the female figure who transgresses sex norms is punished, as well as a rejection of the limiting gender roles of the marriage model in favor of the queer expression of *vestida* identity. The metaphor of the nose and desire for rhinoplasty (standing in for the male genitalia and sex reassignment surgery, respectively) might be read as too obvious or clumsy. I would suggest, however, that this obviousness be read as an intentional use of a simple metaphor that is meant to parody figurative writing in general and the Mexican literary tradition in particular. Indeed, the use of such metaphors, along with an attitude of *relajo* towards literary and cultural conventions and a generally grotesque and carnivalesque style, is present in all of Velázquez's work. The cartoonish metaphor of the nose used in this case ultimately suggests that *vestida* identity should be valued for what it is—a queerness that transcends gender norms, which is quite a radical proposal in itself.

This queerness is evident in the unresolved tension between the masculine and feminine in Alexia's persona. The notion that Alexia is neither a man nor a woman but a *vestida* who combines physical and social aspects of both is reiterated several times in the story, frequently with humor based on a masculine/feminine script opposition. For example, the narrator notes that she satisfies Wilmar's desire for an "Eva Longoria mangueruda" ["well-hung Eva Longoria"] (46). At the same time, her decision to hold him to his promise to pay for her rhinoplasty is portrayed as a masculine behavior connected to notions of virile honor:

> lo que Wilmar no atendía de su ofrecimiento es que Alexia no era una mujer. A una mujer le puedes prometer, le puedes fallar, la decepcionas y siempre estará ahí. Su naturaleza es perdonar.
> A una "vestida" tienes que cumplirle.
> No se trata de amor. Es un pacto. Entre hombres.
>
> [what Wilmar wasn't noting about his offer was that Alexia was not a woman. You can promise things to a woman, you can fail her, disappoint her and she'll always be there. Her nature is to forgive.
>
> You have to keep your promises to a "vestida."
> It's not love. It's a deal. Between men.] (48)

This script opposition becomes operational thanks to Alexia's performance of gender which, like Brenda Berenice's, involves the parodic reinscription of mass-media portrayals of femininity. For Alexia, the ultimate model is the character played by Marga López in the film *Salón México* (Emilio Fernández, 1949),[13] and she likens herself to this woman who "se arrastra por un mísero peso" ["drags herself through the street for a measly peso"]. In contrast to the character in the movie, Brenda does not sacrifice herself to pay for her sister's schooling but rather to pay for her nose job (40). When she falls in love with Wilmar, she transfers this sacrificial behavior from herself to him, deciding to "arrastrarse, venderse, anegarse por la causa del otro" ["drag herself through the street, sell herself, negate herself for the sake of the other"] (54).

This performance of femininity, which reflects Alexia's sentimental education and worldview, is *cursi* in its reiteration of melodramatic language and view of life as tragedy circumscribed by women's duty to sacrifice themselves. The *cursi* humor in this story is also closely connected to the desire to be modern and the notion of a failed attempt to imitate the tastes of higher social strata. Alexia's face is described early on as that of a "modelo europea de imitación" ["imitation European model"] (37), solidifying in her body the racialized modern/un-modern script opposition that underlies this type of humor. Her notion of modernity, connected in her mind with the success represented by winning the Miss Gay pageant, is also based on the idea of participating in bourgeois consumer culture. This is amply illustrated by her fantasies about London suggested by the air freshener hanging from the rear-view mirror in Wilmar's car, which says "Inglaterra" ["England"]:

> Londres, era en lo único que pensaba Alexia en su segundo servicio a Wilmar. Vino a su mente el Big Ben al ver el enorme miembro del cubano. Aunque no lo conocía, mientras era pentrada recorría con su imaginación Camden Town. Se situaba frente a un aparador de Oxford Street enfundada en un abrigo atrigrado.
>
> [London was all Alexia thought about during her second servicing of Wilmar. Big Ben came to her mind when she saw the Cuban's enormous member. Although she'd never been there, she imagined walking through Camden Town as she was penetrated. She saw herself standing in front of a shop window on Oxford Street wearing a tiger-stripe coat.] (46)

However, Alexia becomes conscious on a certain level of the contradiction inherent in the subaltern subject's desire to participate in this type of modernity. She realizes that Wilmar, a black man who probably lived in extreme poverty in Cuba, is a sort of social class "vestida" who now participates in bourgeois consumerism but cannot overcome the cultural baggage of his humble origins. As such, he will never really fulfill the role of Pedro Armendáriz (i.e., the classic, chivalrous, relatively white *galán* of Mexican Golden Age cinema) in her life (62).

This observation demonstrates the opposition of traditional gender roles to the lived experience that underlies some of the conflicts in Alexia's character. While her goal is not "la réplica del hogar heterosexual" ["a copy of the heterosexual home"], she is also capable of being a perfect "ama de casa" ["housewife"] (40). That is, her transgressive sexuality and gender nonconformity are expressions of disidentification with the dominant norms in society that also hinge on the reproduction of traditional feminine roles and her willingness to play the role of wife for Wilmar. In the end, she subverts the traditional feminine role of abnegation and reiterates the dissident aspects of *vestida* identity: "Chingue a su madre Marga López, dijo. Arriba la D'Alessio" ["Fuck Marga López, she said. Long live D'Alessio"] (58).[14]

Her rejection of the marriage model is also a rejection of the aspiration to middle-class respectability. As an older *jota* from her neighborhood advises her: "El matrimonio es para los jotitos que son hijos de familia. Eso no es para nosotros" ["Marriage is for the little faggots from nice families. It's not for us"] (61). This is a reference to the Pacto Civil de Solidaridad [Civil Solidarity Pact], a type of civil union that was legalized in the state of Coahuila in 2007, making it one of the first states in Mexico to recognize same-sex unions. The story suggests that despite this official recognition, economic inequality and the persistence of traditional gender roles in the marriage model make this sort of union of limited benefit to marginal queer subjects such as *vestidas*. By deciding to maintain her working-class identity, Alexia rejects the *cursilería* of attempting to imitate a higher social class in favor of celebrating the camp *cursilería* that identifies her positively as a *vestida*—an economically marginal and queer subject who carves out her own space in northern Mexico. At the end of the story, her physical triumph over Wilmar and literal and symbolic appropriation of the phallus subvert the traditional melodramatic plot in which a woman who strays from the "proper role" (marriage) is violently punished. In this way she disidentifies with the myth of Mexican womanhood that Bartra refers to as "Chingadalupe:" the paradigmatic female figure that combines both sides of a virgin/whore dichotomy.[15]

Though a relatively short text, this story is complex in its signification. A combination of paranoid and reparative reading practices can help understand the value of the portrayal of Alexia's narrative of disidentification and liberation in the face of the violence and oppression of which she is a victim. Alexia's victimization and perpetration of violence might be seen as problematic since it reiterates stereotypes of *travestis* as marginal victims as well as perpetrators of violence (Vargas, "Travestis"). However, the level of violence in the story can also be taken as a critique of the high levels of violence suffered by gender-nonconforming individuals in Mexico. A similar critique could be made of the heavy use of caricature in her characterization, which tends to exaggerate the degraded and corporeal aspects of her persona. However, this is part of Velázquez's general style, which does not discriminate when it comes to the portrayal of grotesque bodies. Furthermore, the agency of Alexia and overall sympathetic portrayal of her as the heroine of the story temper the negativity of this portrayal. As caricatured as she might be, she is still the protagonist who comes to love herself because of her queerness and Latin American working-class positionality.

"La jota de Bergerac" is similar to *Brenda Berenice* in several ways. First, both texts portray *jota* or *vestida* subjectivities that are constructed with camp and *cursi* elements from mass media texts. The way that these two characters consciously base their identities on mass-media portrayals of femininities echoes observations of real-world *travesti* subjectivities in studies such as that of Prieur and in documentaries like the Cuban film *Mariposas en el andamio* ["Butterflies on the Stage"] (Bernaza and Gilpin, 1995). Emilio Bejel has commented on this film's portrayal of the constitution of *travesti* subjectivities through the recycling of mass-media tropes, noting that it often involves the reproduction of stereotypes that have served, in many cases, to oppress both women and queer men but that such parodic reinscription also entails a possibility for subversion and liberation: "The injurious interpellation not only gives rise to a subjugated subject; it also demands that the subject form its subjectivity based on that interpellation. For this reason, the subjugated subject is frequently forced to use the colonizer's categories in establishing the possibility of a dissident identity that leads to a solution of the conflicts" (Bejel 210). This observation explains quite well the tension between subversion and conservation of the dominant social order that is present in all uses of camp and *cursi* discourse to express queerness.

The story of Alexia is also similar to that of Brenda Berenice in the protagonist's insistence on revising allegorical narratives of Mexican identity. In this case it is not the literary tradition, but mass culture, specifically Golden Age cinema, that is rewritten queerly. This is not insignificant, as Golden Age cinema is a major discourse for the transmission of the myths of 20th-century Mexican national identity, and in particular the sentimental education related to normative gender roles.[16] Film is another discourse in which bodies are reduced to signifying others that are meant to uphold the dominant social structure. In allegories of sexual transgression, such as *Salón México*, violations of sexual mores undertaken by a "bad woman" must be punished by death. Alexia refuses this version of the story and instead chooses life. In this way the construction of her subjectivity is inseparable from the rewriting and reinterpretation of those *cursi* texts of national symbol and allegory, much like Molina in Puig's *El beso de la mujer araña* [*Kiss of the Spider Woman*]. In the end, Alexia represents a rejection of misogyny and a celebration of the irruption of femininity and queerness into mainstream Mexican culture.

The second story by Velázquez that I will consider here also involves a queer parody of pop culture discourses that often serve to uphold the dominant social order. "La marrana negra de la literatura rosa" contains a highly caricatured portrayal of the emergence of a queer subjectivity through a parody of a traditional "romance" narrative. The *marrana* in this story is the sexually voracious and emotionally demanding Leonor, who dictates gay-themed novels to her owner Manolo, the narrator, who then publishes them under his name. Manolo is attempting to nurture a budding romance with his childhood friend Claudia, but he is pressured by Leonor to keep up a gay public image in order to sustain the critical and commercial success of the novels. Meanwhile, Manolo is pursued by the owner of Valente, a stud hog who regularly satisfies Leonor's sexual appetite. When Valente dies, Leonor becomes depressed and eventually commits suicide. At the (very camp and very *cursi*) funeral, the pig farmer openly declares his love for Manolo, permanently alienating Claudia. By the end of the story, the narrator, who has given up the economic success brought by the novels and now dresses only in women's clothing, reconciles with the swineherd and accepts his proposal for marriage.

As in the case of Alexia's nose, the pig here is another ironically obvious metaphor, representing in this case the emergence of Manolo's unconscious, which obliges him to accept his homosexuality (Beltrán 89). This aspect of the plot in and of itself is a parody of psychoanalytic discourse (and paranoid reading practices) that expresses the effects of internalized homophobia in a highly caricatured fashion. This emergence leads to the construction of a dichotomy that echoes the dualism of "Chingadalupe" that Bartra critiques in the mythification of Mexican femininity: while Manolo performs the traditional, submissive, virginal female role (the "good" woman), Leonor enacts the opposing, rebellious, sexually active role of a man-eater (the "bad" woman). This opposition is not dialectically resolved by the end of the story because Manolo's acceptance of the farmer's marriage proposal seems to give precedence to the Virgin paradigm in his performance of femininity, even though he does come to accept his sexual orientation and gender identity. While this could be read as a reiteration of gender norms, I would prefer to emphasize the subversive readings possible when we consider how the text parodies the narrative conventions of both *literatura rosa* (Harlequin-type romance literature) and what Doris Sommer calls the "national romances" of 19th-century Latin American literature that allegorize the resolution of social conflicts.

The characterization of Manolo throughout the story illustrates how camp and *cursi* humor give expression to the social conflicts that he will embody. There is a clear progression of gender-based humor centered on Manolo's person that culminates with his acceptance of the role of bride of the pig farmer. This humor gradually contributes to the constitution of a masculine/feminine script opposition in his body that reiterates the stereotype of the effeminate homosexual man. Obliged, as he sees it, to cater to Leonor's whims and clean up after her, Manolo describes his dedication to domestic work as a performance of stereotypically feminine activities: "Actuaba como Robotina, la sirvienta de Los Supersónicos" ["I acted like Rosie, the Jetsons' maid"] (125). This notion is echoed by the swineherd: "Es usted más hacendoso que mi mujer" ["You're more house-proud than my wife"] (125).

Manolo considers a relationship with Claudia as his last refuge from being labeled homosexual and is dismayed when she discovers the first novel dictated by Leonor since he believes that this text will make her assume that he is gay. Ironically, he describes his reaction to the situation as stereotypically feminine: "Cuando Claudia se fue me encerré en mi cuarto. A llorar. Como una hembra sin su Juan. Como una mujer de la colonia Nuevo Repueblo" ["When Claudia left I locked myself in my room. To cry. Like a female without her man. Like a woman from Nuevo

Repueblo"] (127).[17] This depiction highlights the growing association of the narrator with the stereotype of the effeminate gay man, as does Leonor's veto of his involvement with Claudia (related to him in a dream): "La oí claramente, como si le hablara a una señorita de familia a la que le prohíben casarse con un comerciante. *Ese hombre no es de tu condición. Una señorita a la que no le permiten elegir un amor*" ["I heard her clearly, as if she were talking to a girl from a nice family who's been forbidden to marry a poor shopkeeper. *That man is not your equal. A young lady who is not permitted to choose her love*"] (127).

Manolo's performance of femininity continues when the farmer attempts to kiss him, and he reacts in a manner that parodies feminine speech: "se me sienta a comerse sus tamales. Calladito. Sin moverse de la silla. Y se los acaba. Y cuidadito con dejarme comida en el plato. Pos este. Aprovechado. Lo ven a uno solo" ["sit down and eat your tamales. Quietly. Without getting up. And eat everything. Don't you leave anything on your plate. Fresh. They see that you're alone"] (129). That there is a certain ambiguity in this utterance (he is ostensibly outraged but also concerned that the man should eat) suggests that he might not actually be totally repulsed by the farmer's overture. In fact, this is part of the performance of "good" virginal femininity, which must reject sexual proposals outside of marriage. The climax of the story occurs at Leonor's funeral, where the farmer shows up unexpectedly and kisses Manolo, convincing Claudia once and for all that he is gay. Manolo angrily rejects the farmer with the same language Claudia uses against him: "los hombres son todos unos cerdos" ["all men are pigs"] (133). After this, the protagonist returns to his old neighborhood to sell tamales and, he says, never again dresses in men's clothing. S/he finally deigns to be courted by the swineherd, but refuses sex before marriage with yet another feminine cliché: "Yo tengo que salir de blanco" ["I have to wear white"] (134). The farmer proposes, and Manolo accepts, completing the constitution of the stereotype of the effeminate homosexual man with the assumption of the role of bride.

This performance of traditionally modest and virginal femininity is contrasted with Leonor's brazen sexuality: "[A Valente] [l]o deseaba locamente. Deseaba revolcarlo en lodo. Hundirlo en su pasojo. Mancillarlo como a una mazorca. Humillarlo de deseo. *The bitch was so hot*" ["She desired him [Valente] madly. She wanted to roll him in mud. Bury him in her manure. Sully him like a corn cob. Humiliate him with desire. *The bitch was so hot*"] (123). The scatological elements of this quote associate sex with filth, feces, and pollution. This is part of the characterization of

Leonor as the embodiment of "dirty" (that is, openly desiring and erotic) female sexuality. This continues with a description of her evolving paraphilias: "Las perversiones de Leonor cada día eran más sofisticadas. Incluían dildos, disfraces, ropa de cuero y ropa interior comestible. Incluso me ordenó en una ocasión que los filmara mientras tenían sexo" ["Leonor's perversions became more sophisticated by the day. They included dildos, costumes, leather clothes and edible underwear. Once she even ordered me to film them while they had sex"] (124–25). Once again, Leonor embodies an exaggerated version of active female sexuality, with her kinks implying a greater deviation from sexual norms. In this sense, Leonor performs her own camp femininity, but it is an exaggeratedly "bad" and sexually active femininity that contrasts with the "good," virginal femininity performed by Manolo at this point in the story.

The characterization of Manolo as effeminate and of Leonor as the personification of unbridled female sexuality also involves a great deal of *cursilería*, especially in the sense of melodramatic discourse and behavior. The main sources of Manolo's sentimental education are hinted at when he relates how Leonor, angry because he will not show the manuscript of the first novel to Claudia, defecates all over his collection of *TV y Novelas* magazines (124).[18] His own behavior is often melodramatic, as when he weeps after Claudia discovers the first novel (see above) and at Leonor's carnivalesque funeral (133). This feminine *cursilería* mixes with the notion of failed attempts to imitate higher social strata (the "bad taste" of poor and provincial Mexico) in Manolo's description of how he decorated Leonor's room for her weekly romantic encounters with Valente: "Mi deber era decorar el espacio *so romantic*, con velas, pétalos de rosa. Destapar una botella de Sidra Villareal, encender incienso de canela y colocar sábanas de seda" ["My task was to decorate the space so romantic, with candles, rose petals. Open a bottle of Sidra Villarreal, light some cinnamon incense and lay out some silk sheets"] (124). The substitution of cheap cider for champagne, as well as the use of English adjectives, highlights the modern/unmodern script opposition that underlies the humor of this description of the pig's love nest, arranged in Manolo's government-subsidized apartment. Leonor's insistence that Manolo publish her novel derives in part from her desire to ascend socially, as represented by her insistence that he dress in designer clothes ("*Yo de Dior, con algo de Dolce & Gabbana y tú vestido como un macuarro*" ["Me in Dior, with a little Dolce & Gabbana and you dressed like a bum"]) and their subsequent move to a more expensive apartment, where their neighbors are television celebrities (128–30).

At the end of the story, Manolo moves back to his old apartment in the housing project and accepts the working-class farmer's marriage proposal. This dénouement could be read as indicative of Manolo's rejection of Leonor's social climbing and his embrace of working-class *cursilería* and traditional femininity as an expression of his dissident homosexual identity. This would make the end of his story very similar to that of Alexia in "La Jota de Bergerac" since she also comes to accept her queerness and social class as part of her identity. Reading in this sense, the story seems to be a narrative of self-realization and self-acceptance, which takes place through the identification with gender nonconformity as an expression of dissident sexuality and class-conscious regional identity. However, Manolo's story is different from Alexia's in that there is no subversion of typical female roles (recall that Alexia rejects the insistence of melodrama that she be a martyr punished for her "bad" sexuality). In this case, it almost seems as if the emergence of repressed sexual desire in the "perversions" of Leonor is completely sublimated in the assumption of the role of virginal bride-to-be. Such a reading would be, however, too superficial.

The "happy ending" of the marriage between Manolo and the pig farmer is a parody of the conventions of the romance novels of the type that Leonor parodies in her dictations to Manolo. This adds another, metanarrative level of irony to the plot since the story itself is a queer version of a romance narrative about a character who writes queer versions of romance narratives. This can also be read as a parody of the Latin American narrative tradition of "national romances" in which marriage serves as an allegorical solution to social conflicts such as racism and class division (Sommer). In this way, the text both ironically engages with that tradition at the same time that it brings it low by referencing not the classics of Latin American national literatures but the "feminine" and *cursi* genre of *literatura rosa*. The parody of the "feminine" genre of Harlequin romance recalls Manuel Puig's revolutionary use of feminine mass-culture texts such as magazines, films, and popular music, in the construction of his narratives. This story is very aware, however, that several decades separate it from Puig's work, and it signals this with a tongue-in-cheek reference to the marketability of the queer: "Nuestro segundo título, *Los hombres están muertos*, terminó por consolidar a Leonor como la Fernando Vallejo de la literatura rosa. Fue inevitable que surgieran las comparaciones con Pedro Lemebel y Reinaldo Arenas" ["Our second title, *The Men Are Dead*, consolidated Leonor as the Fernando Vallejo of romance literature. It was inevitable that comparisons would be made with Pedro Lemebel and Reinaldo Arenas"] (128).

This high level of irony, along with the emphasis on grotesque caricature, distances the narrative from the conventions of realism. For example, Manolo's subjectivity looks less like a believable portrayal of *travesti* subjectivity than a cartoon exaggerated for humorous effect. Even the subjectivity of Alexia in "La Jota de Bergerac" is much more developed, despite the caricature. This level of irony and abstraction complicates the reading of this text from a reparative perspective. Up to now, in my reparative approaches, I have highlighted how characters express, through the construction of their subjectivities, how camp and *cursi* humor can serve to transcend negative affect and constitute collectives through sympathetic identification with others. I have also indicated, however, that reparative reading can also include attention to the way that texts irreverently challenge Mexican literary tradition and insist that it include portrayals of queerness. While "La marrana" may lack a very realistic portrayal of queer subjectivity, it most certainly presents a gleefully *relajiento* subversion of the literary tradition. In the context of the rest of Velázquez's oeuvre, this story forms part of a project insisting that marginalized identities in Mexico—the queer, the northern, the dark-skinned, and poor—are a necessarily offensive part of (or challenge to) dominant narratives of national identity.

Travesti, vestida, jota, loca and other related identities that are based on male-to-female cross-dressing are among the "queerest" of Mexican sexualities since they perturb binaries of both gender and sexual orientation. The individuals who identify in this way face a great deal of discrimination, marginalization and violence in Mexican society, making the politics of their representation highly critical to their survival and fight for social equality. Although, as Vek Lewis argues, it is important to be wary of the ways in which figurative portrayals of cross-dressing subjects can lead to the erasure of *travesti* and related subjectivities, it is also important to consider how such texts can disidentify with the allegorical literary tradition of Latin America in ways that permit readings focused on questioning the dominant social structure and contributing to the development of dissident subjectivities and collectives. In *Brenda Berenice* and "La jota de Bergerac," there is a portrayal of the construction of subjectivities that also engages, quite ironically, the allegorical literary tradition in Mexico. In *La hermana secreta de Angélica María* and "La marrana negra de la literatura rosa," the subjectivities represented might be more figurative than realistic, but there is also an ironic engagement with literary and cultural traditions that permits readings that celebrate queerness. As with all texts that employ humor as a rhetorical device in the portrayal of subaltern expressions of disidentification, there is a great deal of ambiguity in these portrayals with regards to the subversion and reiteration of negative stereotypes. However, as I have argued in earlier chapters, the social possibilities of such texts depend to a great extent on how they are read. With regards to the four texts above, the examination of their uses of camp and *cursi* humor from a perspective combining paranoid social critique and a reparative celebration of queerness is a highly productive way of reading their interventions in the Mexican literary tradition.

Chapter 4

Having your Cake and Eating it Too

Bisexual *Bildungsromane* from Dismodern Mexico

In this chapter I examine three novels in which dismodern Mexican parodies of the classical European *Bildungsroman* genre employ camp and *cursi* humor in ways that question norms of sex and gender as well as Mexico's relationship to modernity. The main characters in these works portray subjectivities that are defined, to a great extent, by bisexuality. Like homosexuality and heterosexuality, bisexuality is a term that originates in 19th-century sexology. It has variously been used to describe intersexuality or hermaphroditism (the combination of maleness and femaleness in an organism, as in biology and medicine), the combination of masculinity and femininity in the human psyche (as in psychoanalysis), and the combination of heterosexuality and homosexuality in a person (Storr 3–4). This last definition, which is dominant in contemporary discourse, will be the starting point for our discussion here, as it has profound effects on how the protagonists of the texts below construct their identities.

As the definitions cited above indicate, bisexuality focuses on indeterminate positions between two opposing concepts, with the result that it tends to undermine both the stable definition of itself and that of the binary terms that it eludes. This problem is amply illustrated by attempts to measure human sexual orientation, such as the linear scale used by Alfred Kinsey in his famous midcentury study *Sexual Behavior in the Human Male* (1948). On this scale, based more than anything on self-reports of sexual behavior, 0 is exclusively heterosexual, and 6 is exclusively homosexual. Kinsey argues that the entire rest of the scale could describe nearly half the male population of the United States at some point in their lives (Kinsey, Pomeroy, and Martin 36). Though Kinsey does not use the term "bisexuality" to describe these behaviors, his study does illustrate the diversity of practices that could be described by that term.

Attempts to improve upon Kinsey's scale of sexual orientation have led to even more complex views of bisexuality. For example, the Klein Sexual Orientation Grid (KSOG), developed by bisexual psychiatrist Fritz Klein in the 1970s, takes into account not only sexual behavior but also reported sexual attraction and fantasies, emotional and social preference, self-identification, and lifestyle over an individual's lifetime and into their projected future (Udis-Kessler 52–56). The KSOG, then, attempts to measure several of the variables that make it difficult to define bisexuality as an "authentic" sexual orientation, including sequence, frequency, situation, and self-identification. The challenge these variables pose to a stable definition of bisexuality become clear if we imagine hypothetical attempts at classification. Can a man who had a sexual relationship with another man during his youth but afterward only had sexual relationships with women be said to have a bisexual orientation? What about a woman who is attracted to both men and women, but who identifies as a lesbian and decides only to have sex with women for personal and political reasons? What about a man who identifies as bisexual on the basis of attraction to both sexes but has only ever had sex with women (or with men)? Can genderqueer or nonbinary-identified individuals be considered bisexual if they identify with neither gender?

The difficulty of answering such questions speaks to the essentially ambiguous and unstable nature of bisexuality but also to that of homosexuality and heterosexuality. It is not surprising, then, that the bisexual identity has neither been widely adopted nor found much acceptance among people who tend to identify with relatively stable identities based on sexual orientation, such as lesbian, gay, and straight. Biphobia, or aversion towards bisexual people, manifests itself in the rejection of bisexuality as an authentic sexual orientation, the opinion that it is a temporary phase, an index of latent homo- or heterosexuality, a symptom of a lack of political commitment, or simply bad faith.[1] The institutionalization of the bisexual orientation by HIV/AIDS epidemiology focusing on sexual behaviors has contributed to the scapegoating of bisexuals for the spread of STDs and stereotypes of them as sexually promiscuous and as sexual predators (Ault 182). The frequent use of bisexuality in television and film as a metaphor for or index of duplicity, corruption, and/or moral turpitude reiterates stereotypes of bisexuals as untrustworthy.[2] It bears repeating that the roots of biphobia are in the destabilizing effects that it exerts on notions of sexual orientation and the anxiety that this generates in many people.

The destabilizing effect of bisexuality has also led to its development as an epistemology that is opposed to categorization on the basis of sexual orientation and is generally seen as incompatible with stable identities, though there have been attempts to bridge the gap between epistemology and identity (Ault; Däumer; Hemmings, "Extracts"; Storr 8–9). In its tendency to undermine stable notions of identity, bisexual epistemology is similar to queer theory. It differs, however, in its insistence on the importance of signaling the inescapable effects of the gender and sexual orientation binaries on our conception of human sexuality. Theorists of bisexuality sometimes posit this distinction as an improvement over queer theory's alleged tendency to erase sexual diversity and reconstitute an overarching queer/heterosexual binary (Ault 178; Cohen 75; Johnson 100).

While I do recognize these dangers in queer theorizing, I do not believe that the queer should necessarily be replaced by bisexuality. Rather, these concepts can complement each other. In the Latin American context, for example, bisexuality can be seen as a form of queerness, that is, as a form of disobedience to hetero- and homonormativity (Sifuentes-Jáuregui, *Avowal* 5). It can be productively invoked in those instances where the hetero/homo binary blurs but where the importance of signaling the effects of gender is paramount. In such cases, although bisexuality secures the oppositional view of sexual orientation, it also disrupts it and, thanks to its epistemological and historical genealogy, reminds us of the salience of the binary construction of gender in society and its relation to sexuality and power (Angelides 63, 70; Michel 57).

Bisexuality in Mexico and the "Penetration Paradigm"

Probably the main area of conflict and discord surrounding bisexuality in Mexico is the widely held notion that men who identify as heterosexual can have sex with other men without being considered effeminate or homosexual as long as they play the penetrative ("masculine") role.[3] This notion is famously expressed by Octavio Paz in *El laberinto de la soledad* [*The Labyrinth of Solitude*] (1949) as part of his allegorical explanation of the conflicts of Mexican culture. Later social scientific work on bisexuality in Mexico and other regions in Latin America, beginning with the work of Carrier in the 1970s, has generally tended to corroborate widespread practice of bisexuality among men and a certain permissiveness regarding it as long as the man in question plays an active role (Almaguer; Domínguez-Ruvalcaba, *Translating* 126–27; Liguori 137–41).[4] However, this work has also shown that the masculinity of the insertive partner in male-male sex is not always beyond question. For example, Prieur's interviews with working-class Mexican men indicate a great deal of anxiety and discretion around their homosexual liaisons, since there may always be doubt about whether they have played the receptive role in penetrative sex and therefore diminished their masculinity (206–7, 256–58). Carrillo's observations seem to uphold this notion: "the risk is that people might also begin to think of such men as *anormales* (abnormal) and link them to those men who are effeminate" (*Night* 57). These studies suggest that there is a generalized pollution belief that functions with homosexuality as a concept in Mexico—the man who is penetrated loses masculinity, and any man who comes into contact with him also has his masculinity threatened. As Carrillo shows, these conflicts and anxieties reflect the uneasy coexistence of gender- and object choice-based sexual orientation categories in contemporary Mexico (*Night* 60–61).

At the same time, the contemporary bisexual identity is no more popular in Mexico than in the Global North. Similar to the frequent rejection of bisexuality in the Anglo-American context, Mexican collectives of sexual dissidence are often skeptical of the bisexual identity and see it as a way of enjoying heterosexual privilege by denying one's "true" sexual orientation (Salinas, *Políticas* 324). In 1990s Guadalajara, Carrillo found that both hetero- and homosexual-identified people judged "normal" (heterosexual-identified) people who occasionally had same-sex relations much less harshly than those who identified as bisexual, citing the "perception of their permanent ambiguity and the notion that *bisexuals* [are] opportunistic, oversexed, and deceitful" [original emphasis] (*Night* 77). The manifestation of biphobia through the reiteration of stereotypes is a point of similarity between the United States and Mexico and indicates that the destabilizing effects of bisexuality are a barrier to its use as an identity in both contexts.

As far as I know, there has been no bisexual epistemology similar to that of Hemmings, Däumer, Ault, and Angelides theorized in Mexico. There is, however, a Mexican tradition of cultural criticism that places male bisexuality at the center of national culture, as well as a queer Latino American criticism that returns to the Mexican tradition to read it in a subversive fashion. I am referring here to Ben. Sifuentes-Jáuregui's suggestion that we read Paz's *Laberinto de soledad* as a foundational queer text (*Avowal* 10–11). Paz argues that a common attitude about male homosexuality among Mexican working-class men is the notion that an active (insertive) partner in male-male sex may retain his masculinity, while a passive (anally or orally receptive) partner is feminized and placed in the same inferior social position as women. Paz links this idea to a generalized dichotomy in Mexican culture between penetrated/penetrator in which the active position is identified with violent power and masculinity, and the passive, with violated, weak femininity (43). This dichotomy is expressed with the verb *chingar*, which means to rape, violate, or visit violence upon, with the operative positions being that of the *chingón* (subject) and the *chingado/a* (object) (ibid.). Paz's explanation of this aspect of male sexuality in Mexico has been criticized for being dubious (it is not based on scientific research nor firsthand knowledge) and for subordinating female and queer subjectivities to the figurative depictions of Mexico in terms of masculinist crisis (Irwin, *Mexican* xxiv; Quiroga 14). Such critiques, which are informed by feminist and queer theory critiques of essentialism, also join the Mexican critical tradition, exemplified by Bartra, that criticizes the way that Paz abstracts signifying others (working-class and peasant men, women, homosexual men, etc.) in his allegories of the nation.

However, as Sifuentes-Jáuregui reminds us, Paz's essentialism and homophobia do not prevent us from undertaking queer readings of his texts. In this view, Paz's emphasis on the body and his attempt to describe gender in bodily terms that are not performative reflects a major difference between genders and sexualities in the Global North and South, namely, the "*priority of the body in the construction of Latino American gender and sexual identities*" [original emphasis] (*Avowal* 10–11). A major tenet of Judith Butler's theorization on the performativity of gender is that the body does not contribute to the initial construction of gender. Sifuentes-Jáuregui argues, *pace* Butler, that in Latin America, the body does indeed pre-exist the construction of gender in important ways. In chapter 3, I examined the portrayal of *travesti* and related identities that show how the historical domination of bodies in Latin America influences both a regime of social norms and identities based on sexual dissidence and gender nonconformity.

Similarly, Sifuentes-Jáuregui sees Paz's argument about the feminization of the penetrated man, which he calls the "penetration paradigm," as an opportunity to retheorize how male sexuality is understood and represented in Latin American cultures: "Male homosexuality is defined here through a relationship that cuts across the bodies [. . .] Male homosexual identity is not simply written on the body, it is not only about how one body relates to another, but rather—more aggressively—it is about how one body traverses the other, how gender and sexuality are written through the body" (15). In other words, it is about how one body violently *makes* the other one homosexual by violating (penetrating) it. The violent regulation of bodies that was central to the colonial social structures thus influences the construction of genders and related identities, even up to the present.

To a certain extent, these Latin American cultural traits share similarities with genders and sexualities in the Global North. Notably, Paz's notion that penetration renders a male subject "homosexual" through feminization anticipates by several decades work on this theme by early queer theorists. Foucault, for example, describes similar social relations in the highly gendered male sexualities of the Helleno-Roman period (*History of Sexuality Vol. 1*). Focusing on contemporary notions of homosexuality, Leo Bersani argues in his influential psychoanalytic text "Is the Rectum a Grave?" that the anxiety produced by male homosexuality is a fear of the death of the (masculine) self through penetration. While Paz's "penetration paradigm" anticipates both this theoretical notion and the greater focus on bodies ushered in by Foucault, it also signals a key cultural difference, highlighted by Sifuentes-Jáuregui's emphasis on violence—the role of coloniality in the construction of Mexican genders and sexualities.

This is particularly evident in the way that Paz's theorization about penetration in *El laberinto de la soldead* intersects with his treatment of *mestizaje*, or racial mixing, as a central element of Mexican identity. In effect, Paz narrates *mestizaje* through the allegory of what he describes as the rape of la Malinche, the Indigenous interpreter of Hernán Cortés, by the Spanish conqueror. In this sense, Mexicans are all *hijos de la chingada*, children of a raped mother whom they alternately idealize and vilify through the figures of the Virgin of Guadalupe and the treacherous Malinche, blamed for her own victimization. This, it is implied, is a central impediment to the full participation of Mexico in modernity. As the historian Federico Navarrete wryly summarizes, this version of *mestizaje* affirms "incluso que nuestro papá violó a nuestra mamá y que nuestros acendrados complejos de inferioridad provienen de esa violencia fundadora de nuestra identidad familiar y nacional" ["that our dad even raped our mom and that our perfect inferiority complex comes from this violence that founded our family and national identity"] (*México* 97). What is most important here is the way that the violence that is visited upon the mother, which gives birth to the racial difference of "all" Mexicans, is the same violence that is capable of feminizing and making a homosexual out of any man who may fall victim to it (but not the one who perpetrates it).

Reading Paz queerly, as Sifuentes-Jáuregui suggests, we can see that Paz places male bisexuality at the center of his national allegory, as a privilege afforded to the dominant masculine subject (*chingón*) that has as its ultimate model a white European male conqueror. This bisexuality reinforces the masculinity of the *chingón* at the same time that it threatens it through contamination by the dominated feminine object (*chingado/a*) that has as its ultimate referent the female Indigenous victim. A large part of Mexican identity, in this view, rests on the imposition of masculine dominance and white supremacy and the suppression of homoeroticism, the feminine, and indigeneity. While this may be a highly figurative abstraction, it is ultimately based on real social practice, and thus gives expression to social anxieties regarding gender, sexuality, race, and modernity in Mexico. We have seen numerous examples of the way that humor related to homosexuality (camp) intersects with humor based on an always already racialized marginality from modernity (*lo cursi* and *lo naco*). As we will see in the novels discussed below, camp humor can also serve to represent bisexuality and frequently intersects with humor related to *cursilería* and *naquez*. Before beginning the close readings of these texts, however, it is worth considering how humor often functions to make sense of male bisexuality in Mexico.

Humor and Bisexuality in Mexico

As befits a practice that entails such a conflicted and fraught web of significations, there is a great deal of humor in Mexico that serves to make sense of male bisexuality. The researcher Ana Luisa Liguori notes that there is much humor in Mexican popular culture that explicitly or implicitly references both the privileged insertive position and the abject receptive position in the male homosexual encounter, always privileging the former (133).[5] Many examples of this type of humor can be seen in the amateur documentary film *Amor chacal* ["Chacal Love"] (Juan Carlos Bautista, 2001), about straight-identified men in the coastal town of Alvarado, Veracruz, who assume the active role in sex with gay-identified male tourists. These men, known as *mayates* or *chacales*,⁶ play a social role similar to that of the "trade" man (heterosexually identified man who has sex with other men) in Anglo-American culture.⁷ They are opposed to the *puto, joto* or (in a regional variation), *choto*,⁸ which are terms that refer to the supposedly effeminate homosexual or gay-identified receptive partner in male-male sex. As Domínguez-Ruvalcaba observes, the festive, carnivalesque atmosphere surrounding *mayate-joto* sex in Alvarado, which includes jokes and other forms of verbal humor, ultimately reinforces the homo/hetero and masculine/feminine binaries at the same time that it legitimizes the gay consumption and fetishization of "exotic locals" (*Modernity* 144; *Translating* 162–63). While discussing Mexican humor on male bisexuality, it is also worth recalling a well-known joke paraphrased by Bartra in his critique of the portrayal of gender in discourses of national identity (including that of Paz): a man who wants to demonstrate his heterosexuality allows himself to be penetrated by another man periodically in order to prove to himself that he does not enjoy it (202).⁹ In these examples of humor, the basic operative script opposition is masculine/feminine, where masculinity is equivalent to heterosexuality and femininity to homosexuality, and it is the incongruous combination of both in the body of one man that leads to the perception of humor. Ultimately, this type of humor usually serves to maintain the dominant social order by reducing anxiety about bisexuality and reaffirming the privilege of the masculine gender over the feminine, of men over women, and of "heterosexual" over "homosexual" men.

Aside from this type of popular humor, which tends to reinforce the dominant social order, there are also Mexican cultural products that portray male bisexuality with irony and humor in ways that can generally be said to challenge or undermine that order. Examples include films like *Doña Herlinda y su hijo* [*Doña Herlinda and Her Son*] (Jaime Humberto Hermosillo, 1985), where the social conveniences of maintaining heterosexual privilege as a bisexual man are at the center of the plot, and *Y tu mamá también* [*And Your Mother Too*] (Alfono Cuarón, 2001), where the climactic scene in which two friends/rivals have a sexual encounter "underline[s] the unequivocal position of same-sex desire in strongly homosocial masculine gender systems" (Venkatesh, *New* 146). In the literary realm, Ana Clavel's novel *Cuerpo náufrago* ["Shipwrecked Body"] (2006) approaches bisexuality through a playful rewriting of Virginia Woolf's *Orlando*, while in Enrique Serna's novel *La doble vida de Jesús* ["The Double Life of Jesús"] (2014), the bisexuality of the main character serves to satirize shifting norms of masculinity in an allegorical tale of political corruption (Venkatesh, "*La doble vida"*). A similarly allegorical use of bisexuality appears in Juan Villoro's highly ironic coming-of-age tale *Materia dispuesta* ["Ready Materials"] (1996). Tamara Williams reads this novel as a contemporary version of the *Bildungsroman* in which the main character's lack of clear direction in life (which includes his bisexuality) is an allegory of the ideological instability of postmodern Mexican society (362). I find a similar use of bisexuality in the three novels examined below, all of which I also read as postmodern (or, rather, dismodern) parodies of the *Bildungsroman* genre that replace the clear didactic function of such modern narratives with questions that embrace unresolved social conflicts. These texts distinguish themselves from *Materia dispuesta*, and indeed from all of the examples cited above, by their high frequency of camp humor, which intersects with *cursilería* in the characterization of their protagonists. As we will see, this use of camp mainly serves to signal homosexualities and/or gay culture, thus placing the conflict between gender-based and object choice-based theories of sexual orientation at the center of an examination of gender, sexuality, and race in Mexico.

Bisexual *Bildungsromane*

As I already mentioned, the novels examined below all take the form of a parody of the coming-of-age novel or *Bildungsroman*. Although the paradigmatic example of this genre is *Wilhelm Meister's Apprenticeship* (1795) by Goethe, other 19th-century European works like Dickens's *Great Expectations* (1861) and Stendahl's *The Red and the Black* (1830) may also be considered examples of it. Its distinguishing characteristics include a focus on a single protagonist and his or her development within a social order, the portrayal of that order through the protagonist's experiences, an ironic distance with respect to these experiences on the part of the narrator, and a clear didactic function (Hirsch 296–300). The *Bildungsroman* posits a possible social adaptation that may either be accepted or rejected by the protagonist, but that always ends with that main character providing a clear evaluation of his or her place in society (298). In the *Bildungsroman*, then, the construction of the protagonist's subjectivity, undertaken with the narrative conventions of romanticism and/or realism, also allegorizes social conflicts.

The three novels included in this chapter share several of the characteristics of the pan-European *Bildungsroman*, particularly the protagonist's conflict with society and the ironic distance of the narrator. However, there are also several key differences. Rather than a clear resolution regarding social adaptation, there is an unresolved tension regarding the protagonist's place in society. Furthermore, the didactic function is replaced by what I call a "questioning function" that undermines stable notions of sexuality and gender identity and that offers an ambivalent appraisal of the desire to achieve modernity. The ironic relation of these texts to the 19th-century *Bildungsroman*, as well as their skepticism towards master narratives, signals what we might call a postmodern relationship with the original genre (Eco 659; Lyotard xxiv). However, their position of enunciation in Latin America, evidenced especially by their *cursi* humor and related expressions of racialization, marks them rather as dismodern parodies that reflect Mexico's historical marginalization from discourses of (post)modernity (Bartra).

In *Mátame y verás*, by José Joaquín Blanco, the protagonist narrates the disintegration of his familial and professional life, the result of his own actions. A self-identified heterosexual, he is haunted by a sexual encounter he had with another man in his youth, the source of a fear of contamination by effeminacy and homosexuality. His internal conflicts reflect his desire to preserve the privileges of hegemonic masculinity and simultaneously attain modernity by adopting contemporary discourses about sex. The novel's portrayal of a heterosexual subjectivity predicated on the repression of bisexuality and a fear of being *naco* satirizes, through allegory, neoliberal pretensions to modernity in early 1990s Mexico. In *Púrpura* by Ana García Bergua, the narrator-protagonist relates his personal quest for modernity and a stable gender/sex identity in highly ironic terms. He struggles with the notion that his homoerotic inclinations feminize him at the same time that he longs to join the upper classes in "progress" and alpha males in hegemonic masculinity. Ultimately, however, he comes to accept an undefined sexual orientation and an ambiguously *cursi* social position in this allegory of Mexico as a society defined by indefinition. Finally, in Enrique Serna's novel *Fruta verde*, the protagonist's bisexuality becomes a point of contention where social conflicts about gender, sexuality, and modernity are expressed. A figurative resolution of the main conflicts in the narration presents not a dialectical solution but rather an acceptance of incongruity made possible by the reparative functions of humor. In all three texts, bisexuality plays a central role in structuring the internal and social conflicts of the protagonists, which figuratively represent social conflicts in Mexico. Their use of camp and *cursi* humor likewise provides opportunities for approaching them from a perspective combining paranoid and reparative reading practices that question the dominant social structure.

Mátame y verás

Blanco's novel *Mátame y verás* makes use of a first-person narrator who, through means of a confessional autobiography, betrays internal contradictions that reflect key social conflicts of late 20th-century Mexico. Sergio Peña performs a cynical and unsentimental masculinity that he opposes to the effeminacy and *cursilería* of women and effeminate gay men. The novel contains a broad use of humor related to *lo cursi* and *lo naco* in which the intersection of social class and race is very evident. The main character's conflicted subjectivity is clearly marked by bisexuality and internalized racism, embodying in this way social conflicts related to gender, sexuality, and modernity that arose in the early 1990s, the time of the definitive shift of Mexico to neoliberal policies like NAFTA that would insert it more completely into the global market. Reparative uses of camp and *cursi* humor are modeled by the gay men and are admired, to an extent, by Sergio. This reparative use of humor, however, does not lead to any resolution of the conflicts presented. Instead of a clear social adaptation, Sergio's narrative ends with the main character stuck in the same limbo in which he has found himself during the entire narration, suggesting that there is no easy solution to the conflicts of Mexican society, a message that lends itself to paranoid approaches. However, the complex and sympathetic portrayal of all the characters foments readerly identification and empathy, thus offering ample opportunities to combine paranoid and reparative reading practices in the consideration of its complex social satire.

Mátame y verás was originally published in installments from February to April 1994 in the Mexican magazine *Etcétera*. The title may be a reference to the play *Muérete y verás* ["Die and You'll See"] (1837) by the Spanish author Manuel Bretón de Herreros, which parodies romantic literary conventions and satirizes contemporary Spanish mores. One of this play's major themes is the notion of death as a transcendent state from which one could achieve a deeper self-knowledge were it possible to survive it. In a similar fashion, the protagonist of Blanco's novel experiences a sort of social death that gives him the opportunity to reflect on his life up to this point and the manner in which he has adapted to society. This perspective of ironic retrospection and contemporary abjection recalls not only the play mentioned above, but also the *Bildungsroman* genre. Although Sergio's own self-knowledge is dubious, it provides the opportunity for an exploration of the values of middle-class gay and heterosexual men in late 20th-century Mexico, which entails a great deal of ironic and contradictory reflection on the ambiguous notions of modernity extant in Mexico at the time. His subjectivity is full of contradictions that reflect his desire to become modern but also to preserve traditional privileges associated with masculinity.

Sergio is a 40-year-old businessman whose executive lifestyle has collapsed in the face of the aggressive divorce proceedings of his wife, Carmela. Stripped of money and status, he hides out from the police, his brothers-in-law, and his wife's attorneys while he waits for his own lawyer to mount a defense. In a train station, he runs into an old college classmate—Juan Jácome, the gay boy who was picked on by all the *machos*. Their social positions are now reversed, as "Juanito" is obviously materially successful, while Sergio has just lost nearly everything. Sergio manages to get himself invited to spend the Christmas holidays with Juanito and some of his friends at a vacation house outside of Cuernavaca.[10] There Sergio begins writing the story of his downfall on his laptop, saving the text in a file named "LIMBO."

The book presents itself as this document, in which the protagonist narrates the trajectory of his family and professional life, alternating with descriptions of his fellow travelers and their lives. The basis for Sergio's social death is the fact that his wife has accused him (accurately) of misappropriating securities held by both of them. Having met at the university in the 1970s, their courtship was initially based on the flouting of social conventions: she was wealthy and promiscuous, and he was an ambitious social climber. Their mutual cynicism brought them together in a marriage of convenience. In the early years of their marriage, Carmela and Sergio had a nonmonogamous relationship, after which they settled down to have children but with a tacit agreement that they would continue to have discreet extramarital sexual relations. According to Sergio, Carmela has broken this agreement by beginning an emotional relationship with another man, an action that he sees as a plan to eventually substitute him with a younger, whiter version of himself. His theft of the securities is thus defended as a sort of preemptive strike needed to protect himself.

The vacation that Sergio takes with Juanito and his friends forms a counterpoint to the above narrative, and the lives of the gay men become a mirror in which Sergio contemplates himself. Juanito's own life trajectory has been a journey towards mainstream acceptance through the acquisition of wealth. The ugly duckling of the university, he was ostracized by the other young men, including Sergio (with whom he did, however, once have a sexual encounter). Now Juanito is a confident professional with tangible symbols of class status and monetary gain, such as the vacation house in which the group is staying. Another indicator of Juanito's success is his younger and more attractive boyfriend, Aníbal, a beautiful but shallow young man who dreams of a career as a model and actor. Juanito's other friends are of the same generation as he and Sergio. El Jirafón is a tall, twitchy, bespectacled cinema geek with a fetish for working-class men, while Rubén—also known as "la Nenuca"—is a bodybuilder who affects a masculine "clone" style of dress and behavior and spends all day perfecting his suntan. The group is completed by the arrival of Melba, an eccentric 60-year-old woman whose work as an actress in her youth gives her a certain bohemian cachet among her gay friends.

Throughout the novel, Sergio's own narrative parallels sarcastic depictions of the others' lives. The caricature and sarcasm of his descriptions are balanced somewhat by his attention to the experiences that have shaped the lives of the gay men. For example, after a fight with Rubén, he learns that this character's apparent cool and nonchalance hides the deep scars of a trauma he suffered when his lover César died of a brain tumor. At another point Melba relates that Jirafón was molested by an uncle as a young boy and never recovered from the sense of rejection he felt when his uncle repented and refused to see him anymore. The inclusion of such scenes in Sergio's narrative indicates a certain level of sympathy or identification with the gay men.

The apogee of this sentiment is the drunken Christmas party/drag pageant that caps off the vacation. This is the high point of identification between the characters, when Sergio comes to see value in the gay men's disidentification with mainstream society—their use of camp and *cursi* humor in order to transcend negative affect and express solidarity with each other. The identification disintegrates, however, when Sergio attacks Juanito in a burst of paranoia. Although this interpersonal conflict is resolved relatively quickly, it is clear by the end of the book that Sergio's internal conflicts regarding his masculinity, sexuality, race, and social status are not resolved in any way and that the novel is not a story of rapprochement between gays and straights in Mexico. The social conflicts presented here find no easy resolution.

This satire is filtered through the perception of Sergio, whose character is shot through with contradictions that reflect ethical and moral ambivalence as well as contradictory ideas about, sex, gender, race, and modernity. While he generally comes off as cynically self-absorbed and smug, it is also evident that he has been deeply hurt by his wife's emotional infidelity. This is one of the contradictory aspects of his subjectivity that make him a believable character and invite the reader to sympathize with him, up to a point, despite his obvious faults. Sergio is alternately judgmental and sympathetic, sarcastic and self-pitying. His ideas about sex and gender are equally contradictory. While he evinces sympathy for the gay men and seems to reject certain heteronormative ideals as unmodern, he holds on to many misogynist and homophobic prejudices that constantly resurface in his discourse. Sergio targets women and effeminate men with humor in order to defend against threats to his masculine privilege. His use of camp humor often demonstrates the internal contradictions inherent to the dominant order of sex and gender in Mexico.

For example, although Sergio generally characterizes Juanito as effeminate, at certain moments, his descriptions reflect the ambiguous nature of socially determined masculine and feminine traits and how he ultimately sees his old classmate. For instance, he assumes that because of his superior social position to his boyfriend, Aníbal, Juanito must play the active, or masculine, role in sex: "Sospecho que el rol de macho, si todavía entre los putos hay el rol de macho, en estos tiempos ya no se sabe, le toca a Juanito. Nunca lo hubiera imaginado. ¿Las palomas se vuelven gavilanes con la edad?" ["I suspect that the masculine role, if it still exists among fags, nobody knows these days, corresponds to Juanito. I never would have imagined. Do doves become hawks with age?"] (41). At one point, Sergio compares Juanito's laugher to the clucking of a hen, but at another point he says that his old classmate's "carcajadas cantineras de mariachi" ["raucous barroom mariachi guffaws"] are the only masculine thing about him (22–23). In these contradictory depictions, the masculine/feminine script opposition is presented in two different ways: Juanito as a masculine body that performs feminine scripts; Juanito as an essentially feminine body that performs masculine scripts. In both cases, Sergio's comments reflect a confusion about sexual identity categories and a defensive posture regarding masculinity, which he sees as threatened by the ambiguous nature of Juanito's gender performance.

This defensive posture is exacerbated by the fact that he and Juanito once had a sexual encounter during their time at the university. Sergio attempts to minimize the importance of this experience, suggesting that it was a case of situational bisexuality that had no further meaning beyond satisfying a momentary physical need (20). However, the fact that he has never spoken of it suggests that the memory of this experience is a threat to Sergio's sense of masculinity. The reality of this threat for Sergio becomes very apparent when, during the Christmas party, he suspects that Juanito has tricked him into singing a song so that Carmela can listen through the telephone.[11] Attacking Juanito, Sergio accuses him of conspiring with Carmela and of telling her about their sexual encounter (138–40). From Sergio's perspective, women and gay men are plotting against him to undermine his masculinity, which he dangerously compromised in his youth by having sex with Juanito.

Sergio also observes how aggressive and self-deprecating camp humor of the type described by Novo in his autobiography and by Blanco in his essay "Ojos que da pánico soñar" is an integral part of the culture of the gay men. For example, although Rubén has obviously adopted an object-choice based sexual identity, rejecting the traditional notion that gay men must be effeminate, his friends ironically refer to him as "la Nenuca" in order to undermine that assertion. Rubén himself occasionally shows a certain ambiguity about his gender identity, as when he jokes that he wants to spend his vacation sunbathing until he is good and burnt, "la reina de los cangrejos" ["the queen of the crabs"] (27). Much of this humor, particularly when self-directed, functions in a reparative manner, helping them to inhabit uninhabitable days and years, as Blanco puts it ("Ojos" 189). For example, when confronting Sergio for not having invited him to his wedding years ago, Juanito ironically states, "Ni que fuera a presentarse uno en bikini a la iglesia, qué te crees" ["It's not like I was going to show up to the church in a bikini, what do you think?"] (23). This is a clear example of how Juanito uses self-deprecating camp humor in order to deal with the pain of discrimination and disidentify with the values of mainstream Mexican society.

Although Sergio generally criticizes the gay men's reparative uses of humor, which he considers to be an attitude towards life too defined by *relajo* to have any real meaning, he also envies it and even identifies with the men to the point that he enjoys their extremely camp and *cursi* Christmas celebration, which is a sort of queer pageant fueled by alcohol and the carnivalesque parody of traditional portrayals of the season. He also learns to see from the perspective of the gay men, to an extent: "Con Rubén, el Jirafón, Aníbal, Juanito, Melba todo tendría que ser necesariamente grotesco, un tanto patético (desde mi punto de vista, claro, quiero decir: desde sus ojos, los patéticos somos otros, de quienes se burlan), como un travestismo" ["With Rubén, el Jirafón, Aníbal, Juanito, Melba everything would have to be grotesque, a little pathetic (from my point of view, of course, that is: in their eyes, we're the pathetic ones, that they make fun of) like a travesty"] (133). As I mentioned above, however, Sergio's appreciation of their disidentification only lasts until he suspects that Juanito has called Carmela to listen in while Sergio plays her favorite song on the guitar. It is at this point that any view of queer disidentification as a possible discourse of reconciliation between Sergio and the others disappears.

Closely related to Sergio's prejudices regarding gender are his ideas about race, class, and modernity. Just as he critiques the gay men's effeminacy and is especially perturbed by the incongruous combination of masculine and feminine scripts in their behavior, he exhibits a generally negative view of *cursilería*, in the sense of the open expression of sentiment and of failed attempts to imitate higher social strata, which he tends to label as *naquez*. Just as his prejudices about women and gay men betray anxieties surrounding a fragile sense of masculinity, his ideas about social class and race show his fears regarding his own social origins. These contradictions, expressed mainly through satire, allegorize social conflicts related to the definition of modernity in Mexico, particularly at the dawn of the country's neoliberal era. While Sergio attempts to cynically distance himself from his feelings through the sarcastic use of humor, his emotions often show through. This is most evident in the chapter in which Sergio drunkenly rants about the collapse of his marriage and in which he oscillates between angry nihilism and the desire to recover what he has lost. He accuses Carmela of being unmodern in her sentiment and lack of coolness and especially for violating their tacit agreement about adultery by falling in love with another man: "Habíamos llegado a las películas C, maduras, civilizadas, coloradonas, ¡y zas, Carmela, regresaste al canal de las telenovelas! Carmela, heroína de 'Vivir de nuevo.' Tantos Rolling Stones para volver a los Dandys" ["We'd reached the C-rated films, mature, civilized, brightly colored, and pow, Carmela, you went back to the soap opera channel. Carmela, heroine of 'Vivir de nuevo' [Live Again]. All that Rolling Stones just to go back to los Dandys"] (104–5). In this humorous metaphor, he juxtaposes mass-media examples of modernity (imported rock music, adult-themed films) with Latin American production associated with *cursilería*. Despite Sergio's implicit juxtaposition of Carmela's emotional female *cursilería* with his cool, levelheaded modernity, it is clear that he is emotionally hurt by her and is, at least in this section, using no less exaggerated and melodramatic discourse to expound on this topic.

As the comments cited above make clear, aside from the open display of sentiment, Sergio also criticizes *cursilería* in the sense of cultural anachronism. However, he expresses a particular disdain for failed attempts to imitate higher social strata, which in this case might be more accurately described as *naquez*. He identifies this in the consumption patterns of Juanito, who seems to believe that his trips to Europe give him access to a cultural authenticity that is not available in Mexico: "—Pero aquí todo es falso, rancherote. Claro que aquí hay champaña, la misma marca, pero es Jojutla: nomás no te lo crees, aunque sea lo mismo nomás no lo disfrutas igual" ["But here everything is fake, country boy. Of course there's champagne, the same brand, but it's Jojutla: believe it or not, you don't enjoy it the same way"] (113). Sergio's sarcastic reaction to this attitude criticizes what he sees as Juanito's pathetic attempts at social climbing:

> Me reí al imaginarlo en un buen restaurante parisino, recomendado por su agencia de viajes, con traje de etiqueta y servicio de plata, tieso de miedo de cometer una impropiedad y de que los demás clientes le chiflaran y lo mandaran a cenar a la cocina: "¡A la sección de nacos, maricón!"

> [I laughed when I imagined him in a fine Parisian restaurant recommended by his travel agency, in a formal suit, with silver service, rigid with the fear of committing an impropriety and that the other diners would whistle at him and send him to eat in the kitchen: "Get to the *naco* section, faggot!"] (114)

Here the caricature of Juanito has to do with the incongruous combination of someone who is attempting to be what he is not and is failing; he is unavoidably unmodern in a modern setting. Sergio's use of the term *naco* clearly racializes this characterization, ultimately reflecting his own anxieties about his racial identity and humble origins.

According to Sergio, he and Carmela's marriage was originally a cynical agreement that would provide him with social mobility and her with freedom from her family. His entire discourse around this arrangement is symptomatic of an impostor syndrome that is ultimately based on race. He relates that during their university studies, he felt inferior to Carmela and her friends, who (he assumes) saw his face as "un tanto 'étnica,' es decir, aztecoide," ["somewhat 'ethnic,' that is, Aztecoid"] and who (he imagines) referred to him as her "ligue antropológico" ["anthropological pick-up"] (68–70). He also recalls feeling inferior to his father-in-law, referring to himself as the "yerno del gremio folk" ["son-in-law from the folk"] (73). This sense of lack of legitimacy is depicted metaphorically through Sergio's encounter with an older man who is asleep standing up in the metro. Sergio perceives that the sleeping man perturbs the other riders because of the incongruous combination in his person of outward signs of respectability (he is older, well-groomed, wearing a suit) and inappropriate behaviors (he is asleep standing up in the metro):

> La gente siente algo disfrazado, travestido en el Catrín Dormilón: un crápula con facha de decente, un joven maquillado de viejo, un pobre que se atilda como rico. Todos lo miran con desconfianza.

> [The people sense something masked, disguised in the Sleeping Dandy: a drunkard with a respectable façade, a young man masquerading as old, a poor man dressed as rich. They all regard him with distrust.] (48)

Of course, "un pobre que se atilda como rico" is the very definition of *naco*, and it is not surprising that the man appears again at the end of the narrative or that Sergio ultimately identifies with him. In this case, the notion of *naquez* is a metaphor for Sergio's anxiety about his own class and racial origins. This anxiety, along with his ambivalent relationship to *cursilería*, allows us to read Sergio's story as an allegorical portrayal of several conflicts in late 20th-century Mexican society, most notably the desire to modernize the country through integration with the world economy and the fear that the country still might not ever achieve that modernity, even with such changes. The racial component of Sergio's anxiety brings to mind the fears of 19th-century elites that Mexico's participation in modernity would be hindered by the supposed racial inferiority of its largely Indigenous population. This fear, a hallmark of the "liberal" period of Latin American economic history, is repeated here in the "neoliberal" period, thus demonstrating how internalized racism has never actually been overcome by discourses of cultural nationalism such as *mestizaje*.[12]

As I argued above, Sergio's anxieties regarding modernity intersect with his ambivalent view of gender, inasmuch as he desires to have modern attitudes regarding sex but continues to reproduce traditional behaviors associated with machismo and with the fear of feminine/homosexual pollution located in his sex act with Juanito in their younger days. Although he does not identify with a bisexual orientation nor seem to consider such an orientation as a possibility, his subjectivity is constructed bisexually, inasmuch as his early experience with Juanito functions as a sort of trauma that obliges him to constantly reinforce the homo/hetero and male/female binaries through his attempt to perform hegemonic masculinity. Notably, Sergio's story never resolves any of the conflicts portrayed—there is no resolution of the problem of his bisexuality nor of his desire to be modern, which he seems to consider doomed by his essential *naquez*. His expulsion from his normal life gives him the ironic distance to undertake a consideration of his life story similar to that in a *Bildungsroman*, but there is no resolution regarding his social adaptation nor any clear didactic message.

It should be evident from what I have cited above how this novel provides ample opportunities to exercise paranoid reading practices in the interpretation of its satire of social norms and unresolved conflicts. However, the realistic, if somewhat caricatured, portrayal of the characters also invites reparative approaches to the novel. I generally agree with Rafael Pérez Gay that the ambiguity in the characterization of Sergio manages to make him seem somehow both repulsive and endearing: "la astucia literaria puede lograr que un personaje detestable se convierta al cabo del tiempo en alguien comprensible, incluso querible" ["literary ingenuity can make a detestable character change, over time, into someone comprehensible, even lovable"] (96). This is thanks in part to Sergio's own humanizing and sympathetic view of Juanito, Rubén, El Jirafón, and Aníbal. Though often disdainful, Sergio also comes to grudgingly admire these characters and seems to sympathize with them to an extent. At the very least, he acknowledges their perspectives and how their traumas have shaped their personalities. These characters also model the ways that self-deprecating camp and *cursi* humor can be used as reparative coping strategies and as human portrayals of queer lives. These are also lives that, while still affected by homophobia and marginalization in many ways, are significantly less marginal than those portrayed in other works on queer themes, like *Vampiro* or *Brenda Berenice*. In that sense, *Mátame y verás*, despite its pessimism, does have a side that denotes social progress in the sense of a greater acceptance of sexual diversity, as intersected by consumerism as this acceptance may be.

Furthermore, Serio himself, despite his misdeeds, expresses his own human suffering in ways that invite identification with him. Like most people, he does not find a way out of his own contradictions, but he expresses them in the only way he knows how. As an imperfect example of humanity, he also invites a certain level of identification from readers. In the end, his subjectivity can be seen as an allegory of Mexico itself at the dawn of the neoliberal era: shot through with social contradictions that are the result of the persistence of coloniality but also capable, at least sometimes, of self-awareness, empathy, and identification with its Others. A similarly ambiguous view of Mexican society's unresolved conflicts appears in Ana García Bergua's novel *Púrpura*, in which the struggles of a protagonist caught up in the desire for masculinity and modernity figuratively portray social conflicts about gender, sexuality, and what it means to be modern in Mexico.

Púrpura

Púrpura is narrated in the first person by Artemio González, a young man who revisits a series of events in his life that led to several important revelations, including the discovery of his artistic vocation, the hypocrisy of the Mexican ruling class, and his own bisexuality. The action takes place largely in a fictitious capital city that evokes the Mexico City of the 1920s and 1930s without suggesting any specific historical moment. In the employ of his successful cousin Mauro, Artemio travels from the provinces to the capital, attempting all the while to *progresar* [progress] according to his understanding of the notion, gleaned mostly from 19th-century French novels. Spending his cousin's money freely, he insinuates himself into high society, travels the city as a *flâneur*, and begins to write a novel. Sexual attraction and romantic relationships form an important part of Artemio's process of self-discovery, and the objects of these attentions fluctuate during the course of the plot.

At the beginning of his narration, Artemio's advances are rejected by the female secretary of the factory where he works as a clerk. When he goes to work for Mauro and begins to live in his mansion, the attraction he feels for his cousin becomes a source of anxiety that reaches a head when he accidentally discovers that Mauro and his friend Dr. Lizárraga are actually lovers. To avoid any possibility of a scandal, Mauro quickly sends Artemio to the capital with improvised errands to run. On the train ride there he meets Alejandra Ledesma, the view of whose ample bosom allows him to assure himself that he is more attracted to women than to his cousin. Alejandra, who is a pianist and a member of the high society of the capital, becomes the object of Artemio's romantic attentions, which eventually culminate in a rather disillusioning sexual encounter.

Aside from Alejandra, Artemio will also have sex with Freddy Santamaría, a film set designer hired to decorate Mauro's temporary residence in the capital, and Lola, a young prostitute. He also forms an ambiguously homoerotic friendship with a young actor named Ramón Navarro (a reference to the homosexual Mexican film star Ramón Novarro). At the climax of the novel, after Artemio learns that his cousin has been involved with some sort of illegal activity involving the smuggling of opium,[13] he has an abortive sexual encounter with Mauro (he kisses him on the mouth). In the end, he abandons the corrupt high life of the capital and moves to Hollywood, where he works as a screenwriter and apparently lives in a *ménage-à-trois* with Lola and Ramón.

Some critics read Artemio's behaviors, and this ending in particular, as an indication that he should be considered a homosexual or gay character.[14] However, I would argue that the closing scene of the novel, taken in conjunction with the protagonist's conflicted presentation of himself in terms of gender identification, makes a reading of him as bisexual more productive. As in *Mátame y verás*, in this novel the main character's subjectivity is constructed on a basis of bisexuality that represents social conflicts about gender and sexuality, race and modernity. The main character, Artemio, is also highly sympathetic, even more so than Sergio in Blanco's novel. His ironic perspective on his past self, in particular, models a reparative consideration of one's own past errors, a use of humor in order to distance oneself from previously traumatic or negative experiences. In this case, once again, the character's ambivalent social position is not resolved. Rather, the narrator-protagonist of *Púrpura* seems to disidentify with many of the dominant values of Mexican society by embracing camp and *cursilería* as integral parts of his own ambivalent identity.

The primary function of camp humor in this novel is to signify Artemio's ambiguous sexual orientation. Niamh Thornton has argued that Artemio's exaggerated emotional reactions (blushing, fainting, etc.) can be read as a camp performance of feminine gender that signals a gay identity ("*Púrpura*" 228). While I agree that many of Artemio's behaviors can be read as feminine, I would argue that other examples can be read as masculine, while others can be read as masculine and/or feminine—that is, ambiguous in terms of gender. For example, many of his sentimental behaviors could actually fall under what Bartra describes as the myth of macho sentimentality, ascribed by writers like Paz to the modern Mexican working-class man who stands in for the entire nation (135–41). This does not signify a gay identity or latent homosexuality but rather a lack of stable sexual and gender identity that both reifies and undermines the homo/hetero and masculine/feminine binaries; in other words, bisexuality. Artemio's bisexuality, in this case, figuratively portrays just how central abject femininity actually is to the construction of Mexican masculinities.

When Artemio's soul is filled with "el más horroroso sentimiento de confusión" ["the most horrible feeling of confusion"] by the music of Beethoven and the poetry of Béquer at his cousin's house (20), or when he tapes a letter from Alejandra to his chest, right over his heart (89–90), his behavior can be read as either a parody of melodramatic femininity, of romantic masculinity, or of both. When Artemio's jealousy leads him to offend Alejandra on their first outing together and she leaves in a huff, his response is to get drunk, a behavior that could be seen as masculine in the social context established in the world of the novel (68). However, the next morning, he gets into the shower in order to "llorar a gusto" ["have a good cry"], which could be seen as either a stereotypically feminine expression of emotion or a masculine alcohol-induced outburst. Later, he uses his cousin's money to buy a Packard in order to incarnate what he sees as the masculinity appropriate for the social class to which he aspires. When he takes Alejandra to a meeting of society ladies and she asks him to wait outside, he is offended and returns half drunk, angrily telling her to call him the next time she needs a chauffeur (129–30). While the acquisition of the car and the gentlemanly act of transporting a woman in it clearly correspond to a masculine role, his offended response to Alejandra, which he calls an "arranque sentimental" ["sentimental outburst"], might be characterized as a show of masculine pride, feminine emotion, or both. In a context in which the protagonist expresses recurring doubts about his own sexual orientation and gender identity, this ambiguous gender performance signals an indeterminacy of both gender and sexual orientation.

Having Your Cake and Eating It Too 139

This indeterminacy is usually expressed by the protagonist as internal conflict. For example, after his first sexual encounter with Freddy Santamaría, Artemio is tormented with guilt and shame for having given in to his desire. Walking in the garden of the house he has decorated for Mauro's arrival in the capital, he observes the gardener's shed, where he had slept while the house was completed, fantasizing about playing the gamekeeper to Alejandra's Lady Chatterley. This reverie is interrupted, however, by the arrival of the attractive young gardener:

> No pude evitar, al ver al muchacho que se acercaba, de sonrisa franca y juvenil, pensar en la escena a la lady Chatterley que había concebido yo alguna vez con Alejandra cuando habitaba la covacha, pero ahora era al revés: si acaso quien debía encarnar a lady Chatterley era yo. Una vergüenza muy grande se apoderó de mí, y me regresé a la casa, furioso.
>
> [Seeing the approaching boy, with his frank and youthful smile, I couldn't help but think of the lady Chatterly scene that I'd once imagined with Alejandra when I lived in the shed, but now it was reversed: if anyone should be lady Chatterly it should be me. I was overcome with a great shame and went back to the house, furious.] (127)

This self-caricature illustrates the overlap of gender and sexuality in Artemio's world: a man cannot feel desire for another man, much less be penetrated by one (as he is by Freddy), and have his masculinity remain intact. This incongruous combination of masculinity and femininity in the body of Artemio is perhaps best illustrated by his rueful remark that the bed where he first had sex with Freddy is where he lost his "doncellez masculina" ["masculine maidenhood"] when Freddy penetrated him (120). This playfully ambiguous phrase incongruously suggests both the loss and gain of masculinity through penetration and illustrates once again how the gender-based humor in this novel contributes to the sense of indeterminacy that surrounds Artemio's sexuality.

The camp humor in *Púrpura* intersects with *cursilería* regularly. Artemio is *cursi* both in his desire to imitate a higher social stratum and in his reiteration of culturally anachronistic tropes. Once again, the narrator presents the younger version of himself in a humorous light, highlighting the contradictory aspects of his *cursilería*—the humor of which is based on an opposition of modern/unmodern (implicitly, white/un-white) scripts. Many of the behaviors I cited above as ambiguously masculine and feminine (crying, taping the letter to his chest, etc.) can also be read as *cursi*, inasmuch as they are also melodramatic exaggerations of sentiment. This recycling of romantic conventions is also closely connected to the desire to imitate the upper classes. This can be seen when Artemio reproves himself for not having brought a memento for Alejandra the first time he visits her at her home:

> Se mandan cartas, se envían gardenias y bombones; así cuando recuerdan a alguien tienen a mano un mechón de cabello, una flor prensada en un libro, un papel garabateado con lágrimas y tinta violeta o azul . . . Nunca había leído que un rico, alguien de la sociedad, no se ayudara de algún objeto para recordar al ser amado; y eso era porque antes, al encontrarse con éste, habían intercambiado aunque fuera un lazo de seda los lujuriosos, un misal bendito los más católicos, o una mísera rama fragante los románticos, por no contar los coches, las casas o las tiaras de diamantes que entre ellos serían moneda de lo más corriente.
>
> [They send each other letters, send each other gardenias and bonbons; that way when they remember someone they have something at hand, a lock of hair, a flower pressed in a book, a paper scrawled with tears and purple or blue ink . . . I'd never read that a rich person, a society person, didn't use some object to remember their loved one; and this was because when they'd met before they had at least exchanged a silk bow (if they were lustful), a blessed missal (if they were Catholic) or a miserable fragrant bouquet (if they were romantic), not to mention the cars, houses or diamond tiaras that would be the most common currency among them.] (62)

This exemplifies how Artemio's reading of 19th-century French literature has influenced his notion of how upper-class people interact. He desires to imitate them in order to become part of that class, but his view is also Eurocentric and anachronistic. Indeed, this aspect of Artemio's personality can be read as a caricature of the tastes of Porfirian elites, the imitative aspects of which continue to operate to an extent in the era of postrevolutionary cultural nationalism, as Novo describes in *La estatua de sal*. The ultimate effect of this is to create a modern/unmodern script opposition in which the unmodern Artemio gains a certain level of access to high society, but never really feels like he actually belongs.

In fact, this failed attempt to imitate a higher social stratum is the main motor of the plot since Artemio first leaves his village and goes to work for his cousin Mauro because he wants to *progresar* [progress]. Much of Artemio's internal conflicts have to do with the shame that he feels because of his indeterminate social position—he is essentially Mauro's employee, but he is treated with a great deal of indulgence because he is also family. This indeterminacy also extends to his racial identity. Although never mentioned explicitly, it is clear from textual clues that internalized racism plays a large part in Artemio's self-conception. The oblique references to race echo the indirect portrayal of Artemio's queer sexuality and contribute to the overall tone of ambiguity in the novel. For example, on the very first page, the relative whiteness of Mauro is contrasted with Artemio's own social condition and physical appearance, which sets up the racialized modern/unmodern script opposition for the first time:

> Mauro era el orgullo de mi abuelo, de su padre y hasta del mío, que siempre nos miraba con cierta decepción por no haber salido como él, pero es que la materia prima del esplendor de Mauro fue su madre, que venía de Bélgica: de ahí salieron sus ojos azules claros, de tanta distinción, y esa altura con la que a todos nos hacía sentir tan poco y a la vez nos llenaba de admiración. Mauro fue siempre nuestra referencia de un mundo mejor.
>
> [Mauro was the pride and joy of my grandfather, of his father and even of my father, who always looked at us with a certain level of disappointment for not being like him, but the fact is that the raw material of Mauro's splendor was his mother, who came from Belgium: that's where he got his light blue eyes, that were so elegant, and that height that made us all feel so small but at the same time filled us with admiration. Mauro was always our example of a better world.] (11)

This sense of racial inferiority intersects with Artemio's sexuality, as whiteness becomes a trait that is equated with sexual desirability. Thus, he speaks ironically of Mauro's blue eyes as seductive even to someone who is not homosexual: "Y eso que sus ojos azules eran de los más bonito que yo había visto, sin ser maricón, pero es que deveras, ni las muchachas más lindas que conocía y que me gustaban mucho, ni Pura la secretaria de la fábrica tenía esos ojos" ["And his blue eyes were the most beautiful thing I'd ever seen, without being a fag, but it's true that not even the best-looking girls I knew that I was really attracted to, not even Pura the secretary from the factory had eyes like that"] (16). Here the narrator's tongue-in-cheek reference to his earlier disavowal of his homoerotic tendencies sets up a homo-/heterosexual script opposition to humorous effect at the same time that it signals the desirability of whiteness.

In a similar fashion, Artemio's attempt to win over Alejandra is posited by him as an attempt to both exercise his homoerotic demons (to displace his desire for Mauro) and to penetrate a higher (whiter) society. The fact that Alejandra's whiteness is questionable becomes clear when Artemio picks her up from a train station after a trip and is completely disillusioned when she appears wearing a huipil (a traditional Mexican Indigenous dress), without her usual level of makeup (104). This disillusion is repeated when he finally has sex with her after a long, frustrating and very *cursi* courtship: the fact that her pubic hair does not have a "rizo dorado" ["golden curls"] makes him realize that she is essentially the same as the other nonwhite women he has already had sex with (143). In these episodes, the modern/unmodern script opposition that is centered on Alejandra's racialized body ironically signals how Artemio the contemporary narrator has come to recognize the socially constructed and relational nature of whiteness in Mexico (Moreno Figueroa 396–99). Thus, he laughs at his younger self's foolish investment of whiteness with masculinity and modernity.

Artemio's realization of this seems to build over time as he relates several scenes where race is implied as a perceived impediment to modernity. For example, the first time Willie Fernández takes him to see Alejandra in concert at the Palacio de Bellas Artes, he is shocked by how the audience does not meet his expectations:

> Por una parte eran mucho más deformes que los habitantes de Tonalato; había una mayor proporción de chaparros, un sinfín de gordos y muchas güeras pintadas, pero ¿cómo decirlo? Tenían más *chic*, se veían más leídos, con más gracia, o por lo menos eso quise ver.

[On the one hand they were much more deformed than the inhabitants of Tonalato; there were more short guys, an endless number of fat guys and a lot of bottle blondes, but, how can I explain it? They had more *chic*, they seemed more well-read, more elegant, or at least that's what I wanted to see.] (40)

Here once again the modern/unmodern script opposition serves to ironically distance the narrator from his younger self's equation of whiteness with modernity and the possibility of being modern in Mexico.

After several such experiences, Artemio eventually becomes completely disillusioned with the corruption and duplicity of the society to which he aspires. His most symbolic disappointment occurs when he discovers that the sumptuous decoration that Freddy Santamaría prepared in Mauro's house is nothing more than a huge movie set built from cheap materials that will fall apart as soon as Mauro leaves: "Igual a mí todo me parecía suntuoso; ¿pues en qué escala de las cosas vivía yo, o más bien en qué escala tan pequeña, que me era imposible distinguir lo real de los disfraces? Si esto era sólo un escenario efímero, ¿qué era todo lo demás?" ["Even so everything seemed sumptuous to me; at what scale must I be living, or rather, at what a small scale must I be living, if I couldn't distinguish what is real from a costume? If this were only an ephemeral stage, what was everything else?"] (119) At this point he realizes that he will probably never truly belong to this social class, but also begins to reflect that perhaps he does not want to after all, thus beginning a process of disidentification with the values of the Mexican elite.

By the end of the novel, Artemio has indeed abandoned his desire to form a part of Mexican high society. Having discarded the possibility of running off to the provincial state of Campeche with Alejandra, he is left with two options: return to his home town or remain in Mexico City working as an actor in the movies with Freddy and receiving money from Mauro. He chooses the second route, but only initially. In the end he prefers to cut himself off from Mauro rather than be involved in his shady dealings, and he forgoes the job of actor for that of screenwriter. In the last pages of the novel, we learn that he has moved to Hollywood with his friends Ramón and Lola. At this point the narrator/protagonist, following the convention of the *Bildungsroman*, seems to make an evaluation of his place in society. However, this evaluation is ambiguous. He recalls seeing a photograph of Alejandra Ledesma in Paris with a young French writer in a recent newspaper:

> La idea de que ese joven pude haber sido yo, quizá, me persigue desde entonces en mis insomnios, mientras miro por la ventana las estrellas de estas noches calientes de California, y Ramón y Lola duermen como niños en el king size.
> Lo bueno es que sufro pocos insomnios.
>
> [The idea that that young man could have been me, perhaps, bedevils me since then whenever I suffer from insomnia, while I look out the window at the stars of these hot California nights, and Ramón and Lola sleep like babies in the king size.
> The good thing is that I very rarely suffer from insomnia.] (171)

These lines close the novel with indeterminacy. Is Artemio relieved at having escaped the role of the young writer in the photo, does he long for it, or both? He seems to be grateful to have escaped from the limiting roles that a young social climber could aspire to in that milieu but also nostalgic for the illusions believed in by his naive younger self. He has, in other words, an ambivalent attitude towards his own *cursilería*, which is portrayed with a mixture of self-deprecating irony and nostalgia.

Artemio's ambivalent attitude towards *lo cursi*, which is expressed through the narrator's ironic perspective, intersects with the ambiguous camp gender performance that signals his bisexuality and the racial position from which he strives for the relative privilege available in *mestizo* Mexico to those who identify with whiteness. It is this ambiguity in particular that subverts the traditional ideology of the *Bildgunsroman* genre. *Púrpura* has a clearly parodic relationship with this genre, and particularly with *The Red and the Black* by Stendahl (Bencomo, "La imaginadora" 85). Here, the sense of indeterminacy replaces the modern didactic function of the *Bildungsroman* with a dismodern one of questioning. That is, with one that reflects the persistence of the coloniality of power, gender, and sex in Mexican society and the desire to disidentify with those discourses that reinforce it.

Ana García Bergua, the author, has affirmed that the frequent play with *albures* and double-entendres in this novel is meant to reflect the way that discourse functions in Mexico in all strata of society (Güemes 31). In other words, part of the author's communicative intent was to depict Mexican culture as infused with ambiguous signification. Artemio himself embodies ambiguity through his bisexuality and his attitude towards the *cursi* aspects of his personality, his racial identity, and Mexican culture and society. Traditional gender roles can be limiting, but their very definition often includes, upon closer examination, an ambiguity that can signal fluid sexual desire. *Lo cursi* might index the illusion of reaching hegemonic notions of modernity through acquiring social and cultural capital, including whiteness, but it can also be a nostalgic discourse of great import for personal identity and even intersect with gender nonconformity and sexual dissidence. This ambiguous position of disidentification, one that includes both critique and celebration, is what allows us to approach this novel with a combination of paranoid and reparative reading practices. In this way we can examine *Púrpura*'s incisive critique of the ways that the desire for modernity and ambiguous signification uphold the dominant social order in Mexico at the same time that we can see the beauty of camp and *cursilería* in the expression of queer subjectivities.

Regarding the portrayal of subjectivity, it should be noted that the narrator in this novel speaks with such ironic distance and in such playfully ambiguous terms (keeping with the tone of the entire narration) that it is difficult to take him as a completely "reliable" narrator, in the most realistic sense of the term. This does not mean, however, that his self-presentation prohibits reparative approaches to the text. On the contrary, it is precisely this playful, *relajiento* attitude towards signification in general that models a reparative, ironic distancing from one's own previous attitudes and struggles, as well as a bittersweet nostalgia for the *cursilería* of one's own culture. The last novel I will examine in this chapter, Enrique Serna's *Fruta verde*, employs a similar narrative strategy in order to portray how a subjectivity defined by bisexuality can be apprehended with ironic distance. Serna's use of camp and *cursi* humor in this portrayal similarly allows for a combination of paranoid and reparative approaches to reading the queer practices of disidentification in his work.

Fruta verde

Fruta verde by Enrique Serna is a semi-autobiographical coming-of-age novel set in late 1970s Mexico City that narrates an important formative period in the life of Germán Lugo, a young aspiring writer.[15] As Germán enters the university and the working world, he begins to differentiate himself from his mother, Paula, and forms an intense intellectual, emotional, and sexual relationship with Mauro Llamas,[16] an older man. While

Paula, who inculcated her son with a love of reading from an early age, continues to encourage his literary ambitions (the novel open with a scene of her typing a short story that her son will submit to a newspaper), Germán struggles against what he sees as her overly rigid sexual morality. As part of his new responsibilities as a young adult, Germán gets a job at an advertising agency, where he attempts to emulate the cultural knowledge and sophistication of his gay male coworkers.

His most important teacher in this second school is the flamboyant playwright Mauro Llamas, who attempts to seduce Germán from the very first day they meet. Despite his initial disgust at these advances and subsequent contretemps in their relationships, Germán eventually falls in love with Mauro and they begin a romantic sexual relationship. Paula suspects that Mauro wants to seduce her son, and her relationship with Germán becomes increasingly strained until he moves out of her house. Meanwhile, Paula herself struggles with the moral question of whether to respond to the attentions of Pável, a young friend of Germán who has fallen in love with her. In the end, despite her obvious desire for sexual fulfillment, Paula rejects her young admirer and remains ensconced in the celibacy she had imposed on herself since her divorce from Germán's father eight years before. Mauro, disappointed by Germán's reticence to define himself as gay and his continuing interest in women, comes to realize that he cannot control Germán's sexuality any more than Paula can.

The twenty numbered chapters of the novel are followed by a coda titled "Ofrenda" ["Offering"], in which Germán, some thirty years after the action that takes place in the first part of the novel, receives the news of Mauro's death. A successful novelist, Germán had remained a close friend of Mauro even after their romantic relationship came to an end. After participating in the funerary events, Germán finally feels that he is able to undertake a challenge posed to him years before by Mauro: to write the story of his life. After Germán finishes the manuscript, he leaves it on a Day of the Dead alter he has made in remembrance of his mother, who had died fifteen years before from uterine cancer. At night, he sleeps well for the first time in weeks and dreams that his mother and Mauro appear close to the altar, chatting amiably, finally reconciled as friends. In this way, the novel proposes a figurative resolution to the author's internal conflicts, which themselves are indicative of broader social conflicts. This notion of coming to terms with his past evokes the way the main character usually takes stock of her/his place in society in the classic *Bildungsroman*. Upon closer examination, however, it becomes clear that this is not a true resolution of conflicts but rather an acceptance of their unresolvable nature. The ironic perspective of the narrator combines with a focus on the reparative uses of camp and *cursi* humor in the portrayal of Germán's bisexual subjectivity, which embodies social conflicts about gender, sex, race, and modernity in contemporary Mexico.

In the first twenty chapters of the novel, a third-person narrator focalizes the narration through the three principal characters (Germán, Paula, and Mauro), often transcribing their speech and interior monologues, while also maintaining an ironic distance from their perceptions. This mode of narration is interrupted at times by the insertion of different textual styles. For example, when Paula catches her guest Kimberly, a distant relative from Seattle, making love with one of Germán's friends in a hammock, she publicly shames her the next day in a sort of unofficial trial that is presented as a play. At other times, there are epistolary exchanges, such as those between Pável and Paula, and at one point, Germán begins to keep a diary, the entries of which form the majority of several chapters. The "Ofrenda" that makes up the last section of the book is narrated in the first person by the older Germán who, it is implied, is the author of the first part of the novel. Much of the humor in the novel derives from the narrator's use of free indirect style to satirize the behaviors and beliefs of Germán, Paula, and Mauro from an ironic distance. A large part of the humor is based on camp gender nonconformity, which serves to signal the homosexuality of Mauro and the bisexuality of Germán.

The first appearance of Mauro highlights the incongruous combination of masculine and feminine scripts in his body (he has a very virile voice but feminine body language), connecting this self-presentation with Mauro's expression of a dissident gay identity (45). However, it is in the body of Germán himself that the most significant uses of gender-based humor by Mauro occur, since the combinations of the masculine/feminine script opposition in his body undermine traditional gender roles and, metonymically, homo- and heterosexual categories of identity. For example, Mauro compares Germán to a stereotyped vision of a young woman who is playing hard to get, with himself in the role of masculine seductor:

> De hecho, en las últimas semanas se comportaba como esas criadas rejegas que al ir por el pan, esquivan a manotazos los toqueteos del novio, rezongando con voz queda: "Estate sosiego, Lencho." Un rechazo tan tibio en realidad era una invitación a ir más lejos, como bien sabían los padrotillos de barrio.

[In fact, the last few weeks he'd been acting like those reluctant housemaids that, on their way to buy the day's bread, swat away their boyfriend's touches, quietly grumbling: "Calm down, Lencho." Such a tepid rejection was in fact an invitation to go farther, as the barrio pimps knew well.] (161)

Later, however, when Mauro is elated to have received a job writing a *telenovela*, he imagines Germán in the role of a man and himself in the role of a woman:

Como buen héroe de película mexicana, [Germán] se había entregado por amor, sin esperar nada a cambio, a una corista pobre y remendada, la tabasqueña Maura Llamas, sin sospechar que el día menos pensado [. . .] la rapazuela de quinto patio se convertiría en vedette de fama internacional.

[Like a good Mexican film hero, [Germán] had surrendered himself for love, without expecting anything in return, to a poor and ragged chorus girl, Maura Llamas from Tabasco, without suspecting that one day [. . .] the girl from the ghetto would become an internationally famous star.] (226)

In these two examples, Germán is imagined first as a feminine and then as a masculine figure by Mauro, who imagines himself in first masculine and then feminine roles. Germán's indeterminacy, in other words, highlights a similar indeterminacy in the way Mauro conceives of his own sexuality and gender identity.

For his part, Germán learns from Mauro and his friends how to disidentify with mainstream gender norms by using camp humor reparatively as an in-group identity marker and psychic self-defense, and he employs it in ironic and self-deprecating reflections on his ambivalence about his sexual orientation and the gender roles he feels that society expects him to play. For example, he compares himself to the stereotyped figure of a good-looking woman who is courted by an unattractive man (Mauro): "como tantas mujeres guapas conquistadas por feos encantadores yo había tenido la gentileza de regalarle mi cuerpo en recompensa por su largo y devoto cortejo" ["like so many good-looking women conquered by ugly, but enchanting, men I'd had the courtesy to give him my body in compensation for his long and devoted courtship"] (218). Germán also feels a very strong attraction to camp humor as expressed by Mauro and his intellectual friends. He notes in his diary that he has a "licencia para jotear" ["license to camp"] that he is daring to use with his "hermanas" ["sisters"] in the office, who give him the nickname "Sor Juana" because of his disciplined study habits: "Cuando le digo 'manita' a la Chiquis o nos ponemos a hablar con la letra 'i' en las juntas de la oficina ('quí bírbiri mijir') me siento como pez en el agua" ["When I call la Chiquis 'sister' or we start talking with the letter 'i' in office meetings ('quí bírbiri mijir')] I feel like I'm in my element"] (263–64).[17]

However, he also expresses a sense of divided allegiance between the gay fraternity and the heterosexual mainstream, between hegemonic and "effeminate" masculinities, which he expresses through a metaphor that disidentifies with both hetero- and homonormativity by setting up a script opposition in his own body: "Preferiría tener una sola cara con bigote y rimel en las pestañas, en vez de cambiar de papel según el público que me observa" ["I would prefer to have one face with a mustache and mascara, rather than change roles according to the audience that's observing me"] (264). This sense of indeterminacy returns at the end of the novel. In the "Ofrenda," we learn that all of Germán's subsequent sexual relationships have been heterosexual, and, we can surmise, he has passed for heterosexual in society. This changes, at least momentarily, with the death of Mauro and his assumption of the role of widow, which he earns for having been part of the longest and most stable relationship of Mauro's life: "No me molestó desempeñar ese papel durante el velorio, ni me sentí un impostor al recibir los pésames en la capilla ardiente, porque la viudez es un vacío espiritual, más que un estado civil, y yo traía el alma tan enlutada como Juana la Loca" ["It didn't bother me to play that role during the wake, nor did I feel like an imposter while receiving condolences while he was lying in repose, because widowhood is more of a spiritual emptiness than a marital status, and my soul was more grief stricken than Juana la Loca's"] (296). With this camp assumption of femininity, Germán reiterates, metaphorically, his bisexuality. This indeterminacy with regards to sex and gender roles, expressed through camp humor, intersects with an equally ambivalent use of *cursilería* in the novel.

In this novel, *lo cursi* appears as the failed attempt to imitate higher social strata and cultural anachronism (romantic, sentimental, melodramatic discourse). The young Germán initially rejects both of these in an attempt to constitute his own identity, although he later accepts them as somehow inevitable. To a great extent, this means rebelling against what he sees as his mother's *cursilería*. However, Germán the author seems to have a more nuanced view of *lo cursi* and explores many of its more contradictory aspects in his characterization of Paula, Mauro, and the young Germán. Therefore, much of the humor derives from young Germán's ignorance of his own internal contradictions, which themselves are often the result of his lack of awareness of his gender, class, and racial privilege. In the end, the novel presents an ambivalent evaluation of *lo cursi* that highlights both its limitations and its creative and liberating possibilities. This ambivalence implies a dismodern parody of the pan-European *Bildungsroman*—there is no clear evaluation of the protagonist's place in society, but rather a meditation on its inherent ambiguity that itself reflects social conflicts in Mexican society and the value of *cursilería* as a sort of sensibility that expresses Mexico's position in the Global South.

For the young Germán, eager to rebel against the authority of his mother, his Marxism-laden college curriculum gives him a vocabulary to criticize her modest desires for material comforts (she is happy when Germán's father helps him buy a car; she dreams of owning her own house), which he considers shamefully *cursi* (101). More than anything, however, Germán considers his mother to be unmodern because of her insistence on preserving traditional sex and gender norms. In Germán's mind, this is cultural anachronism connected to traditional religion and melodrama—he compares his mother to a "beata de pueblo" ["sanctimonious small-town churchgoer"] (27), argues that her arguments are "melodramas" and that she is a "mojigata" ["prude"] with medieval values (205–6). To him, his mother's insistence on traditional values is particularly contradictory since she is very well read. He cannot understand why her opinions are not more similar to his (in part because he is incapable of understanding her social position as a woman in Mexico).

The older Germán, from his perspective of greater knowledge and experience, offers us a much more nuanced portrayal of Paula and her internal conflicts. This is evident in the humorous depiction of her disillusioning encounter with her cousin Baldomero from Spain, whom she imagines as very traditional but who turns out to be living in a ménage-à-trois with his wife and niece: "No podía ser verdad lo que estaba oyendo. Baldomero, su primo hermano, el rústico leñador de Piloña a quien había imaginado inocente y puro como un manojo de albahaca, le confesaba tan tranquilo una intimidad repugnante" ["What she was hearing couldn't be true. Baldomero, her first cousin, the rustic woodcutter from Piloña whom she had imagined as innocent and pure as a bunch of basil, was shamelessly confessing this repugnant personal matter to her"] (239). This is particularly significant for Paula since she imagines her mother's home village of Piloña, Asturias as an idealized, Arcadian space where traditional values of sex and gender are preserved. This clashes with the sexual liberation of post-Franco Spain in a frustration of expectations based on a modern/unmodern script opposition.

However, Paula also perceives that Baldomero is obligating his wife to accept this in a reaffirmation of traditional masculine privilege disguised as modern liberation. This is illustrative of one of the major contradictions in her character: though she views her mother's village as the space of *cursilería* with nostalgia, she also realizes that the traditional values of this space are very oppressive to women (they were, in fact, a major reason her mother left the village in the first place). Paula is offered an escape from such traditional gender roles when Pável falls in love with her and courts her with very *cursi* letters. However, she ultimately decides to remain true to her identification with the traditional role of decent, abnegated mother, unable to abandon that position.

A similar juxtaposition of the perspectives of the younger and older Germán can be seen in the characterization of Mauro. The young Germán criticizes Mauro's decision to write *telenovelas* in order to make money, interpreting it as a waste of his talent and a pathetic attempt at social climbing that makes him just like Germán's mother, *la cursilona* ["the big *cursi*"] (228). While the implied author (older Germán) does indeed lightly satirize Mauro's tendency to get himself into financial difficulties in order to keep up appearances (54, 56), he also seems to validate Mauro's opinion that one can strike a balance between making money and making art. In this view, even the mass-produced melodrama of *telenovelas* can be a space for artistic creation (265–67). Significantly, this is connected to Mauro's life experiences and self-expression: "Y aunque detestaba los cartabones morales del melodrama, su educación sentimental lo predisponía a intensificar emociones, a simpatizar con las víctimas: no en balde había visto cine mexicano toda su infancia" ["And even though he hated the moral strictures of melodrama, his sentimental education predisposed him to intensify emotions, to sympathize with victims: not for nothing had he watched Mexican movies all through his childhood"] (226). The modern/unmodern script opposition is in play here as Mauro, a subject who strives to be modern, recognizes that he must call on his familiarity with unmodern *cursilería* in order to achieve the financial stability that he needs in order to live a modern lifestyle. This quote also appears on the same page as the one cited above in which Mauro imagines himself in the role of vedette and Germán as the cinematic hero. In that case, camp and *cursi* humor intersect in Mauro's ironic reinscription of his own lived experience as a sort of melodrama. Ultimately, Mauro's view of *lo cursi* as a source and outlet of artistic self-expression is accepted by Germán, who adopts this perspective and reparative use of *cursilería* in his rendition of the novel.

As the examples cited above suggest, Germán the author maintains an ironic view of his younger self's perspectives on *cursilería*. Indeed, we might view his entire characterization as a tongue-in-cheek expression of a modern/unmodern script opposition, since Germán rejects *cursilería* but is himself *cursi*. For example, while he criticizes Paula and Mauro's desire for economic stability in Marxist terms, he is unable to recognize that his own pseudosocialism is itself predicated on the imitation of a European discourse of modernity. Similarly, his belief in "art for art's sake" is based on ideals that originate with romantic European notions of aesthetic autonomy and is, therefore, both a repetition of European discourse as well as a cultural anachronism. This is recognized by Mauro, who literally labels this attitude as *cursi*, noting that Germán is only able to demand such purity from art because he has always enjoyed the financial security of his middle-class family (265).

Germán has a similar blind spot with regards to his racial privilege (like the writer Enrique Serna, he is descended from refugees of the Spanish Civil War), which is contrasted with Mauro's experiences as a clearly racialized subject from the provinces of Mexico. Early in the novel, Germán is represented as idolizing the lifestyles of the vaguely leftist Mexican hippies of the time: "Esos rebeldes con causa habían elegido el mejor antídoto contra el culto a la moda: ir a todas partes con morral y camisa de manta, es decir, vestidos de indios, en abierto desafío a los prejuicios de una sociedad clasista y racista" ["Those rebels with a cause had opted for the best antidote to the cult of fashion, going everywhere with a woven bag and a coarse cotton shirt, that is, dressed like Indians, in open challenge to the prejudices of a racist and classist society"] (33). Shortly after this, Mauro remembers that when he first came to Mexico City from Tabasco dressed just like that his friends started to call him

> la Olmeca, un apodo cariñoso pero veladamente racista, que por fortuna había logrado sacudirse con el paso del tiempo [. . .] Elegía la ropa con más cuidado, sin renunciar a los vivos

colores del trópico, pues había comprendido que en los círculos
intelectuales de México sólo los criollos podían darse el lujo
de vestirse como indios.

[the [lady] Olmec, an affectionate but implicitly racist nickname
that he had fortunately been able to lose over time [. . . now
he] chose his clothes more carefully, without abandoning the
lively colors of the tropics, since he had understood that in
the intellectual circles of Mexico City only whites enjoyed the
privilege of being able to dress like Indians.] (47)

This highly ironic juxtaposition is built on the modern/unmodern or white/
unwhite script opposition, and it ultimately highlights how the countercultural appropriation of Indigenous iconography not only does not combat racism, it usually ends up reinforcing it through social exclusion. Young Germán's ignorance of this contributes to his ironic characterization by his older self as naive.

Similarly, the younger Germán is also characterized as a highly emotional person who identifies with romantic and melodramatic expressions of sentiment, despite his criticism of such attitudes in his mother. When he complains that her mind has a "lógica visceral de melodrama barato" ["visceral logic of cheap melodrama"] (73), he is himself also struggling against the siren call of a melodramatic song that might lead him to wallow in self-pity: "Y aunque ahora mismo, en el radio de la combi, José José cantara las delicias de un fracaso amoroso, debía taparse los oídos con cera, como el astuto Ulises, para no resbalar por esa pendiente de masoquismo" ["And even though right now, on the bus radio, José José was singing the delights of a romantic failure, he needed to plug his ears with wax, like the clever Ulysses, to avoid slipping down that slope of masochism"] (73). This tendency towards sentimentality is evident in other actions of his, such as crying when he identifies with the protagonists of a melodramatic film he watches with Mauro (166–67) or deliberately searching out passé popular music and bars in order to feel decadent:

No entienden [mis amigos] cómo puede gustarme oír boleros nostálgicos en la penumbra de un bar, entre borrachines astrosos y putas decrépitas. Si supieran cuánto amor coagulado tengo aquí adentro, tal vez comprenderían por qué pertenezco a ese mundo.

> [[My friends] don't understand how I can enjoy listening to nostalgic boleros in the shadows of a bar, among raggedy drunks and decrepit whores. If they knew how much curdled love I have inside, maybe they'd understand why I belong to that world.] (193)

All of these behaviors contribute to Germán's comic characterization as a walking script opposition—he is both modern and unmodern at the same time and cannot help but be so. The ambiguous *cursilería* of young Germán, which parallels his ambiguous sexuality, reflects the book's generally ambivalent evaluation of *lo cursi* as both a reflection of the coloniality of power, gender, and sex and a positive expression of Mexican sensibility.

By the end of the novel, we learn that Germán the author has taken the advice of his friend Mauro and written a book about his own life. It can be read, in part, as older Germán's reflection on his sentimental education and the role played in it by his mother and Mauro. In this sense, it contains a deeply ambivalent assessment of the value of *cursilería*. On the one hand, the example of Paula shows how *lo cursi* is intimately connected to traditional social values that can be very oppressive and limiting. Although Paula has the opportunity to transgress these values, offered to her in *cursi* language by Pável, she ultimately does not do so because of the weight of traditional gender norms in her notion of self. Mauro, on the other hand, is able to tap the wellspring of *cursilería* that forms the basis of his own sentimental education in order to find an outlet of self-expression through art. Germán attempts to do this in the end as well, also recognizing how *cursi* texts (such as the bolero "Fruta verde," which was playing when Mauro succeeded in seducing him) helped him to transgress social norms of sex and gender.

Germán's comic portrayal of the *cursilería* of himself, his mother, and Mauro intersects with camp humor that, more than anything, expresses his bisexuality. This lack of a clear orientation perturbs the norms of sex and gender that rule both the heteronormative mainstream represented by Paula and the homonormative gay culture in which Mauro participates. Germán's ironic depiction of himself at Mauro's funeral, where he plays the role of widow, illustrates the intersection of camp and *cursi* humor in the novel, but it also depicts the ambiguity with which gender, sexuality, and the relationship with modernity signaled by *lo cursi* are treated. Read as a parody of the pan-European *Bildungsroman*, the novel can be said to replace the genre's didactic function with one of questioning. The ironic perspective of the protagonist's older self does not include a clear evaluation of his current place in society, but rather it leaves the reader with questions to which there are no clear answers. Which is more authentic: Germán's role as an ostensibly heterosexual man or his role as Mauro's queer "widow"? Should his sexual orientation be considered heterosexual, bisexual, queer, or none of the above? Is *cursilería* ultimately a more liberating or a more limiting discourse from which to imagine nostalgia and identity?

Perhaps, as with attempts to define bisexuality, such questions should not be answered as either/or, but as both *and* neither. This lack of epistemological clarity is dismodern. That is, it reflects the persistence of the coloniality of power, gender, and sex in Mexican society and a desire to disidentify with Mexico's dominant social structure. Like *Mátame y verás* and *Púrpura*, *Fruta verde* parodies the *Bildungsroman* genre, expressing unresolvable social conflicts about sex and gender, race, class, and modernity in the protagonist's explanation of his process of gaining self-knowledge. In all three of these novels, bisexuality structures those subjectivities, thus illustrating the centrality of gender to the construction of sexualities in Mexico as well as the highly unstable basis of hegemonic masculinity there. The works all portray reparative uses of camp and *cursi* humor that are part of queer strategies of coping, disidentification, and resistance, and that ultimately accept ambiguity and the unresolved tensions of coloniality as a central part of Mexican identity. These uses of humor, along with the novels' incisive satire of the injustices of Mexican society, make them very apt texts for reading with strategies that combine paranoid and reparative perspectives in a critical and subversive view of the possibilities of literature.

Chapter 5

Machorra Camp and Lesbian *Cursilería*

Sexuality, Gender, and Humor in Narratives by and about Queer Women

All the texts we have seen up to now have centered on male bodies engaging in camp and *cursi* humor, and especially on camp as gender nonconformity, a willful performance of effeminacy that signifies queerness. In the system of humorous signification I have been explaining thus far, even *travesti* and *vestida* identities, with their queer evasion of gender and sex binaries, are ultimately based on the perception of a male body performing feminine gender. In this chapter, I will examine some works of literature that employ camp and *cursi* humor in the portrayal of women characters who engage in gender nonconformity and sexual dissidence. As I explain below, these portrayals are often closely connected to lesbian sexualities and cultures. As in the previous chapters, here the use of camp and *cursi* humor gives expression to social conflicts. Below I will consider the ways that the queer women characters in these texts use this humor to disidentify with mainstream Mexican masculinities and femininities and how these portrayals can be approached from both paranoid and reparative reading perspectives.

To begin, we should ask why there are so few of these texts in comparison with the ones featuring male characters. Recall that the connection between male gender nonconformity and homosexuality has a sort of moment of irruption in Mexican culture: the scandal of the 41 in 1901. There is no analogous moment of crisis for female homosexuality and gender nonconformity. In part, this is due to the historical androcentrism of discourses of social control in the region. José Quiroga has noted a general dearth of attention to female queer sexualities in Latin America in the early 20th century: "In a context that repressively (and predominantly) indexed men, lesbians were consigned to an effacement that in itself belied the male-centered concerns of institutions of power" (13). This reflects the double discrimination (based on gender as well as sexuality) that lesbian and/or queer women have long faced in Mexico (Alfarache, "La construcción" 127), as well as the long tradition of representing the Mexican nation figuratively as a male figure and through male homosocial and homosexual relations (Domínguez-Ruvalcaba, *Modernity* 75–93, 99; Irwin, *Mexican* 4–5, 47).

This does not mean, however, that women's gender nonconformity and lesbian sexuality have not been visible in Mexican culture. The sexuality of women, along with that of men, became an increasingly scrutinized topic of scientific discourse in the early 20th century (Irwin, *Mexican* 50–58). In literature, characters engaging in lesbian sex appeared as early as 1886 in José Tomás de Cuéllar's novel *Baile y cochino . . .* ["Dance and Pig"], and lesbian sexuality is treated as a social ill in Federico Gamboa's *Santa* (1903), the classic text of Mexican naturalism (Reséndiz 140). Women's gender nonconformity was common during the Mexican Revolution, particularly among the *soldaderas*, women who participated in military actions in various ways (Arce; Salas). The *soldadera* figure was the topic of yet another naturalist novel, *México marimacho* ["Butch Mexico"] (Quevedo y Zubieta, 1933), which explicitly linked feminine masculinity to lesbian sexuality, understood as a symptom of social degeneration and a threat to the nation (Ruiz Alfaro). The scholar María Elena Olivera notes a later tendency towards existentially pessimistic portrayals of lesbian characters in novels like *Los muros de agua* ["The Walls of Water"] (1941) by José Revueltas and *Figura de paja* ["Straw Figure"] (1964) by Juan García Ponce, which does not change until the publication of Rosamaría Roffiel's *Amora* (1989), widely considered to be Mexico's first lesbian feminist novel (85–90; 94–97). This book was followed by more narrative texts with explicitly lesbian themes, such as Sara Levi Calderón's novel *Dos mujeres* [*The Two Women*] (1990); *Infinita* ["Infinita"] (1992) by Ethel Krauze; *Con fugitivo paso* ["With Fugitive Steps"] (1997) by Victoria Enríquez; *Réquiem por una muñeca rota* ["Requiem for a Broken Doll"] (2000) by Eve Gil; *Con la boca abierta* ["With Open Mouth"] (2006) by the Cuban exile writer Odette Alonso; and the three works that I will examine in this chapter: *¿Y qué fue de Bonita Malacón?* ["Whatever Happened to Bonita Malacón"]

(2007) by José Dimayuga; *Del destete al desempance* ["From Weaning to the Digestif"] (2008) by Gilda Salinas; and *Contarte in lésbico* ["Tell You in Lesbian"] (2014) by Elena Madrigal.

In Mexico, films and television programs that have openly portrayed lesbian sexuality have been even more rare than the literature, likely reflecting the tendency of heteropatriarchy to erase lesbian existence (Rich). Venkatesh argues that some films, such as Jaime Humberto Hermosillo's *Amor libre* ["Free Love"] and María Luisa Bemberg's biopic of Sor Juana Inés de la Cruz, *Yo, la peor de todas* [*I, The Worst of All*], may not be explicitly homoerotic but do "portray tactics and positions that decenter [. . .] heterosexist structures," thus opening them to queer readings (*New* 54). Bemberg's film, in particular, has become a central text in the debates about the possibility of reading Sor Juana as a lesbian figure.[1] Some recent films have been more explicit in their portrayals of lesbian relationships, though not necessarily more nuanced. According to María Castro Ricalde, "semi-Sapphic" films such as *Así del precipicio* [*On the Edge*] (Teresa Suárez, 2006) and *Todo incluido* [*All Inclusive*] (Rodrigo Ortúzar, 2008) open the possibility of lesbian visibility at the same time that they close it through their heteronormative scopophilia and reduction of relationships to an aspect of neoliberalism (209, 214–17). In this sense, they are similar to films that center gay male identity as part of neoliberal modernity, such as *La otra familia* (Venkatesh, *New* 186–87). A similarly heteropatriarchal portrayal of lesbianism can be seen in *Las Aparicio* [*The Aparicio Women*] (Moisés Ortiz Urquidi, 2015), based on the telenovela of the same name, while *Todo el mundo tiene a alguien menos yo* [*Everybody's Got Somebody . . . Not Me*] (Raúl Fuentes, 2012) includes a problematically pessimistic portrayal of a dysfunctional lesbian relationship (Smith 89–94). The HBO Latin America television program *Capadocia*, a gritty women-in-prison show with complex portrayals of lesbian relationships, reiterates some stereotypes but also offers a more complex portrayal than most of the films mentioned above (Smith 128–33).

As this summary indicates, lesbian identities and sexualities in Mexico tend to be much less visible than those of homosexual, bisexual, gay, and gender-nonconforming men. While this may mark a similarity with the Global North, there are also important cultural differences regarding the perception of lesbian sexualities in Mexico. In the English-speaking world, the term "lesbian," which had acquired a pejorative meaning by the early 20th century, was appropriated in the 1960s and 1970s as a positive form of identification associated with feminism. In a seminal 1980 essay, Adrienne Rich critiques the compulsory heterosexuality imposed on women and proposes instead a respect for "lesbian existence," which refers not only to sexual attraction between women but, more importantly, to the notion of making affective relationships with women a central part of one's existence and one's resistance to the impositions of patriarchy. While lesbian feminism certainly is at the center of certain expressions of lesbian identity in Mexico, such as Roffiel's novel *Amora*, it does not have as large an influence on lesbian sexualities as it does in the Global North.

Writing from the US context, Amy Villarejo has recently noted a tension in lesbian visibility between a tactical essentialism that is necessary for political progress and a destabilizing queerness that undermines all notions of essential identity (14). In Mexico and the rest of Latin America, for numerous reasons, queerness often outweighs essentialist identity politics in cultural portrayals of lesbian sexuality. As Sifuentes-Jáuregui notes, essentialist notions such as the "closet" and exiting it are not as important to homosexualities in Latin America as they are in the United States (*Avowal* 66, 70, 80). The short story "Five Windows on the Same Side" by the Cuban-American author Sonia Rivera Valdés (from the collection *The Forbidden Stories of Marta Veneranda*) illustrates this difference clearly. In this story a Cuban-American woman has a brief affair with a female in-law from Cuba. The protagonist, whose view of female-female sexual relations are influenced by US identity politics and the object choice-based theory of sexual identity, begins to gravitate towards a lesbian identity. The Cuban woman, in contrast, considers the relationship an expansion of heterosexual desire that does not affect her sexual identity (*Avowal* 222–23). We will see a similar Latin American queerness at work in the portrayal of lesbian sexuality in Dimayuga's *Bonita Malacón* below.

While Dimayuga's novel shies away from directly naming lesbian sexuality, the works by Salinas and Madrigal, both self-identified lesbian authors, take lesbian sexuality and identity as their main themes. Even these works, however, demonstrate key contrasts with comparable works from the Global North. For example, there are marked differences in the work of these Mexican authors and Chicana lesbian writers from the United States. Although they do share certain cultural affinities, their texts demonstrate divergences in US and Mexican lesbian cultures as well as the social positionalities of the writers themselves. In the 1980s, Chicana lesbian activist writer/scholars such as Gloria Anzaldúa and Cherríe Moraga allied themselves with women of color feminism in the first major expression of US Latina/o/x LGBT visibility (Almaguer 90; Torres 1). Their work, which tends to be formally experimental and multigeneric, focuses specifically on the intersection of different aspects of their identities borne of resistance to oppression—namely gender, sexuality, race and social class (Garza).[2] A major part of this experience, amply illustrated in the work of Moraga, is an internal conflict between identification with the patriarchal Chicano family culture (seen as a bastion of resistance to racial and class discrimination in the United States) and with the Anglo-American lesbian feminist culture that provides an opportunity for self-realization but also pressures her to assimilate to white US culture (Almaguer 91–95). This sense of cultural conflict is also present in the multilingual nature of the Chicanas' texts, which can best be described as English-language works where occasional interjections of Spanish are a stylistic element that serves to disrupt monolingual writing/reading practices (Fagan).

This contrasts with the largely middle-class, mostly unicultural and monolingual (Spanish) perspectives portrayed in much Mexican literature on lesbian themes written by lesbian-identified authors, such as the works by Salinas and Madrigal included in this chapter.[3] As we will see, while these texts do directly identify themselves as "lesbian," discussions of race, class and politics are largely absent from their pages, a fact that reflects the positionality of their authors as upper-middle-class women in urban Mexico. On the other hand, the work by Dimayuga, a gay man from the provinces, centers race and social class at the same time that it shies away from specifically using the term "lesbian," thus reflecting a more rural and traditional, but at the same time somewhat queerer, perspective on female sexuality.

While there may be several differences between the ways that Chicana and Mexican lesbian writers approach their identities and expressions, one thing that they all share is a history of colonization (Torres 4). Even in Mexican texts with few direct references to race and class, the expression of coloniality is evident through the use of *cursilería*. As in the texts we've seen above that feature male protagonists, here *lo cursi* intersects with camp in humorous portrayals of gender-nonconforming characters. The humorous figures present here have an analogue in one of José Muñoz's main examples of disidentification: the work of the Cuban American performance artist Alina Troyano, "Carmelita Tropicana." Muñoz reads Carmelita's performances as "*cubana* dyke camp," which includes elements of gender parody, such as the cross-dressed character "Pingalito," an exaggerated caricature of a macho Cuban exile (124). This performance in particular ironically satirizes Cuban and Cuban American racism and sexism at the same time that it disidentifies with camp itself (originally a white, masculine, Anglo-American discourse) through the intersection of lesbian camp and Cuban *choteo*, or ritual insult humor (133, 138). In other words, Carmelita's "*cubana* dyke camp" places coloniality at the center of a performance that questions discourses of Cuban identity from a lesbian perspective. In a similar manner, the texts below posit a disidentification with mainstream Mexican masculinities and femininities in the portrayal of women's queerness by combining forms of lesbian camp (particularly the performance of female masculinities) and humor based on *cursilería*.

While camp has generally been associated with male homosexuality (and especially with gender parody and effeminacy), there is also a critical tradition of reading camp as done by women, particularly among lesbian collectives.[4] This current arose with the queer recovery of camp as a liberating discourse and focuses especially on potentially subversive readings. Some theorists, such as Butler and Case, have focused more on the most obviously nonconforming examples, such as drag kings and butch identities, while others, like Robertson and Hemmings, have focused more on the performance of femininities in women's camp. Hemmings in particular worries that excessive attention to female masculinities can reinforce the reduction of lesbian sexualities to traditional gender models (160–62). While I agree that it is important to consider this danger, and that this argument makes sense in the US context, I disagree that this perspective is necessarily the best way to consider much Mexican cultural production on lesbian themes.

In particular, the texts I analyze below seem to demand a clear focus on the performance of what might be called *marimacho* or *machorra* [tomboy, bull dyke] camp, from two of the words frequently used to disparage "masculine" women in Mexico. A common stereotype of women who engage in same-sex relations in Mexico, somewhat analogous to that of the effeminate homosexual man, is that of the masculine lesbian. Epithets such as *marimacho*, *machorra* or *trailera* [truck-driving dyke] are symptomatic of the association of lesbian sexuality with stereotypically masculine behaviors and activities (Muñoz 58–59; Alfarache 132). This stereotype is widespread in Mexican society and is the most frequent way that lesbian characters are portrayed in the mass media (Mancera 188). The figure is essentially satirical (critically humorous) and generally appears to serve the dominant social order by reducing anxiety about sexuality and gender and by stereotyping, ostracizing, and ridiculing lesbians.

Reading this stereotype as an example of humor, the *machorra* embodies a masculine/feminine script opposition in which an ontologically female body performs masculinities through stereotypically macho activities like drinking, womanizing, and fighting. Notwithstanding the very real repressive functions of this stereotype, we must also recognize that certain types of gender nonconformity can serve as reparative expressions of *lesbiana* and/or queer identities. One of the most famous practitioners of such reparative performance was the singer Chavela Vargas, whose own persona was based on an appropriation of macho elements of midcentury hegemonic masculinity in Mexico, including heavy drinking and womanizing (Bustamante). This is not to imply that there is no "feminine" camp done by Mexican women. The subversive theater of Jesusa Palancares, for example, often includes a great deal of camp and *cursi/naco* humor involving parody of the female gender. However, what stands out as a source of humor in the texts below, where it is clearly associated with lesbian sexuality, is the humorous figure of the *machorra*, the woman who can be just as macho (if not more so) than any man.

Why might this figure appear in these texts? To begin with, there is a real-world referent for this figure in Mexican lesbian cultures. Anahi Russo has recently recorded gender-based labeling practices in the lesbian collectives of Mexico that distinguish the more masculine *azul* from the more feminine *rosa* in a manner analogous to butch and femme labels in the United States ("The Emergence" 83; "El ambiente"). Aside from the mimetic aspect of these portrayals, I would argue that there are at least three other major reasons that this figure appears in these texts: the primacy of the body in the construction of gender in Latin America; the historical androcentrism of Mexican culture; a tendency in recent literature to deproblematize lesbian sexuality and women's gender nonconformity through the use of humor.

In previous chapters, I have echoed Sifuentes-Jáuregui's argument that the body pre-exists the construction of gender in Latin America (*Avowal* 10–11). One effect of this is the way that the interpellation of subjects often includes a preconceived notion of bodies as racialized and gendered. That is, in Latin America subjectivities are constructed through and against the coloniality of power, sex, and gender (Domínguez-Ruvalcaba, *Translating*; Lugones). One effect of this is the close association of men's sexual dissidence with effeminacy. There is a similar association of lesbian/queer female sexualities with masculinities that feeds stereotypes but that also contributes to the construction of dissident identities. In fact, the willful performance of masculinities by women can be read as a challenge to the historical androcentrism of Mexican culture. It was certainly seen that way by the author of *México marimacho*, who seems terrified of this challenge and its implications for the social order (Ruiz Alfaro). This type of gender nonconformity also seems to be central to the individual and collective identities of many queer women in Mexico. The texts that I analyze below, particularly those written by lesbian authors, reflect an approach to this and other social conflicts through camp and *cursi* humor.

These texts form part of a relatively small corpus of works produced in Mexico that portray female queer and/or lesbian sexualities. Chicana lesbian feminist writers such as Gloria Anzaldúa and Cherríe Moraga, whose work has been very influential in the United States, have little or no connection to most lesbian-themed literature and criticism that has been produced in Mexico in Spanish. More recent studies that continue to develop the Latina lesbian feminist/queer tradition, such as those of Danielson, Soto, and Rueda Esquibel, also focus almost exclusively on US-based, English-language Latina culture. In contrast, there has been a relatively small amount of scholarship focusing on this topic produced in Mexico in recent years. The most exhaustive study is that of María Elena Olivera, who analyzes all significant portrayals of lesbian characters in narrative but privileges those texts that, according to her criteria, offer the most possibilities for lesbian readers to find both expressions of sexual dissidence and possibilities for what I am calling reparative reading practices (29).

Olivera notes a shift from existentially pessimistic portrayals of lesbian characters, as in *Figura de paja* [Straw Figure] (1964) by Juan García Ponce, to more reparative portrayals beginning with Rosamaría Roffiel's 1989 novel *Amora* (85–90, 94–97). She identifies this work as Mexico's first lesbian feminist novel thanks to its clear ideological orientation towards the vindication of the rights of women in general and lesbians in particular (113, 125–27). This shift in the portrayal of lesbian characters recalls a similar shift in the portrayal of homosexual male characters that began with *Vampiro de la colonia Roma* (Schneider 87–88; Westmoreland 45). *Amora* differs from these novels, however, in that it contains a lower frequency of humor and a high frequency of overtly didactic content that portrays lesbian culture and relationships in an almost entirely positive light. Olivera notes that this didacticism has often been criticized on aesthetic grounds, and she endeavors to defend the value of the novel based on its ideological content and its importance to lesbian readers in Mexico as a foundational text for their culture (109-30).

Whatever its relative merits, *Amora* contains relatively few examples of humor. Mexican narrative on lesbian themes with higher frequencies of humor begins to appear in the late 1990s and 2000s with texts such as the short story collection *Con fugitivo paso* (1997) by Victoria Enríquez; *Réquiem por una muñeca rota* (2000) by Eve Gil; some of the stories included in *Con la boca abierta* (2006) by the Cuban exile writer Odette Alonso; *¿Y qué fue de Bonita Malacón?* by José Dimayuga; *Del destete al desempance* (2008) by Gilda Salinas; and the stories in *Contarte in lésbico* (2014) by Elena Madrigal. Generally speaking, these texts are more varied than *Amora* in their portrayal of lesbian sexualities and identities—they do not limit themselves to positive portrayals, but they include highly complex and contradictory representations that can be read both from more positive and more critical perspectives. It is no surprise, then, that they are willing to use the *machorra* stereotype as a primary material.

The Mexican lesbian writer Artemisa Téllez sees this shift as a generational difference between lesbian feminist writers like Roffiel and younger, "postfeminist" writers like herself whose aesthetic projects transcend the earlier ideology (180-84). Indeed, Téllez argues against the tendency, expressed in Olivera's study, to only legitimate those texts that contain positive portrayals of lesbian characters, arguing instead for an acceptance of more nuanced portrayals and greater artistic experimentation alongside the necessity to argue in favor of identity politics. I agree with Téllez in this respect. In fact, I believe that this acceptance of ideological complexity and varying possibilities of reading is necessary in order to consider texts such as the ones that I analyze below. This implies searching for a balance of paranoid and reparative approaches rather than simply rejecting every text that does not have an obviously positive signification about lesbian identity politics. This is especially true for texts that use the inherently ambiguous form of humor and that trade in stereotypes such as the *marimacho*. As we will see, it is the very recycling of these stereotypes that permits the disidentification with dominant social norms, and with lesbian feminism, that is posited in these texts.

Below I will consider three of these recent works in which the stereotyped figure of the *marimacho* or *machorra* appears as a source of humor described through camp and *cursi* discourse. In *¿Qué fue de Bonita Malacón?* women's camp forms part of the portrayal of an entire provincial town as a fountain of *cursilería* in which the desire for mediated modernity intersects with the queerness of everyday life. In *Del destete al desempance: Cuentos lésbicos y un colado* by Gilda Salinas, a first-person narrator regales us with her carnivalesque adventures as a hard-drinking, womanizing *machorra* who ultimately finds reparative possibilities in *cursi* culture and feminine values. Finally, in some of the stories from Elena Madrigal's collection *Contarte en lésbico*, ironic humor focusing on *azul/rosa* gender roles forms part of a generally reparative portrayal of various aspects of lesbian subjectivity. As has been the case in the texts with male protagonists, here camp and *cursi* humor intersect in the portrayal of characters whose sexual dissidence and gender nonconformity imply both the construction of dissident subjectivities and the embodiment of social conflicts.

¿Y qué fue de Bonita Malacón?

In José Dimayuga's novel *¿Y qué fue de Bonita Malacon?* (2007) various residents of a fictional town in the southern Mexican state of Guerrero relate their memories of Bonita Malacón, the town's most famous resident, to a silent interlocutor who is filming their responses as part of his university thesis.[5] Bonita, who rose to fame as an international beauty queen and film actress, married a drug trafficker and then presumably died in a police raid on one of his properties, functions less as a protagonist than as a unifying theme for the townspeople's recollections of their own personal and collective histories. This structure, which resembles that of Juan Rulfo's novel *Pedro Páramo*, makes it possible to read the town of Palma Gorda as the true protagonist of the novel and Bonita, like the central figure of Rulfo's novel, as a metaphor for social forces and cultural practices. If Pedro Páramo represents the destructive effects of *caudillismo*, Bonita can be said to incarnate the contradictory desire both for the maintenance of cultural tradition and for capitalistic modernity, as intersected by questions of race, sexuality and gender.

Not incidentally, there are several queer characters at the center of this story. Perhaps the most central is Pedro Isabel, also known as "Chabelis," a gay bar owner of humble origins who idolizes Bonita and dreams of building a museum dedicated to her. Another, more secondary, queer character is the Argentine movie star Fabio Tesso, a friend of Bonita who has long-term relationships with two men from Palma Gorda. Describing

Tesso's relationship with the *mayate* (trade man) El Mirlo, Chabelis reports, "A cualquier palmagordeño le quedaba claro esto y nos valía madre; porque aquí a todos, de una y otra forma, nos gusta la culiandanga" ["This [their relationship] was clear to every Palma Gordian and we didn't give a shit; because here everybody, in one way or another, likes to screw"] (114). This illustrates the idea, held at least by Chabelis, that in this tropical, rural region sexual orientation can be rather fluid. While this comment tends to reinforce the stereotype of the southern regions of Mexico as realms of exotic sexuality, it also speaks to the existence of actual sexual practices that do not necessarily line up with metropolitan notions of sexual orientation, such as the *mayate*, arguably the queerest form of masculinity in Mexican sexual culture (Domínguez-Ruvalcaba, *Translating* 162–63).

However, this sexual ambiguity is not limited to the men of Palma Gorda since it extends to some of the female characters as well. Bonita's ambivalent sexuality (she has sex and relationships with both women and men) is read by María Elena Olivera as lesbian, and she sees the portrayal of this character as lesbophobic, inasmuch as Bonita is sexually promiscuous, the victim of violence and appears to have no hope for a better life ("¿Hay homofobia" 167–68). Ernesto Reséndiz disagrees with this assessment, citing the multiple narrative voices that undermine the notion of a single, masculine narrator, the complex characterization of Bonita, and the possibly parodic reading of Bonita as a cult figure for the gay character Chabelis (164). While I agree in principle with Reséndiz that Bonita functions as a cult figure for Chablis and that this novel should not be labeled as lesbophobic, I would also like to suggest that the character who could most obviously be read as lesbian is not Bonita but rather Maya Andraca, a woman who engages in gender nonconformity marked by cross-dressing.

Maya, who owns the local Corona beer and PepsiCola distributorship along with her sister, is a character whose masculine demeanor and dress make her the object of local ridicule and suspicion about her sexual orientation. At the same time, however, her financial power and strong personality are generally admired. Formerly a close friend of Bonita's mother, Maya was banned from the Malacón home by Bonita's father because he was afraid that she would seduce his wife. Dressing in men's clothing, driving a delivery truck, and fist fighting anyone who insults her, she incarnates the stereotype of the butch lesbian, her body the center of a masculine/feminine script opposition that underlies humorous depictions of her by other characters:

Siempre andaba fodonga: la veías metida en un overol guango, color mugre y una camisa arremangada a cuadros [. . .] Tenía un semblante de veras cabrón. No miento si digo que los huevos más grandes del Estado eran de Maya Andraca. A todos en Palma Gorda no nos cabía la menor duda de que Maya era una machorra hecha y derecha. Incluso, tuvo una novia simpática en Agua del Perro.

[She always dressed like a slob: you would see her in baggy, dirt-colored overalls and a plaid shirt with the sleeves rolled up [. . .] She really looked like a bad-ass. I wouldn't be lying if I told you Maya Andraca had the biggest balls in the state. None of us in Palma Gorda had the smallest doubt that she wasn't a full-fledged bull dyke. She even had a pretty girlfriend in Agua del Perro.] (24–25)

This description, which comes from Chabelis, emphasizes the townspeople's clear association of her gender nonconformity with lesbian sexuality (it is worth remembering that the only "proof" in the novel that Maya had a relationship with another woman is gossip related by an unreliable narrator). It is likewise Chabelis who relates how Maya also fell in love with a man and began to adopt more feminine dress and behaviors:

La Maya irreconocible, tú. Dio un cambio de quinientos ochenta grados si no es que de más. Me acuerdo bien cuando se puso un vestido verde limón con escarola amarilla en los puños y en el pecho que le cosió doña Mary. Se veía muy bien la Maya, lo que sea de cada quién; se le veían setenta años menos. No es cierto. Pero sí amuchachada y femenina. Cupido le ordenó que echara a la basura su overol jediondo y las camisas cuadradas.

[Maya was unrecognizable. She changed five hundred and eighty degrees if not more. I remember perfectly when she put on a lime green dress with yellow ruffles on the cuffs and the decolletage that doña Mary sewed for her. Maya looked good, to each his own; she looked seventy years younger. I'm kidding. But she did look girly and feminine. Cupid ordered her to throw away her nasty overalls and plaid shirts.] (27)

This comic description is also based on another masculine/feminine script opposition, but with the concepts inverted: here it is her ostensibly ontological feminine masculinity that is incongruously combined with her performance of feminine gender. Chabelis's somewhat contradictory depiction of her (she goes from a "full-fledged bull dyke" to a feminine straight bride in just a few lines) makes Maya perhaps the queerest character in the entire novel at the same time that it highlights the connection of gender nonconformity with female homosexuality in the Mexican imaginary. This portrayal, while it does play with stereotypes, is not simply lesbophobic because, like many other residents of Palma Gorda, Maya has a backstory that fleshes out her behaviors and provides depth to her characterization.

This "humanizing" element of Maya's story is the melodramatic dénouement of her marriage, which intersects with *cursi* humor in a tragicomic fashion: Maya does marry the man, but he runs off immediately after the wedding with millions of pesos she had given him to build a nail factory. Later, the story appears on a national television program that dramatizes real-life stories sent in by women.[6] Chabelis, because of his fondness for writing fan letters to famous actors, is accused of sending in the story, but he denies it was him. The pathetic story of Maya's lived experience is thus converted into spectacular melodrama of the type that informs the townspeople's own sentimental education. This sort of humor based on *cursilería* and *naquez*, which is very prevalent in the novel, repeatedly emphasizes the incongruous combination of modern and unmodern elements in the worldview of the residents of Palma Gorda, highlighting their provincial distance from, and peripheral engagement with, discourses of modernity that they perceive largely through the mass media. Of course, there is a racial component to this feeling of marginality, which they frequently express through discriminatory disavowals of their Indigenous ancestry. Chabelis brings this into play when he complains about the townspeople's opposition to his plan for building a museum about Bonita: "Pero mis paisanos, ay, mis paisanos, se resisten a dejar las plumas y el taparrabos; quieren continuar y morir en la ignorancia, la incultura y en el atraso" ["But my townspeople, oh my townspeople, refuse to take off their feathers and loincloths; they want to keep on until they die in ignorance and backwardness"] (82). Chabelis's mother, on the other hand, is described by Maya as "una señora chaparra, chinita chinita y de ojos bizcos" ["a short lady, very *china* and with crossed eyes"] (96).[7] This *naquez* intersects with the queer sexuality of these characters, thus illustrating how social conflicts related to gender, sexuality, race, and modernity connect in contemporary rural Mexico. As in many of the other texts I have considered in this study, this novel demonstrates an ambivalent orientation towards *lo cursi* as a marker of cultural difference that can be interpreted simultaneously in positive and negative ways, an ambiguity that connects with the portrayal of sexual dissidence and gender nonconformity in stereotyped but also sympathetic portrayals.

Olivera's argument that the text contains a lesbophobic portrayal points towards possible paranoid readings that could highlight the text's reiteration of stereotypes about women in general and queer women in particular. The character Maya Andraca, for example, could be read as a heterosexual woman who is stereotyped as lesbian because of her gender nonconformity or as a lesbian woman who succumbed to the social pressure of compulsory heterosexuality. From a more reparative perspective, however, we might highlight the importance of gender nonconformity to the construction of Maya's identity, which disidentifies with any hetero- or homonormativity. We should also remember the implied author's generally sympathetic portrayal of all of the residents of Palma Gorda, whose provinciality is here portrayed as both endearingly *cursi* and creatively queer. This portrayal differs substantially from the texts that I will consider below, where women authors construct characters who move in urban settings in which explicitly lesbian subjectivities are front and center.

Del destete al desempance

In *Del destete al desempance: Cuentos lésbicos y un colado* ["From Weaning to the Digestif: Lesbian Stories and a Stowaway"] (2008) by Gilda Salinas, the visibility of lesbian subjectivity and lesbian collectives in Mexico City takes center stage. Though presented as a collection of stories, the short narratives that make it up might more accurately be described as vignettes or *crónicas* since they lack a traditional short story plot structure. Taken as a whole, however, the short texts form a longer chronological narrative focused mainly on the experiences of an unnamed first-person narrator, a lesbian woman who looks back on her life experiences from the 1970s to the 1990s. The arc of her personal development leads from a lifestyle of heavy alcohol consumption, sexual promiscuity, and compulsive infidelity to one of moderation and emotional stability in a long-term monogamous relationship. The narrator maintains a humorous and ironic perspective with regards to her younger self's behaviors and attitudes in the majority of the stories, employing a high frequency of humorous slang and ample references to popular music of the time periods represented.

Elena Madrigal notes that much of this language reproduces jargon belonging to the narrator's generation and to the lesbian collectives of Mexico City. In that sense the book can be considered a sort of chronicle of lesbian culture in Mexico ("Un carnaval" 97). Another historical aspect of the narrative is the mention of several bars and nightclubs (such as the Pago-Pago and the Don) that no longer exist but that served as important safe spaces for the emergence of lesbian collectives in Mexico City (Madrigal 96; Russo, "The Emergence"). Madrigal also emphasizes the rhetorical effect of the first-person narrative form, which connects the narrative to the life of the author ("Un carnaval" 95). This perspective makes the text not only a chronicle of lesbian culture but also a clear intent to portray lesbian subjectivity in a realistic or authentic fashion. The reparative uses of camp and *cursi* humor form an important part of this subjectivity. In this text, as in others like *La estatua de sal*, *Vampiro*, *Utopía gay*, and *Brenda Berenice*, the main character models the use of humor as a form of disidentification with mainstream Mexican gender norms that serves the reparative purpose of transcending negative affect and contributing to the construction of collectives.

As I mentioned above, Russo has observed the use of gender-based labeling practices in the lesbian collectives of Mexico that distinguishes the more masculine *azul* from the more feminine *rosa*, which can be described as analogous to the Anglo-American butch and femme labels/identities (Russo, "The Emergence" 83). These two identities form a dichotomy of stereotypically "masculine" and "feminine" behaviors, dress, and discourse that are often presupposed to correlate with "masculine" (active) and "feminine" (passive) sexual behaviors and desires for women labeled with the opposite gender (Walker, et al. 90–93). However, in actual social practice, butch and femme are the extreme poles of a spectrum of labels and identities related to gender, and the sexual activities and desires of women who identify with these labels vary greatly (ibid.). Russo's study indicates that this type of variation is also present in Mexican lesbian identities, along with varying levels of racial and class identity that intersect with sexual orientation ("El ambiente"). This variance between more masculine and feminine gender performance is reflected in the characterization in Salinas's book, while the racial and class identity of the protagonist remains largely implicit.

With regards to gender identity, the narrator of *Del destete* hews more towards the *azul* pole, though she also switches to a more *rosa* role when she so chooses. Central to the portrayal of the narrator's more masculine behaviors is what we might describe as a humorous "macho" script, based on stereotypes of traditional Mexican masculinity. Such stereotypes characterize macho men as "heterosexuales, misóginos, homofóbicos, mujeriegos, valientes y borrachos" ["heterosexual, misogynist, homophobic, womanizing, belligerent and drunken"] (Bustamante 202). In this case, the traits of being *mujeriega* and *borracha* are particularly important to the narrator's self-presentation, and her engagement in these behaviors often creates humor based on the opposition of the macho script and a feminine script since she is a woman (a biologically female body) performing masculinity. This use of gender-based humor functions less as a satire of others and more as a part of the narrator's self-deprecating and ironic portrayal of her younger self, about which she expresses a certain ambivalence. The social functions of humor that subordinate queer subjects to the mainstream and alleviate general societal anxiety about homosexuality are largely absent from this narrative. Instead, what predominates is a personal use of humor on the part of the narrator to constitute an imagined community and transcend the pain of discrimination and self-destructive behaviors.

In "El destete" ["Weaning"], the first story in the collection, the narrator relates how a girl she met at a bar scammed her out of several hundred pesos with the promise of a future liaison. Months later, she sees the same girl working as a stripper at a lesbian club where there is a "septuagenaria muy pero muy poco agraciada de todo, poniendo ojos de babeo por ti, mi reina, y esculcando en el sobre de la quincena para sacar de ahí y meter un billetito entre elástico de tanga y piel" ["not-very-attractive septuagenarian, fixing her lascivious eyes on you, princess, and digging in her salary envelope to take out and place a bill between thong elastic and skin"] (12). Although she initially considers this older woman pathetic, she quickly comes to think that she has no right to judge her since, after all, she engaged in basically the same behavior when she gave the girl money in the hopes of sleeping with her. Here both the narrator and the older woman play the traditional masculine role of treating a woman as a desirable sex object and attempting to achieve sexual satisfaction by exploiting their economic privilege. In this case the macho script is positioned in opposition to a feminine script that contains the notion of propriety (an older woman, for example, should be respectable and chaste, not openly expressive of sexual desire). Although she caricatures the older woman, the narrator eventually identifies with her, establishing a self-ironizing tone that will dominate throughout book. Notably, this story also includes the only open mention of race in the entire work. The narrator racializes the object of her desire by describing her as having the "piel tersa y morena de teibolera" ["smooth and brown skin of a stripper"] (10) and decides that she should not judge the older woman's desire to "sentir la firmeza de esa piel morena moviéndose solo para ella" ["feel the firmness of that brown skin moving only for her"] (12). These brief comments are part of a series of textual clues that point to the economically and racially privileged social position of the narrator (and, by extension, the author). As I mentioned above, the influence of this positionality marks a major difference with the work of Chicana writers such as Gloria Anzaldúa, whose lesbian identity is informed by the experience of class and race prejudice in the United States.

The self-deprecatory mode that the narrator evinces in the previous story is also evident in the depiction of her own womanizing behavior in the short text "Los años verdes" ["The Green Years"], where she identifies with a friend who, like her, is unfaithful to her romantic partner. Responding to the question of what she would do if this were her last day on earth, the friend answers that she doesn't have time to die since the next day she has to take a friend to Puebla, pick up her mistress (present at the enunciation of this plan), drop the two of them off, and then pick up her "wife" from work in time to go to the movies.[8] This character's discourse reproduces the script of the macho who enjoys the masculine privilege of infidelity, an action that serves to dualize the women involved into a chaste wife and a mistress who serves the purpose of sexual release. To this shameless exposition of her philandering, the narrator (who is at that moment also cheating on her partner) can only respond with the rhetorical question: Who was I to judge her?

This "doble vida" is further portrayed in "Entre copas . . . 34B" ["In (34B) Cups"] and "Alaska tropical" ["Tropical Alaska"] where the narrator relates a series of relationships with women that ended because of infidelity. The language used to describe this compulsive womanizing reaches a sort of apex in "El cofre del tesoro" ["The Treasure Chest"], where the narrator recalls being extremely drunk at a party and not wanting to decide between two lovers:

> Ay, qué maravilla que pudiera juntarlas para que las tres fuéramos felices [. . .] Por qué será que cuando estoy con éstra extraño a la ostra y cuando estoy con la ostra también. Y decía eso también porque la peda era tan honda que ya no sabía ni con cuál estaba.
>
> [Oh, how great it would be if I could bring them together so that the three of us could be happy [. . .] Why is it that when I'm with this one I miss the other one and when I'm with the other one it's the same. And I said this because I was so wasted that I didn't even know which one I was with anymore.] (91)

Here it is possible to see the combination of the *borracha* and *mujeriega* aspects of the macho script as enacted by the female narrator. (Alcohol plays a central role in all of the previously cited examples as well.) Her typically "macho" cynicism and lack of respect for her partners is highlighted by the humorous line at the end of the quote, which signals that these women are basically interchangeable for her.

While the examples cited above demonstrate the narrator's stereotypically *machista* behaviors that can be read as humorous oppositions of macho and feminine scripts, there are also some notable episodes where her gender performance includes dressing for the part. In "Cofre del Tesoro," she describes the costume she donned for a friend's party:

> A mí se me ocurrió vestirme de exhibicionista con una gabardina de mi amigo Miguel, camiseta color carne con pelos pintados y un miembro siempre erecto que hasta parece la mera verdad y cuyo nombre es Panchito. Por ahí andaba yo: pelo envaselinado y chichis vendadas, abriéndome la gabardina para enseñarles el pito y decir guarradas sabrosas.
>
> [I had the idea to dress as a flasher with my friend Miguel's trench coat, a flesh-colored t-shirt with chest hair painted on it and an always-erect member that looks like the real thing and whose name is Panchito. So there I was: hair slicked back and tits bandaged, opening the coat to show them my cock and say deliciously filthy things.] (88)

The flasher costume can be read as a metaphor for the assumption of male privilege inherent in some examples of gender parody, particularly since it reproduces a gendered relationship of sexual violence. At the same time, its carnivalesque appropriation of the phallus mocks that very same privilege, exemplifying how a camp text can be read from both paranoid and reparative positions. A similarly contradictory situation occurs when the narrator temporary assumes a femme or *rosa* role in "Roles bimbo."[9] "Mi síster dijo que a mayor oferta mejor demanda, que para eso era la internacionalidad, para cotizarse en la bolsa vigente, no como antes, cuando las ambientalistas se casaban con el rol de machín o el de abnegada mujer mexicana. El chiste era voltearse en el momento necesario" ["My sister said that more supply means more demand, that's what switching is for, to give yourself value in the current market, not like in the old days, when lesbians were married to the role of macho or self-sacrificing Mexican wife"] (81).

This observation would seem to indicate a greater acceptance of fluidity of gender roles in the narrator's generation versus older generations of lesbians in Mexico City. At the same time, her emphasis on the fact that this is not her usual gender expression (she is wearing her only skirt and is uncomfortable in her heels) sets up a masculine/feminine script opposition based on the incongruous performance of femininity by a woman who normally identifies as more masculine.[10] Notably, she claims to be doing this only in order to increase her sexual availability and to cheat on her partner, which places the entire episode within the frame of her macho infidelity. The previously cited examples of humor related to camp gender parody can be read as figurative portrayals of conflicts surrounding gender that arose in late 20th-century Mexico, particularly in lesbian collectives. They indicate that while gender nonconformity may be liberating inasmuch as it provides an escape from the constraints of social norms, it may also lead to the reiteration of certain oppressive or antisocial behaviors, such as heavy drinking and infidelity. A similar ambivalence can be seen in the book's use of humor related to *lo cursi*.

Cursilería appears in *Del destete* most often in the form of the romantic, melodramatic discourse of Latin American popular music and is closely connected to the personal experiences of the narrator and her constitution of a dissident lesbian identity that disidentifies with mainstream gender roles. These are clearly reparative uses of humor that illustrate the importance of *cursilería* to lesbian subjectivities in Mexico. The narrator frequently employs musical references and song lyrics as part of her generally humorous self-representation, evincing a cynical rejection of sentiment that recalls the attitude of the male protagonists in *La estatua de sal*, *Vampiro* and *Mátame y verás*. The humor related to *lo cursi* usually derives from a modern/unmodern script opposition, inasmuch as sentimental language can be considered *cursi* and unmodern while a cynical rejection of sentiment is considered modern (Monsiváis, "La cursilería"). As I have argued in previous chapters, Latin American *cursilería* is always implicitly racialized. In this book, however, the racial aspects of it remain largely implicit, which realistically reflects the way that relative whiteness is experienced as a normalized site of privilege in Mexican society (Moreno 387). A rather dismodern use of *cursi* discourse involves the camp recycling of mass culture texts by dissident collectives that incorporate melodrama into their self-representation. For example, the *travesti*, *loca*, and *vestida* characters from the texts in chapter 3 all make use of *cursilería* in the construction of their identities. In *Del destete*, the narrator betrays a certain ambivalence towards this raw material, suggesting that it might be both benighted and tacky but also personally relevant to her as a lesbian woman in Mexico. This is most clear at the end of the book, where she makes an explicit connection between *cursilería* and her identity. However, this attitude is also evident during the entire course of the narration.

In "El destete," the story I mentioned above, the narrator meets the young woman who will end up scamming her at a bar where the singer Chavela Vargas is performing. Vargas is best known for interpreting *rancheras* written from a masculine perspective, and lyrics from many of her signature songs punctuate the narrator's humorous portrayal of the somewhat carnivalesque ambience of the bar and her naiveté with regards to the intentions of the young woman. Notably, the refrain "Que no somos iguales, dice la gente" ["We're not equal, that's what people say"] from the song "Vámonos" ["Let's Go"] by José Alfredo Jiménez appears twice. The original song is the lament of a young man who is prevented from being with his beloved because of class prejudice. In both instances the narrator uses it humorously, first to foreshadow the conflict caused by the class difference between the her and the young woman, and later to ironically reinforce her identification with the older woman she sees at the strip club. The citation of this song in particular signals lesbian identity, since Vargas's version can be read as a lament about societal proscriptions of homosexuality and is something of a lesbian anthem in Mexico (Bustamante 207). It also establishes a modern/unmodern script opposition by reinterpreting serious melodramatic discourse as humorous and suggests a tension between sentimental expression and the cynically humorous rejection of sentiment in the narrator's self-presentation. This tension is also evident in other humorous uses of *cursilería* in *Del destete*.

In "Entre copas . . . 34 B" the narrator cites the Argentine folk song "Cuando pa' Chile me voy" ["When I Go to Chile"] in part of her relation of how she followed her lover to Chile in order to repair the relationship (43). Later, in Santiago, she joins members of the lesbian community in the local bars:

> bailamos y cantamos a la D'Alessio a grito pelado: Lo siento mi amor / pero hoy te lo voy a decir / aunque puede faltarme el valor al hablarte a la cara. / Lo siento mi amor / pero ya me cansé de fingir / y pretendo acabar de una vez para siempre esta farsa.
>
> [we danced and sang to D'Alessio at the top of our lungs: I'm sorry my love / but today I'm going to tell you / although I might not have the courage to tell you to your face. / I'm sorry my love / but I'm tired of pretending / and I want to end this farce once and for all.] (43)

In this case, the lyrics have more than a passing reference to the relationship that is about to end, but they are also used to illustrate an aspect of lesbian culture.[11] The fact that the women in the bar sing along *a grito pelado* suggests that the song has emotional importance for them as an identity marker. In the examples cited above, *cursi* sentimental texts are recycled within the narrator's humorous, cynical discourse, thus establishing a modern/unmodern script opposition. In the first example, she is merely indicating that she traveled to Chile with her lover. In the second example, we can see both a portrayal of queer cultures and a possible tension between the camp (and emotionally distant) recycling of *cursi* texts and the suggestion that such texts might actually have emotional import for those who repurpose them as part of their disidentification with heteronormativity. This reflects the narrator's own ambivalence towards *cursilería*, which can be clearly seen in the contrasting tones of the last two texts in the collection.

In "Achiote de golondrinas" ["Swallow Annato"] she relates, with ironic cynicism, how she attended a Christmas dinner with her chosen family, composed mostly of couples who she predicts will probably be broken up soon due to various infidelities: "si la vida entera es un desmadre esta cena de amor navideño mutuo y compartido es una farsa digna del Óscar [. . .] De todas formas me encanta la convención de hacernos pendejas, aquí puro amor eterno" ["if life is basically a fucking mess this dinner of mutual and shared Yuletide love is a farce worthy of an Oscar [. . .] At any rate I love the convention of fooling ourselves, nothing but eternal love here"] (97–98). The tone of this story is darkly ironic and cynical, and the humor of her comments can be read as a modern/un-modern script opposition inasmuch as she rejects the traditional end-of-the-year toasts of her friends as trite to the point of farce, since the values they espouse (fidelity, friendship) will certainly be violated. This attitude changes completely in "El desempance" ["The Digestif"], the last chapter of the book, in which she puts the earlier stages of her life into perspective with regards to her current situation.[12]

Recalling that the construction of her lesbian identity began with the realization, at a young age, that she was sexually attracted to the Chilean singer Monna Bell (whose music could be described as *cursi*), she then reviews her days of hard drinking and womanizing as a series of youthful indiscretions and ends by explaining how she took up moderation and settled down with a permanent partner: "Estacioné mi vida junto a la suya y me he dedicado a amarla y a regar nuestro amor con montones de abrazos y besos, atizando la flamita de la pasión para que siga encendida bajo la augusta cama" ["I parked my life next to hers and I've dedicated myself to loving her and to watering our love with loads of hugs and kisses, fanning the flame of passion so that it keeps lit under our august bed"] (102). This quote can be read as containing a modern/unmodern script opposition, inasmuch as it parodies *cursi* poetic language ("flamita de la pasión," "augusta cama") in order to describe her relationship, but the tone is notably different from the majority of the examples cited above. Rather than her habitual cynicism, what shines through is a seriousness about the positive evaluation of her current situation. This tone continues until the end of the book, where she presents an overall positive appraisal of her life:

> Hoy, en el desempance, veo mi vida desde el principio y me parece que sí, que fue cuesta arriba, pero rica y divertida y, aunque no tenga diez años, si Mona [sic] Bell me canta la La montaña en un disco compacto sé que reacciono con la misma sensibilidad de la infancia, que la caja de herramientas emocionales está intacta y que mi existencia, toda, ha valido la pena.

[Today, in the time of the digestif, I look at my life from the beginning and I think that yes, it was uphill, but delicious and fun, and even though I'm not ten years old anymore, If Mona [sic] Bell sings La montaña [The Mountain] to me on a CD I know that I react with the same sensitivity of my childhood, that my emotional toolkit is intact and that my existence, all of it, has been worth it.] (105)

With its retrospective view and overall positive tone, "El desempance" frames the rest of the book somewhat ambiguously. Though the narrator does seem to express a certain amount of regret for her earlier behaviors, she generally seems to see them as mere youthful indiscretions and never really expresses concern for the effects of her actions on others. This makes it doubtful whether the narrator intends for the relation of her previous behaviors to be read more as a satire of such behavior or as a carnivalesque celebration of the transgression of social norms. However, the portrayal of her younger self may also be understood as a use of humor in order to transcend the pain of social discrimination and earlier self-destructive behaviors, as well as an attempt to contribute to the construction of a collective with her narration. The behaviors that could be described as self-destructive and ethically questionable are associated with a "macho" script that might also include the cynical rejection of sentiment as *cursi* (unmodern).

However, as we saw above, *cursi* mass-media texts play a very important role in the constitution of the narrator's identity as a lesbian woman in Mexico, and she betrays a certain identification with the sentiment that they express. As the quotes from "El desempance" illustrate, she does not seem to either take *cursilería* seriously nor to completely reject it since it has been such an important part of her sentimental education and dissident identity. This attitude reiterates what Monsiváis identifies as the general Mexican attitude towards *lo cursi*: an ambivalent shame about its unmodernity but recognition of it as something particularly familiar and Mexican ("La cursilería"). Likewise, the narrator's somewhat difficult reconciliation with sentiment, along with her praising of her stable, long-term relationship, might be taken as an ultimate disidentification with machismo, the privileging of stereotypically feminine discourses (open expressions of love, tenderness, an emphasis on domestic life) over masculine ones (cynicism, braggadocio). Ultimately, it is this ambivalent attitude towards camp, *cursilería*, and the narrator's entire life story that permits an approach to these texts that combines paranoid and reparative reading practices. While the main character's performance of masculinities obviously involves the reiteration of certain self-destructive and damaging behaviors that recall the worst stereotypes of *machista* behavior, she also clearly illustrates the reparative possibilities of humor for lesbians in Mexico.

Contarte en lésbico

Another text in which female-to-male cross-dressing and *cursilería* intersect in humorous portrayals of lesbian sexuality and identity is the short story collection *Contarte en lésbico* ["Tell You in Lesbian"] by Elena Madrigal. In "Pensión de viudez" ["Widow's Pension"] the narrator, a lesbian who dresses and acts in a traditionally feminine manner, recounts how she was courted by another woman who embodies many stereotypes of northern Mexican masculinity (loud speech, sexual aggressiveness, heavy drinking):

> Entonces, me decidí a darle un chance a la Quintero, que llegaba trastabillando, tequila en mano, y aullando hasta que se le reventaran los pulmones [. . .] Salí al portón—¡uta!, como en las pelis de rancheros—. Muy sonreída, le recibí las canciones, y cuando se acercó con su ramote de flores, le susurré al oído que mandara la música a otra parte y que pasara un ratito.
>
> [So then I decided to give Quintero a chance and she showed up stumbling, tequila in hand, howling until her lungs burst [. . .] I went out to the front gate—shit!, like in a ranchero movie. All smiles, I listened to the songs and when she came up with her big-ass bouquet of flowers I whispered in her ear to send the mariachis somewhere else and come inside for a while.] (18)

To the narrator's dismay, however, this similarity with men extends to the butch woman's sexual selfishness as well:

> me llevó casi cargando a la cama, se bajó los pantalones, medio se bajó la trusa, se me echó encima; chirrinchinchín, pa'rriba y pa'bajo la cadera. Me enteré de que se había venido cuando los ojos se le pusieron en blanco y . . . sanseacabó. Ni besitos, ni encueradas, ni toqueteos. Nada [. . .] Por mi mente centel-

learon rencorosas las imágenes de torpeza de Fernando, de Agustín, de Horacio, de Arturo [. . .] Antes de irse, se atrevió a preguntarme: "¿Quedaste satisfecha?" No le contesté y me prometí nunca más volver a verla.

[she practically carried me to the bed, pulled down her pants, halfway pulled down her shorts, jumped on top of me; chirrinchinchin, up and down with the hips. I realized that she had come when her eyes rolled back and . . . that was it. No kisses, no strip tease, no touching. Nothing [. . .] The fumbling images of Fernando, Agustín, Horacio, Arturo all flashed angrily through my mind [. . .] Before she left, she had the nerve to ask me: "Are you satisfied?" I didn't answer and I promised myself never to see her again.] (21)

She does see "la Quintero" again, however, and is in fact currently involved in a relationship with her in order to benefit from her widow's pension. In the last line of the story, the narrator tells her interlocutor (with whom she is evidently drinking in a café) not to look at her "like that," indicating a nonverbal communication of disapproval of her cynical behavior.

The two main sources of humor in this story are the narrator's disillusioning discovery of her new lover's sexual selfishness, all too similar to that of men she has known, and her final revelation that she is playing the role of the "wife" of la Quintero out of economic self-interest, which frustrates the interlocutor's and reader's expectations that she will have abandoned la Quintero because her behavior is too similar to that of many men. In both of these events, the masculine/feminine script opposition is central to the humorous effect. In the first case, the script opposition is present in the body of la Quintero, emphasized in her dress, actions, and sexual performance, which is portrayed in a manner that frustrates the narrator's expectations that this woman will be a more attentive lover than a man. In the second case, the narrator's own reiteration of a stereotyped notion of femininity (that of the woman who trades sexual satisfaction for economic stability) appears as another performance of gender, its constructed and arbitrary nature highlighted by the script opposition operational in la Quintero's performance of masculinity. *Cursilería* plays a role in this masculinity, through la Quintero's use of romantic clichés (flowers, serenades), and ultimately presents us with a modern/unmodern script opposition through the frustrated expectations: the lesbian women, whose dissident sexuality one might assume would make them more enlightened in their own sexual and affective relationships, end up reiterating traditional gender roles in a way that leads to sexual frustration for the narrator, who decides to play a traditional role out of self-interest. In this way, the narrator of the story uses irony in order to disidentify with the moralizing discourses of lesbian feminism.

A similar comic situation is the main source of humor in the story "A dos, de tres caídas . . ." ["Two Out of Three Falls"] where another first-person narrator relates how she was courted by a *luchadora* (female professional wrestler in Mexico's *lucha libre*, a type of masked professional wrestling) and how, despite dressing the part of the femme, she comes to dominate the wrestler. This ironic inversion of roles is highlighted by the narrator's mocking description of the wrestler as more of a housecat than a *pantera* ("Panther," her name in the ring) and of the sexual domination that ensues when she lowers the Pantera's jeans and which ends with the Pantera cooking breakfast for her. In this story, the masculine/feminine script opposition underlies the inversion of roles: the Pantera, supposedly more masculine or *azul* because of her profession and dress (which includes jeans and large belt buckle), is dominated by the more feminine, *rosa* partner.

Cursilería has a less central role to play in this story, though the mention of *lucha libre* relates the aesthetics of the story to a cultural practice that is a prime example of *naco* culture, or the "bad taste" of the lower classes. While this type of culture is always racialized, this aspect of it remains implicit in the story. *Lucha libre* is also closely associated with working-class masculinity and in that sense highlights the gender parody involved in the characterization of the Pantera. In both of these stories by Madrigal, then, there are humorous reversals of expectations based on Mexican gender norms that inform lesbian identities and relationships, closely connected to the collection's general theme of a lesbian eroticism based on the experience of the female body. While both the *norteño* persona of la Quintero and the *luchadora* persona of la Pantera include elements that are implicitly racialized, these stories do not openly engage the question of race. Like Salinas's stories, those of Madrigal reflect a Mexican position of relative social and racial privilege in which access to relative whiteness seems largely taken for granted. Reading paranoically, we could signal the somewhat problematic reiteration of negative stereotypes about *azul* and *rosa* identities, as well as the way that the ironic, sardonic humor in these stories tends to distance the reader from the subjectivities of the characters portrayed. A more reparative approach, on the other hand, might highlight the stories' inclusion in a larger collection with the obvious intent to interpolate a lesbian readership with portrayals of dissident subjectivities anchored in the corporeal experience of erotic pleasure that disidentify with the strictures of mainstream society.

The works by the three authors mentioned above are all texts that use camp and *cursi* humor in the portrayal of characters that can be read as stereotypical *marimachos* or *machorras*—women performing feminine masculinities that are based on hegemonic Mexican masculinities. This stereotype has served to oppress lesbian women in Mexico but has also been appropriated as an expression of sexual dissidence and disidentification with hetero- and homonormativity. In *Bonita malacón*, the gender nonconformity of Maya Andraca is more queer than lesbian, but her feminine masculinity is obviously related to the stereotype of the *machorra* in Mexican culture. This forms part of the contradictory relationship with modernity of the town of Palma Gorda, which can be read as an allegory of the contradictions of dismodernity (including racism and the transgression of sex and gender norms) in provincial Mexico. Gilda Salinas's *Del destete al desempance* is a humorous portrayal of the construction of a dissident lesbian identity in the context of late 20th-century Mexico City. The narrator/protagonist presents herself as a stereotypical *machorra* whose ethically questionable behaviors are narrated humorously. Her identification with *cursi* discourse through popular music forms a basic part of her subjectivity, which is posited in the end as a sort of rapprochement with femininity. Finally, the short stories from Elena Madrigal's collection *Contarte en lésbico* present a highly ironic view of *azul/rosa* relationships in which the characters playfully engage with gender stereotypes that are camp but also *cursi* in their specifically Mexican forms. Like the texts we have seen in the previous chapters, all these works can be read as figurative challenges to the allegorical Mexican literary tradition as well as portrayals of subjectivities that give much-needed expression to reparative cultural practices involving humor. All in all, as Artemisa Téllez suggests, these are texts that require readers to balance paranoid and reparative reading practices in order to see their value for collectives of sexual dissidence. While they may not always portray lesbian sexualities in an unswervingly positive fashion, their use of ambiguous humor certainly highlights social conflicts about gender, sexuality, and modernity that are very relevant to queer women and collectives in Mexico.

Conclusions

In 2016 and 2017 two feature-length films that used humor in the portrayal of sexual dissidence were released in Mexico and garnered quite a bit of attention in the media. *Pink: El rosa no es como lo pintan* ["Pink Is Not What They Say It Is"] (Francisco del Toro) was a low-budget attempt to create propaganda against same-sex marriage and adoption, while the mainstream buddy comedy *Hazlo como hombre* [*Do It Like an Hombre*] (Nicolás López) promoted a modern bourgeois masculinity that includes the tolerance of homosexuality. The relative reception of these films and their particular uses of humor to portray sexual dissidence highlight many of the themes that I have raised during this study. In particular, they illustrate the importance of literary texts such as those that I analyzed above to cultural portrayals of queerness in Mexico. Literature can provide alternative, often more complex textual strategies for representing social conflicts than films such as these as well as contribute to a deeper understanding of the sociohistorical context in which all these texts are produced. While it is certainly important to engage with and analyze mass cultural products such as the films mentioned above, they should not be taken as the only, or the most important, representations of queerness in Mexico. Rather, they can be most productively read alongside more complex portrayals such as the literary works I have included in this study.

Pink reflects the ideology of director Francisco del Toro, whose self-produced films on "social themes" espouse an evangelical Christian message. The intended message behind the convoluted plot of *Pink*, which involves a gay couple who adopt a boy and fail to raise him properly, would seem to be that homosexuality is a (bad) lifestyle choice, that marriage is a holy sacrament that should only take place between a man and a woman, and that children raised by same-sex couples are doomed to social maladaptation. In other words, the ideology is almost the complete opposite of that presented in the film *La otra familia* (Gustavo Loza, 2011), where the upper-class gay male couple are presented as better parental figures than their adopted son's heterosexual biological parents. Another major difference between these two films is the use of humor, which is largely absent in *La otra familia* but present in *Pink* in the camp and *cursi* persona of one of the gay parents. This figure, an effeminate, frivolous, sexually promiscuous gay man obsessed with appearances, reiterates many of the stereotypes about homosexuality operative in Mexican society. Somewhat surprisingly, the actor who plays this role is Pablo Cheng, a television personality who is openly gay and who has made his career playing effeminate, camp characters.

Rather unsurprisingly, the film caused a great deal of controversy in Mexico, and it was particularly ill-received by collectives of sexual dissidence, who generally saw it as homophobic propaganda ("Debate derivado de PINK"). The film was briefly available for streaming on Netflix, but it was removed after protests from individuals and gay rights organizations in Mexico and the United States, and Pablo Cheng has responded by apologizing to the LGBTTTI community in Mexico and expressing regret for taking part in the film ("Pablo Cheng"). *Pink* was not a great commercial success. Its run lasted two weeks in some two hundred cinemas in Mexico, with a few more than 40,000 tickets sold ("Película Pink"). The media coverage of the controversy probably generated a bigger audience than the film itself, a fact that would seem to reflect the shifting mores in Mexican society regarding sex and gender in an era of increasing queer visibility and of expansion of civil rights such as marriage equality.

The relative success of Nicolás López's 2017 comedy *Hazlo como hombre*, which became the fifth-most-seen film in Mexican history ("Hazlo como hombre"), might also reflect changing values in Mexican society. In this buddy film, the main character is an upper-class, heterosexual, cisgender white man whose best friend comes out of the closet in his mid-30s. The arc of the story involves the straight man's growing acceptance of his friend's sexual orientation and the progressive abandonment of certain traditional values about sex and gender, especially homophobia. Rather than camp expressions of queerness, the majority of the humor is focused on the protagonist, whose views are satirized as contradictory and benighted and whose lack of self-awareness includes an ignorance of the queer aspects of his homosocial relationships that is often expressed through unintentional reiterations of *cursilería*. In one scene, for example, he sobs in the shower over the loss of his best friend. This recalls Artemio's scene of crying in the shower over a woman in *Púrpura*, which I signaled as a *cursi* behavior that is essentially ambiguous in terms of gender performance. To achieve a comic effect, the film often relies on the reiteration of homophobic insults ("*puto*" figures prominently) and jokes focusing on the fear of anal penetration. The overall message of acceptance, while certainly progressive, is also redolent of what Blanco feared gay rights would become in the late 1970s: a tolerance based on relative purchasing power and conformity to bourgeois social ideals ("Ojos"). In this way, the film transmits a message similar to that of *La otra familia*, *Así del precipicio*, and *Todo incluido*, where the acceptance of economically privileged homonormativity is portrayed as part and parcel of neoliberal modernity (Venkatesh, *New* 186–87; Castro Ricalde 209, 214–17).

Both *Pink* and *Hazlo como hombre* demonstrate the inherent ambiguity of camp and *cursi* humor, the importance of reading intentionally, and the need to compare various portrayals of sexual dissidence in order to have a more comprehensive view of the context of production and of different textual strategies, such as dialogue with the allegorical literary tradition and the portrayal of subjectivities. For example, the fact that *Pink* places the stereotype of the effeminate homosexual man at its center provides an opportunity to reflect on the relevance of camp and *cursi* humor to portrayals of sexual dissidence in Mexico, as well as to the possibility of reading such portrayals from paranoid and reparative perspectives. In fact, the Internet Movie Database entry for the film includes two comments (in English) that neatly illustrate paranoid and reparative approaches to reading this film. The first comment decries it as homophobic propaganda that serves no other purpose than the reiteration of hate in Mexico, echoing the objections of many activists in that country (mymachinedomination). This represents a paranoid reading position, in which the negative elements deserving of criticism in the film are highlighted.

The second comment, however, suggests reading the film as an unintentional comedy, one in which the use of stereotypes is so exaggerated that it actually undermines the director's stated purpose (sugarfreepeppermint). In particular, Cheng's intentionally camp and *cursi* performance makes the entire film an example of unintentional camp that can be laughed at rather than taken seriously. That is, this perspective argues for an ironic reading that looks to purposefully undermine the communicative intent of the film in order to reach a subversive conclusion. In other words, it wants to queer the film. This reading is more nuanced than the first one and suggests not only a paranoid critique of the contradictions of the film's homophobic content, but also a reparative enjoyment of the exaggerated, potentially subversive humor of its portrayal.

Of course, this perspective hinges on the intentional reading of the text from a subversive position. Without this intention, the film can be read at face value as a reiteration of stereotypes that uphold the notion of the inferiority of queer people, something that can be particularly dangerous in a country with high levels of homophobic and transphobic violence like Mexico. As I have argued throughout this study, this type of intentional reading is not only necessary when "queering" or "subverting" a text with an ostensibly heteronormative communicative intent. It is also necessary when reading *any* use of camp and *cursi* humor to portray sexual dissidence and gender nonconformity, even those that are sympathetic. Such portrayals inevitably make use of stereotypes and modes of portrayal that reflect the coloniality of power, gender, and sex in Mexican society. This is, however, unavoidable and is actually a necessary expression of the social contradictions inherent in a postcolonial society founded on white supremacy and heteropatriarchy. Humor, an expression of social contradictions that can be read as semantic script oppositions, is an inherently ambiguous form that can be read, intentionally, from a perspective that seeks to disidentify with the dominant social structure.

As I have suggested, such readings require textual comparisons and contextual knowledge. For this reason, a film like *Pink* can be read in a much more nuanced manner, and its homophobic ideology contested, if it is compared with a work like Calva's novel *Utopía gay*, which also focuses on the conceit of a same-sex male couple with a child. *Utopía gay* not only provides a perspective diametrically opposed to that of *Pink* by celebrating and normalizing, rather than condemning, same-sex unions, but also employs camp and *cursi* humor in a much more complex fashion. The subjective depth of the characters Adrián and Carlos goes far beyond the cartoonish stereotypes in *Pink*, and the novel's self-conscious and self-critical reflection on the effects of gender in same-sex relationships intelligently anticipates a major issue that continues to inform debates about marriage equality today. Other examples of greater representative complexity can be seen in works like *Brenda Berenice* and "La jota de Bergerac" that center the construction of *loca*, *vestida* and *jota* identities. The disidentification of these protagonists with hetero- and homonormativity counters hegemonic portrayals such as *Pink* that leave no room for believable portrayals of queer subjectivities. Finally, even highly metaphorical works such as

"La marrana negra de la literatura rosa" and *Púrpura* engage in a highly sophisticated manner with the allegorical literary tradition in ways that a film like *Pink* simply does not.

Similarly, *Hazlo como hombre* can be productively compared with a novel like Blanco's *Mátame y verás*, where the homophobic protagonist's development over the course of the text leads not to a happy ending of gay/straight reconciliation (i.e., tolerance of homonormative gayness) but rather to an indeterminate, ambiguous ending that reminds readers that there are no simple resolutions to any of the major social conflicts embodied by the characters. *Hazlo como hombre* would seem to posit that the tolerance of sexual diversity is a necessary aspect of cultural and political modernity. This might be a laudable notion, and the use of humor to defend and uphold it through satirizing machismo provides opportunities to approach the film from a reparative perspective. Nevertheless, its narrow, whitewashed definition of modernity has little to do with the actual life experiences of most of the population of Mexico. For this reason, it is worth returning to works like *Mátame y verás*, *Fruta verde*, *Púrpura*, *Vampiro de la colonia Roma*, and *La estatua de sal* where the characters disidentify with the very values that are espoused in *Hazlo como hombre*. All of these books demonstrate how the connections between race, class, gender, sexuality, and modernity in Mexico are much more complex than the plot of this film might suggest and allow us to examine the myriad ways that humor can illustrate these complexities.

Both of the films I have cited above, of course, focus on gay male protagonists. As I noted in chapter 5, queer women enjoy a much smaller level of media presence in Mexico. With regards to lesbian humor in film, it is worth mentioning the prize-winning 2017 independent biopic *Chavela* (Gund and Kyi), which had a much smaller (but more international) distribution than *Pink* or *Hazlo como hombre* and garnered very little media attention in Mexico. Though a documentary and certainly not a comedy, it does contain some examples of Chavela Vargas's often self-deprecating humor and provides an unquestionably sympathetic portrayal of her sexual dissidence. The historical marginalization of lesbians in Mexico clearly makes it imperative to examine portrayals such as *Chavela* as well as literary works like Gilda Salinas's *Del destete . . .* , Dimayuga's *Bonita Malacón*, and Elena Madrigal's *Contarte en lésbico*. These texts illustrate how camp and *cursi* humor is also relevant to the portrayal and discussion of the social conflicts surrounding gender, sexuality, modernity, class, and race experienced by women in Mexico.

As the references to film and television that I have sprinkled throughout the book indicate, the portrayal of queerness in Mexico goes far beyond literature. Fortunately, the traditional conservatism of Mexican mass media has been steadily eroding over the past few decades, opening new spaces for the articulation of queerness, particularly in cinema. The release of David Pablos's dramatic film *El baile de los 41* [*Dance of the 41*] in November 2020 marks a significant point in this history of changing mores. This film's use of lush period sets and beautiful actors centers a tragic story of love, scandal, and betrayal with a clearly sympathetic portrayal of the queer characters.[1] The high national and international profile of this film evidences as much as anything the changes taking place in Mexican society around norms of gender and sexuality.

Nevertheless, I hope I have illustrated that the study of literature can, and should, supplement the study of other forms of cultural production when looking at these themes. Since colonial times, literature has provided opportunities for experimental and often daring explorations of controversial topics and taboo subjects in ways that are often not possible in more mass forms of communication. Furthermore, literature is still arguably the most privileged form of cultural expression in Mexico, as well as one of the main areas of intellectual debate about the meanings of national culture. Even in comparison with other forms of cultural production, literature can provide nuance, context, and alternative modes of portrayal that can enrich discussions of how culture deals with social conflicts. This is certainly the case when we look at the use of camp and *cursilería* to portray queerness in Mexico. While humor has long been used in this context to promote a colonial ideology that includes gender, sex, race, and class discrimination, its inherent ambiguity also permits decolonial uses and readings of it, as the books and stories I have cited above amply demonstrate.

Notes

Introduction

1. This is not to say that homosexuality did not exist in Mexico before this event. It is highly probable that some notions of male homosexuality that were different from the colonial category of "sodomy" already existed in the nineteenth century in Mexico (Sifuentes-Jáureguri, *Transvestism* 26, 38-39). However, this event is a useful marker for indicating a cultural inflection point where modern medico-scientific discourses about sexuality began to have more influence over popular ideas about sex.

2. Translations are enclosed in brackets. Titles of books and films that have been previously translated into English by others appear in italics. Otherwise, they appear in quotation marks. All translations of quotes are mine unless otherwise noted.

3. The stereotype of the effeminate homosexual man appears in Mexican cinema as early as 1939 in Fernando de Fuentes' *La casa del ogro* ["The Ogre's House"] and was central to the success of the actor Mauricio Garcés in such films as *Modisto de señoras* ["The Ladies' Dressmaker"] (René Cardona, Jr., 1969) (Schuessler 133-34). In the 1970s and 1980s, the effeminate homosexual man was a constant figure in popular *fichera* (prostitute/stripper) films, where it was meant to shore up traditional masculinity (de la Mora 107-18; Venkatesh, *New* 28-38).

As Julee Tate has observed, even the homosexual characters that have recently begun to appear in Mexican *telenovelas* have also generally been reproductions of the effeminate stereotype, despite the appearance of a few more nuanced and less caricatured portrayals of gay men. One of these exceptions was TV Azteca's 1999 show *La vida en el espejo* ["Life in the Mirror"] which, according to Paul Julian Smith, featured "the first complex and sympathetic gay character in the history of Mexican television" (118). The same production company (Argos) later produced *El sexo débil* ["The Weaker Sex"] (2011), another *telenovela* with complex and nonstereotyped portrayals of gay male characters, for the upstart Canal 3 (Smith

106–27). Notwithstanding these exceptions, Smith notes the persistence of comic stereotypes of homosexual men in shows like Televisa's *Vecinos* ["Neighbors"], a remake of a Spanish sitcom that did not stereotype its gay characters, and *La hora pico* ["Rush Hour"], a long-running sketch comedy show (107–08). Héctor Domínguez-Ruvalcaba's survey of the portrayal of homosexuality in the programming of Televisa from the 1960s to the present bears out these initial observations of Smith, showing a persistence of comic stereotypes related to homosexuality, including the effeminate man ("Los mecanismos").

The figure of the effeminate homosexual man has also appeared in Mexican literature, from the characters in Eduardo Castrejón's 1906 naturalist novel *Los 41* to the members of the queer Mexico City intelligentsia portrayed in Salvador Novo's *La estatua de sal* to the frivolous character Gus in Fuentes's *La región más transparente* [*Where the Air is Clear*] (1958) (Irwin, *Mexican*).

4. While conservative opposition to such policies might be expected, there is also a great deal of controversy regarding marriage equality within collectives of sexual dissidence and gender identity. In Latin America, such collectives frequently form political coalitions with other groups who fight for social justice within a broad context of social inequality in neoliberal regimes. Often influenced by queer theory and political action, they frequently question the essentializing notions, clientilistic practices, and state control of bodies behind such policies of accommodation (Fiol-Matta 223–26; Figari 235–36). The arguments of Susana Vargas against the support for marriage equality in Mexico highlight many of these issues. She notes that the legal recognition of marriage necessarily privileges those who marry over those who do not, thus reinforcing heteronormative values like monogamy as well as economic inequality, since official marriage is a less common practice among working-class people in Mexico (Vargas, "¿Defendamos al matrimonio?"). I discuss this topic in greater detail in chapter 2.

5. Many of these texts are studied by Paul Julian Smith in his excellent survey of contemporary queer Mexican media, which also includes a look at more marginal types of production, such as web series and pornography.

6. One example of this is Ediciones Quimera, which has published both the work of well-known authors like Luis Zapata and José Joaquín Blanco, as well as younger writers such as Odette Alonso and Juan Carlos Bautista. Another is the LGBT bookstore and performance space Voces en Tinta, located in the Zona Rosa of Mexico City.

7. I use the term "sexual dissidence" instead of "sexual diversity" in order to highlight the disruptive aspects of sexuality. I also generally use the term "collective" instead of "community" in order to refer to groups of people organized around sexual dissidence and/or gender nonconformity. The term "collective" designates a more ephemeral grouping that has less of a clear and stable notion of identity behind it, and is thus less closely allied with the traditional identity politics, such as gay and lesbian (Fiol-Matta 221).

8. Despite recent intents to better track violence against women in Mexico, it is still difficult to obtain very accurate data on this problem. For a treatment of the challenges that face this type of data collection, see Casique Rodríguez.

9. See Balderston, Bejel, Domínguez-Ruvalcaba *Modernity* and *Translating*; Figari, Fiol-Matta, Foster *Sexual* and *Ensayos*; Irwin; Irwin et al.; Lewis, Marquet, Olivera, Quiroga, Schaefer, Schneider, Sifuentes-Jáuregui *Transvestism* and *Avowal*; Venkatesh *The Body*.

10. Venkatesh coins the terms "maricón cinema" and "new maricón cinema" to differentiate Latin American cinema that tends to privilege a scopophilic portrayal of homosexualities from international queer cinema that tends to disrupt sex and gender binaries in a more profound manner. This is another example of how Latin American culture demands the translation of theoretical constructs with origins in the Global North.

Chapter 1

1. See Babuscio, Core, Dyer, Newton.

2. See Babuscio, Britton, Butler, Dollimore, Dyer, Flinn, Robertson, Tyler.

3. This is Sedgwick's term for what Paul Ricoeur calls the "hermeneutics of suspicion," the discursive mode dominated by the need to uncover hidden truths and contradictions. Sedgwick connects this reading practice to the psychoanalyst Melanie Klein's theorization of alternating "paranoid" and "reparative" positions that the subject-in-formation enters into while it is establishing object relations with the mother. Klein's theory shifts the emphasis in psychoanalytic object relations from the Oedipal stage to a much earlier stage when the infant begins to identify with the primary caregiver (usually the mother in Western cultures). This revision provides, among other things, an opportunity to question the androcentrism of Freud's theory.

4. See Cleto, Meyer, *Politics*.

5. The term is of uncertain etymology and there are several myths about its creation. For a thorough discussion of this problem see Valis.

6. The *coloniality of gender* refers to the inclusion, within Quijano's paradigm of the coloniality of power, of the importance of gender as a social construct that is used in social domination. This includes, for example, the definition and privileging of a white, bourgeois femininity that is always superior to other possible femininities as well as a suppression and/or erasure of existing social structures with diverse conceptions of gender, such as Native American "third" genders or the complex gender system of the Yoruba people of West Africa (Lugones 98–99).

The *coloniality of sex* "refers to the punishment of difference as a way of correcting gender expressions and sexual practices" (Domínguez Ruvalcaba, *Translating* 21)

7. Examples include 19th-century liberalism, which advocated private capitalism (as in Porfirian Mexico), 20th-century corporatism, which advocated state management of capital and labor (as in Post-Revolutionary Mexico), 20th-century socialism (as in Cuba), and more recent neoliberalism (as in contemporary Mexico), neosocialism (as in contemporary Venezuela), and neocorporatism (as in contemporary Ecuador) (Schroeder-Rodríguez 11–12).

8. This state of affairs is particularly evident in the implementation of liberal notions of progress, such as under the dictatorship of Porfirio Díaz in Mexico (1875–1910). For example, while Díaz did modernize the national infrastructure to a great extent, this was almost exclusively oriented towards extractive industries and the construction of European-like urban spaces. Meanwhile, rural spaces languished and the economically poor majority of the nation (mostly Indigenous and mestizo agricultural workers) were relegated to a culturally marginalized, politically disenfranchised, and economically exploited condition similar to that of the colonial period. Arguably, despite the constitutional guarantees brought about by the Revolution and its aftermath (including universal suffrage and land reform), Mexico has continued to suffer from the implementation of projects of modernization that align its national interests more with those of international capital and local elites than with the majority of the population.

9. On the debate about postmodernism in Latin America see Beverley; Aronna, et al.; Casullo.

10. Examples include the theorizations of the Brazilian avant-garde in the 1920s, specifically as expressed in the "Manifesto Antropófago" ("Cannibalist Manifesto") by the poet Oswaldo de Andrade. This text famously describes the motor of Brazilian culture as the "cannibalistic" digestion of the cultural production of other regions (mostly Europe) in order to create original cultural works (see Bary for gloss and English translation). A more contemporary theory in this same line is that of neobaroque aesthetics, most famously developed by the Cuban writer José Lezama Lima. This theory sees recent Latin American uses of rhetorical strategies associated with the colonial baroque as alternatives to the dominant discourses of modernity (Schroeder-Rodríguez 305–6).

11. Cornejo Polar argues that social conflicts that took place in the colonial period, such as that between Indigenous and European culture and orality and written discourse, persist up to our times in the form of social contradictions that cannot be resolved dialectically, though several influential discourses of regional identity (*mestizaje*, transculturation, hybridity) have attempted to do so (*Writing in the Air*, "Mestizaje e hibridez," "Mestizaje, transculturación, heterogeneidad").

12. In this symbolic economy, the *naco* is frequently opposed to the *güero* (light-skinned person) or the *fresa*, the contemporary version of the fin-de-siècle *catrín*, now more given to imitating modes of consumption of the United States

rather than the fashions of Paris and London that were the model for the Porfirian elites. The juxtaposition of these two stereotypes can be seen in some of the characters portrayed by the comedian Luis de Alba in his television show *El mundo de Luis de Alba* ["Luis de Alba's World"], which ran from 1978 to 1981 on Televisa (he still occasionally brings these characters out of retirement on Mexican TV). "El Chido," so called because his favorite adjective is *chido* ["cool"], is a stereotypical *naco* who speaks in streetwise slang that often leads to misunderstandings with other characters and wears cheap imitation versions of contemporary fashions from the United States. "El Pirrurris," on the other hand, is the *fresa* son of a millionaire who attends a private university, peppers his speech with Anglicisms, and constantly reaffirms the social difference between himself and the *nacos*, who, according to him, make up the majority of the Mexican population. Monsiváis considers this humor self-hating (*Escenas* 335–41).

The opposition of *nacos* and *fresas* can also be seen in contemporary internet humor that also trades with the stereotypes, such as the series of YouTube cartoons titled "Naco y Fresa" by Víctor Hernández or the faux documentary YouTube cartoon series "El Verguillas" by the group FASComedy. Domínguez-Ruvalcaba has analyzed this particular cartoon as a portrayal of the consumption of disposable bodies that characterizes gendered violence in contemporary Mexico ("Atisbos" 103–8).

13. Their song "Guaca Rock de la Malinche," from this same album, is a decolonial hymn to Mexican coolness that argues "Si lo mexicano es naco y lo mexicano es chido, entonces, verdad de Dios, todo lo naco es chido" [If everything Mexican is *naco* and everything Mexican is cool, then, God's own truth, everything *naco* is cool].

14. The more complete General Theory of Verbal Humor (GTVH) was developed by Raskin and Attardo from the SSTH, adding to the original focus on the script opposition several other "knowledge resources" that contribute to humor, including logical mechanisms, situation, target, narrative strategy and language (223–26). The heavy formalism of the GTVH, as well as its original orientation towards the analysis of short texts (jokes), makes its productive application to narrative humor very limited (Attardo, *Humorous Texts*; Triezenberg). For this reason, my own analysis returns to the simpler focus of Raskin's SSTH in order to identify what I argue are the particular semantic script oppositions underlying humor in the texts that I analyze: masculine/feminine (camp) and modern/unmodern (*lo cursi*).

15. These attitudes are reproduced in a recent video report by Nájar on the *albur* for BBC Mundo.

16. This supposed indifference towards death is another well-known myth dissected by Bartra, who considers it symptomatic of a colonialist search for authenticity in Indigenous cultures. See *Jaula*, ch. 8.

17. This went as far as an appeal in 1934 by various writers to the Congressional Public Health Committee to purge the cultural bureaucracy of homosexuals, whom they considered counterrevolutionary by nature (Monsiváis, *Salvador Novo* 76).

18. All translations from *La estatua de sal* are mine. There is a recent English-language translation of the book by Marguerite Feitlowitz published by the University of Texas Press. This translation is of such poor quality that it is not worth citing.

19. The following verses describe Villarrutia:

Esta pequeña actriz, tan diminuta / que es de los liliputos favorita, y que a todos el culo facilita. / ¿es exageración llamarle puta?

[This little actress, so small / who is the favorite of the Lilliputians [untranslatable pun involving the word "puto"], and who makes her ass available to everyone. / Is it an exaggeration to call her a whore?] (Monsiváis "El mundo soslayado" 62)

Novo's sonnet about himself is the following:

Escribir porque sí, por ver si acaso / se hace un soneto más que nada valga; / para matar el tiempo, y porque salga / una obligada consonante al paso.

Porque yo fui escritor, y éste es el caso / que era tan flaco como perra galga; / crecióme la papada como nalga, / vasto de carne y de talento escaso.

¡Qué le vamos a hacer! Ganar dinero / y que la gente nunca se entrometa / en ver si se lo cedes a tu cuero.

Un escritor genial, un gran poeta . . . / Desde los tiempos del señor Madero, / es tanto como hacerse la puñeta.

[Write just because, to see if perhaps / one can make a sonnet worth more than nothing; / to kill time, and to make appear / an obligatory consonant rhyme.

Because I was a writer, and this is the case / that I was as thin as a greyhound bitch; / my double-chin grew like an ass cheek, / vast of flesh and with little talent.

What can we do! Make money / and let no one interfere / in how you give it to your trade.

A brilliant writer, a great poet . . . / Since the times of Mr. Madero, / is the same as jerking off.]

(*La estatua de sal* 193)

20. Novo did publish many of these poems in the 1970 collection *Sátira: El libro ca* . . . ["Satire: The Bastard Book" (the *ca* . . . is short for *cabrón*)].

Chapter 2

1. These are all examples that portray male homosexuality. There is a general consensus that positive, protagonistic portrayals of lesbian characters do not appear until even later, with Rosamaría Roffiel's *Amora* (1989) and Sara Levi Calderón's *Dos mujeres* (1990) (I explore this theme in more detail in chapter 5).

2. Blanco's claim that the text treats homosexuality in a dignified manner might seem contradictory, given the text's irreverent and scabrous tone, but Blanco seems to be referring to the manner in which Zapata portrays the subjectivity of his protagonist in a highly sympathetic manner.

3. Although Calva's book was published in 1985, we can deduce that the text was largely composed during the late 1970s since a review of the book clearly based on a galley copy was published in 1980. At that time it was slated to be published by Editorial V Siglos in their collection "Terra Nostra," which obviously did not happen (Trejo Fuentes 45–46). In the same review, the title is given as *Utopía gay (en tiempo compuesto)* ["Gay Utopia (in compound time)"]. This title turns out to be important for understanding an inconsistency in the novel: in the prologue Calva claims that the title is formed by three elements, the first being the utopic element, the second the gay element, and the third being one which "alude a un término musical que da idea del ritmo y carácter de la prosa a lo largo del texto" ["alludes to a musical term that gives an idea of the rhythm and character of the prose during the entire text"] (159). This was evidently the "tiempo compuesto" ["compound time" (which in Spanish also means compound tense in the grammatical sense)] that was eliminated from the final title.

4. See Schaefer; Covarrubias; Pérez; López; Ruiz, "Prostitución"; Domínguez Ruvalcaba, *Modernity*; Palma; Medina; Gutiérrez; Schulenburg; Eduardo Ruiz; Aluma-Cazorla; Wind; Sifuentes-Jáuregui, *Avowal*.

5. The title of this essay is a translation of a verse from the poem "The Hollow Men" by T. S. Eliot.

6. Now highly trendy and gentrified, these neighborhoods, which began as upper-class suburbs in the early decades of the 20th century, were relatively decadent and impoverished by the late 1970s when the novel was published.

7. The picaresque is a narrative genre that first appeared in Spain in the 16th century and generally presents itself as the autobiographical discourse of a socially marginal protagonist (the *pícaro*) whose experiences and observations satirize contemporary society. The texts cited in *Vampiro* appear in this order: *Segunda parte de Lazarillo de Tormes* ["Second Part of Lazarillo de Tormes"] by H. de Luna; *El Periquillo Sarniento* [*The Mangy Parrot*] by José Joaquín Fernández de Lizardi; *Lazarillo de Tormes* by an anonymous author; *La pícara Justina* [*The Life of Justina, the Country Jilt*] by Francisco López de Úbeda; *Santa* by Federico Gamboa; *Guzmán de Alfarache* by Mateo Alemán; *La vida inútil de Pito Pérez* ["The Useless Life of Pito Pérez"] by José Rubén Romero; *Vida del Buscón don Pablos* [*The Swindler*] by Francisco de Quevedo.

Lazarillo de Tormes (considered the first picaresque novel), *Segunda parte de Lazarillo de Tormes*, *La pícara Justina*, *Guzmán de Alfarache*, and *Vida del Buscón don Pablos* are all examples of the classic picaresque novel of the 16th and 17th centuries. *El Periquillo Sarniento*, considered the first Latin American novel, was published in the early 19th century and is a satire of the society of late New Spain. *Santa*, published in 1908, is Mexico's most famous naturalist novel and is not generally considered part of the picaresque tradition, although its focus on the life of a character on the margins of society is similar to that of the picaresque. *La vida inútil de Pito Pérez*, published in 1938, satirizes the society of rural post-revolutionary Mexico in a manner similar to that of the classic picaresque novels of the 16th–17th centuries. For a discussion of the picaresque genre and form, see Casas de Faunce; Davidson; González-Echevarría; Guillén, "Toward a Definition," "Genre and Countergenre"; Rico; Scholes; and Wicks.

8. In my direct quotations, the spaces between words greater than one keystroke (which vary in length in the original text) are represented by a single slash (/), while the breaks between lines (which often divide words) are represented by a double slash (//).

9. Gender-based categories of sexual identity are those that assume that sexual orientation is related to the performance of gender; that is, that homosexual men are more effeminate, and heterosexual men are more masculine. Object-choice–based categories are those that assume that it is the choice of the object of desire, rather than gender performance, that determines sexual orientation; i.e., a homosexual man may be effeminate or masculine because what determines his sexual orientation is the sex of the object to which he is attracted. The first category is generally considered more "traditional" and "Mexican," while the second is considered more "modern" (Carrillo, *Night* 60–61). A conflict between what is perceived as more modern and more traditional is clearly evident in Adonis's opinions about sexuality.

10. The English-language quotes cited here are from Lacey's translation of the novel.

11. The idiomatic expression "estar de atar," though similar to the English idiom "fit to be tied" (meaning that someone is angry enough to need to be restrained), means rather that a person is so mentally ill ("crazy" or "loony") s/he should be tied up, or, as Lacey translates it, imprisoned in a "nuthouse."

12. While novels in the picaresque tradition generally do not portray homosexuality openly, it should be noted that recent readings of texts such as the *Lazarillo de Tormes* and the *Periquillo* have argued that certain ambiguous sections of these insinuate that male-male sex is taking place. See Irwin, *Mexican* and Sifuentes-Jáuregui, "Swishing."

13. The character is not described as transgender, transsexual, nor intersex. Rather, the pregnancy is presented as a fluke that cannot be fully explained by modern science, which suggests a parody of the virgin birth of Jesus Christ.

14. The term *travesti* generally refers to men who identify as homosexual and with the female gender, but not as women. I explore the portrayal of such identities in greater detail in chapter 3.

15. The sexual and affective relationship between Oscar Wilde and the younger poet Lord Alfred Douglas (also known by his nickname "Bosie") is often considered a paradigmatically tragic and/or destructive same-sex relationship. The two fought constantly, and Wilde was convinced by Bosie to bring a suit for libel against his father, the marquess of Queensbury, which eventually resulted in the destruction of Wilde's public image and his imprisonment for sodomy and gross indecency. The prologue explicitly contrasts the novel's positive portrayal with the stereotype that all same-sex relationships must be as unfortunate as Wilde and Douglas's.

16. Barker's examples are drawn from the United Kingdom, the United States, Canada, Australia, Israel, South Africa, and several European countries.

17. The Immaculate Conception does not refer to the conception of Jesus in Mary's womb, as is often assumed, but rather to the idea that Mary herself was divinely preserved as immaculate (without sin) from the time of her conception in the womb of her mother, Anne. The fact that Adrian's mother is named Ana is likely an ironic reference to this. The Virgin Birth refers to the miraculous birth of Jesus.

18. See Cleto.

19. There is a pun in this quote that I struggle to render in English. When Carlos says "nomás enredas," he uses the verb *enredar*, which means both to tangle up (like a cord) and, metaphorically, to confuse things. When Adrián says "me dicen la culebrosa," he is making a play on words by relating *enredar* to the slithering action of a snake, using the nonstandard or invented form "culebrosa," which means "snake-like" and also implies, through the use of the feminine article and inflection, a performance of femininity.

Chapter 3

1. The term *travesti* is common throughout Latin America. The precise meaning of this term varies according to the social context. Some major studies of *travesti* and related identities in Mexico and elsewhere that illustrate the diversity among these identities include Carrier, Kulick, Prieur, Núñez Noriega, and González Pérez.

2. The continued presence of the *muxe'* in Zapotec communities is read by Domínguez-Ruvalcaba as a decolonizing gesture, a resistance to the imposition of heteronormativity through the coloniality of sex (*Translating* 32–37).

Although the actor who plays the main character in *Carmín Tropical* is not *muxe'*, the director, who is Zapotec himself, used nonprofessional actors and took great pains to make the cultural portrayals as accurate as possible (Smith 101-04).

3. Serna explores this same idea in the chronicle "Machismo torcido."

4. According to Lewis, texts that do not move beyond a figurative portrayal of such characters include the novels of Reinaldo Arenas, Zapata's *La hermana secreta de Angélica María,* and Santos Febres's novel *Sirena Selena vestida de pena [Sirena Selena].* Those that do include Bellatin's *Salón de belleza [The Beauty Salon],* Aïnouz's film *Madame Satã*, Pedro Juan Gutiérrez's book *El rey de la Habana [The King of Havana],* and various works by Pedro Lemebel.

5. In the original edition of the novel, capital letters appear without diacritic marks. I have preserved the original spellings in my quotations, but added the necessary diacritic marks in my own text.

6. Angélica María Hartman Ortiz (b. 1944) is a Mexican actress and pop singer best known for a series of roles she played in films of the 1960s and 1970s. She was generally typecast as an attractive, white, and somewhat frivolous (though always virginal) upper-middle-class high school- or college-aged girl.

7. See *New Maricón* chapters 5 and 6.

8. David Reynoso is a famous actor known for his masculine persona; La Chilindrina is a female character from the Mexican children's television program *El chavo del ocho* ["The Kid from Apartment Eight"], who talks in a high-pitched, nasal voice.

9. His comment is "tus nalgas bien valen una misa" ["your ass is well worth a mass"], which Brenda jokingly interprets as comparing her bottom to the city of Paris. This is a reference to the phrase supposedly uttered by Henri IV of France after his conversion to Catholicism in order to assume the throne: *Paris bien vaut une messe* ["Paris is well worth a mass"]. This is probably the most obscure cultural reference in the entire book and is obviously meant to emphasize Brenda's erudition.

10. This is unusual for someone who identifies as a *vestida* or *travesti* since these identities seem to be more associated with working-class than with middle-class culture (see Prieur; Vargas, "Travestis").

11. *Brenda Berenice* actually establishes intertextual relationships with both of these texts. Brenda mentions the character of Adonis García at one point, and this novel was obviously influenced by the use of humor in the first-person narrative of Zapata's novel. In addition to the pessimistic ending, it also shares the diary format with *El diario de José Toledo*.

12. Velázquez is a native of this industrial city in the northern border state of Coahuila, and most of his texts, including this one, include geographic and cultural references to this region. His work thus marks a difference from the traditional centralism of Mexican culture, as illustrated by the prominence of Mexico City as either point of enunciation or symbolic space of modernity in every other text included in this study.

13. In this film, a classic of the *cabaretera* genre, the Argentine-Mexican actress Marga López plays a young woman who works as a taxi dancer and prostitute in a cabaret in order to pay for her younger sister's boarding school tuition. Two men vie for her romantic attentions: her exploitative dancing partner and a policeman who wants to rescue her from her dissolute lifestyle. When the former refuses to share the prize money that they have won in a dance contest, she steals it from him. The ensuing conflict ends in a final confrontation in which each kills the other.

14. Lupita D'Alessio is a pop singer in the romantic *cursi* vein who is also an icon for certain queer subcultures in Mexico. See chapter 5 for an example of the appropriation of her music by lesbian cultures in Latin America.

15. Bartra argues that traditional gender roles are reinforced by the persistence in the Mexican imaginary of the myth of "Chingadalupe"—the Mexican version of the traditional Western virgin/whore dichotomy that opposes la Malinche (the Indigenous woman who was Hernán Cortés's interpreter and lover) to the Virgin of Guadalupe (Mexico's brown-skinned patroness, who supposedly appeared to the humble Indian Juan Diego during the colonial period) (211). What makes this myth specifically Mexican are the colonial overtones: la Malinche is conflated with the archetype of *la chingada* ["the raped one"], the paradigmatic national traitor who is blamed for her own rape as well as the figurative rape of Mexico by the Spanish and is imbued with the aspects of carnality and eroticism. The Virgin of Guadalupe, on the other hand, embodies the maternal purity of Mary, but in the form of an Indigenous woman who, thanks to her dark skin, serves to incorporate the colonized Other of Mexico into the Catholic fold (204–210). Similar to myths of Mexican machismo, these myths of femininity illustrate the persistence of the coloniality of gender and sex in Mexico.

16. See Irwin, *Mexican*; Domínguez-Ruvalcaba, *Modernity*; Monsiváis, *Escenas* 103–17, "Ortodoxia"; de la Mora.

17. Nuevo Repueblo is a working-class neighborhood in the northern Mexican city of Monterrey.

18. This is a popular magazine that features news related to the production of *telenovelas*, interviews with actors, and recaps of episodes. It is marketed to

a female readership and widely associated with female consumers and feminine mass culture in Mexico.

Chapter 4

1. See Ault; Bryant; Clausen; Däumer; Denizet-Lewis; Garber; Eadie; Hemmings, "Extracts"; Hutchins and Kaahumanu; Klein; Storr. Bisexual women have reported encountering biphobia in the lesbian community, a phenomenon that is usually interpreted as a reaction to their perceived threat to a stable lesbian identity, c.f. Ault; Clausen; Hemmings, "Extracts."

2. Examples of this can be seen in the Anglo American television programs *Oz* (HBO), *Game of Thrones* (HBO), and *House of Cards* (Netflix) and in the Spanish American programs *Capadocia* (HBO) and *La casa de las flores* (Netflix).

More sympathetic portrayals of bisexual characters may be seen in films such as *Madame Satã* (Karim Aïnouz, 2003) and *Brokeback Mountain* (Ang Lee, 2005). For a list of films from the early 20th century to the mid-1990s that contain both positive and negative portrayals of bisexual characters, see Bryant.

3. Male bisexuality has received a great deal of attention in Mexican studies, while female bisexuality, like female sexuality in general, remains a relatively understudied and underrepresented aspect of Mexican society. This is probably due in part to the patriarchal nature of Mexican society (and Western society in general). The discourse produced in and about Mexico has tended to privilege androcentric perspectives that extend to allegorical portrayals of the nation, such as that of Octavio Paz. When female bisexuality is mentioned in relation to Mexican culture, it is most often as a personality trait of women like the painter Frida Kahlo and not as an integral part of notions of national identity.

Though not often theorized or studied in Mexico, female bisexuality does appear in film and literature. Paul Leduc's 1983 film *Frida, Naturaleza viva* [*Frida, Still Life*] and Julie Taymore's 2002 *Frida* both include scenes that clearly portray Kahlo with a bisexual orientation. Literary portrayals of female bisexuality include the novels *Nadie me verá llorar* [*No One Will See Me Cry*] (1999) by Cristina Rivera Garza, *Réquiem por una muñeca rota* ["Requiem for a Broken Doll"] (2000) by Eve Gil, and *¿Y qué fue de Bonita Malacón?* (2007) by José Dimayuga (see chapter 5). In the novel *Amora* (1989) by Rosamaría Roffiel and in the short story "El cordón umbilical de la Gorgona" ["The Gorgon's Umbilical Chord"] by Gilda Salinas, sequential bisexuality is represented as part of a process in which the telos is the adoption of a lesbian identity. The short story "Arielle" by Elena Madrigal plays with the theme of a housewife seduced by another woman. While some (though not all) of the texts mentioned above do employ humor in their portrayal of bisexuality, they are not included here because they do not demonstrate the same centrality of theme nor the same intersection of camp and *cursi* humor as the novels analyzed in this chapter, which incidentally have male protagonists.

4. Domínguez-Ruvalcaba cites studies that estimate bisexual practices in upwards of 30% of the Mexican male population. He also notes how the blurring of the line between homo- and heterosexuality has complicated responses ot the AIDS epidemic in Latin America (*Translating* 126–27).

5. Liguori reproduces many common jokes and refrains about this topic in her article. For example: "¿Cuál es la diferencia entre un mexicano homosexual y uno que no lo es? Dos copas" ["What is the difference between a Mexican man who is homosexual and one who is not? Two drinks"] (132); "En tiempo de guerra cualquier hoyo es trinchera" ["In wartime, any hole is a trench"]; "Cualquier hoyo, aunque sea de pollo ["Any hole, even if it's a chicken"] (137); "Veracruz es la tierra del aguacate: el que no es puto es mayate" ["Veracruz is the land of the aguacate: whoever isn't a fag is a *mayate* [trade]"] (142); "Siendo agujero aunque sea de caballero" ["As long as it's a hole, even if it's a gentleman's"] (150); "Andando de cacería, de lagartija p'arriba todo es pieza" ["When you're hunting, anything bigger than a lizard is fair game"] (152). The novel *Mátame y verás* by Blanco contains other examples of similar jokes: "a la dama por la hermosura y al caballero por la apretura [. . .] cuando no hay lomo de todo como" ["to the lady for her beauty and to the gentleman for his tightness [. . .] when there's no meat ('loin') I'll eat anything"] (96–97).

6. Prieur and Domínguez-Ruvalcaba argue that the term *mayate* originates in the name for one or more species of beetle whose use of dung as a substratum for their larvae may be a metonymic reference to anal sex and whose shiny color may be an allusion to the loud dress of working-class men (Prieur 27; Domínguez-Ruvalcaba, *Modernity* 133). According to Domínguez-Ruvalcaba, the term *chacal* refers to a species of shrimp that resembles a scorpion and whose edibility and fierce appearance connote "a savage sensuality" (133).

7. See Cagle for an exploration of the "trade" phenomenon in the English-speaking world.

8. The etymology of the term *joto/choto* is somewhat contested. Prieur claims to have heard that it refers to a Spanish dance in which men move in ways considered feminine but also cites the folk etymology that locates the origin of the word in cell block J (*jota*), where the homosexuals were supposedly isolated in the Lecumberri prison in Mexico City (25). Domínguez-Ruvalcaba, on the other hand, claims that the term probably derives from the verb *chotear*, "to make fun of" (*Modernity* 133).

9. The late Argentine cartoonist Roberto Fontanarrosa once brilliantly illustrated this joke in an episode of his comic strip *Boogie el Aceitoso* in which a Mexican character claims that his toughness is the result of being a "*macho probado*"—that is, a man who has proven to himself that he does not like to have sex with men by having sex with men—and who periodically continues to subject his masculinity to this test just to be sure.

10. Cuernavaca, located approximately 50 miles to the south of Mexico City, is the capital of the state of Morelos and the site, since pre-Columbian times, of

properties used by the elite of the metropolis for relaxation. Juanito's vacation home here is thus a symbol of the social status he has achieved.

11. The question of whether or not Juanito actually did this is never resolved, which tends to contribute to the overall lack of closure and resolution of the conflicts planted in the plot.

12. See Navarrete, *México* chapters 5 and 6 for a discussion of how *mestizaje* has functioned to camouflage racism in Mexico.

13. The exact nature of Mauro's shady dealings is never explained in the novel, a detail that contributes to the book's overall ambience of ambiguity and indefinition.

14. See Cázares; Domínguez Michael; Gil; Thornton, "*Púrpura*."

15. Serna has indicated that the novel is based on his experiences as a young man, with the three main characters being based on himself, his late mother, and the playwright and TV writer Carlos Olmos, with whom Serna had a sexual-affective relationship in his youth. This has led some critics to read it as a "coming-out" of the author as bisexual. See Cárdenas; García Hernández, "Irreverencia"; Thornton, "Being Fruity."

16. The fact that he shares the same first name as Artemio's cousin in *Púrpura* appears to be a coincidence.

17. Deformation of "qué bárbaro mujer" ["how awful, girl"].

Chapter 5

1. For more on the theme of reading Sor Juana as a lesbian figure, see André; Bergmann; Rueda Esquibel, chapter 4.

2. See Moraga and Anzaldúa, *This Bridge Called My Back*; Moraga, *Loving in the War Years*; Anzaldúa, *Borderlands/La Frontera*.

3. An exception to this cultural uniformity is Sara Levi Calderón's novel *Dos mujeres*, where the protagonist struggles with her allegiance to her wealthy, insular, patriarchal Jewish community in Mexico City and her desire to live freely as a lesbian woman. In the end she moves to San Francisco and assimilates to the Anglo-American lesbian culture there. Aside from the obvious class difference, the problem of cultural allegiance here is very similar to that expressed by Moraga.

4. See Butler; Case; Hemmings, "Rescuing"; Munt; Nestle; Robertson.

5. This convention of having a silent interlocutor recording the speech of the characters recalls the format used in *Vampiro*. Dimayuga, like Luis Zapata, is a gay writer originally from a small town in the southern Mexican state of Guerrero, and this similarity may indeed be a nod to the work of the older writer.

6. This is called *Mujeres* in the novel. The real-world referent is *Mujer: casos de la vida real* [Woman: Real Life Cases], hosted by the famous actress Silvia Pinal.

7. *Chino* is a term used to describe racial mixing that dates from the colonial period; here it is used to indicate that the woman looked very Indigenous.

8. The time period portrayed here (late 1970s) antedated any official recognition of same-sex unions based on the marriage model. Therefore, the mention of the character's "wife" responds to a social convention not officially sanctioned by the state.

9. The title of this section is a joke that plays on a brand of cinnamon roll sold in Mexico and the notion of portraying a stereotypically feminine role, as a "bimbo."

10. For discussions of women performing femininity as camp, see Hemmings and Robertson.

11. Lupita D'Alessio is a pop singer who is also a queer icon in Latin America; see chapter 3.

12. The Mexican term *desempance* refers to a small drink of alcohol, such as a shot of tequila or anisette, that is drunk after eating in order to aid digestion. It derives from the term *panza* (belly), and refers to the reduction of gases in the abdomen that the drink is supposed to provide. Here it suggests a period of rest after an excess of consumption as well as a focus on bodily pleasure.

Conclusions

1. The film centers on the figure of Ignacio de la Torre y Mier, the son-in-law of Porfirio Díaz, who was, according to Mexican urban legend, the 42nd man arrested that fateful night, spared from ignominy and prison because of his family connections.

Works Cited

Alfarache Lorenzo, Ángela. "La construcción cultural de la lesbofobia. Una aproximación desde la antropología." *Homofobia: laberinto de la ignorancia*, edited by Julio Muñoz Rubio, Mexico City, UNAM, 2012, pp. 125-46.
Almaguer, Tomás. "Chicano Men: A Cartography of Homosexual Identity and Behavior." *Differences: A Journal of Feminist Cultural Studies*, vol. 3, no. 2, 1991, pp. 75-100.
Alonso, Carlos J. *The Burden of Modernity: The Rhetoric of Cultural Discourse in Spanish America*. Oxford U Press, 1998.
Alonso, Odette. *Con la boca abierta*. Madrid, Odisea Editorial, 2006.
Altman, Dennis. "Internationalization of Gay Identities." *SocialText*, vol. 14, no. 3, 1996, pp. 77-94.
Aluma-Cazorla, Andrés. "La Visibilidad Del Homosexual, Sus Cartografías Urbanas y La Tolerancia Del Consumo/Queer Visibility and Its Urban Cartographers as a Result of Consumer Tolerance." *Revista de Humanidades*, vol. 25, June 2012, pp. 121-44.
Alzate, Gastón A. "Albur, 'naquiza,' camp y manierismo en el cabaret de Regina Orozco." *Latin American Theatre Review*, vol. 45, no. 1, 2011, pp. 95-113.
Amícola, José. *Camp y posvanguardia: Manifestaciones culturales de un siglo fenecido*. Buenos Aires, Paidós, 2000.
Amor libre. Directed by Jaime Humberto Hermosillo, CONACINE, 1979.
Angelides, Steven. "The Queer Intervention." *The Routledge Queer Studies Reader*, edited by Donald E. Hall and Annamarie Jagose with Andrea Bebell and Susan Potter, Routledge, 2013, pp. 60-73.
Anzaldúa, Gloria. *Borderlands/La Frontera: The New Mestiza*. San Francisco, Aunt Lute Books, 1987.
Arce, B. Christine. *México's Nobodies: The Cultural Legacy of the Soldadera and Afro-Mexican Women*. SUNY Press, 2017.
Así del precipicio. Directed by Teresa Suárez, Agárrate del Barandal, 2006.
Attardo, Salvatore and Victor Raskin. "Script theory revis(it)ed: joke similarity and joke representation model." *Humor*, vol. 4, nos. 3-4, 1991, pp. 293-348.

Attardo, Salvatore. *Linguistic Theories of Humor*. Berlin, Mouton de Gruyter, 1994.

———. *Humorous Texts: A Semantic and Pragmatic Analysis*. Berlin, Mouton de Gruyter, 2001.

Ault, Amber. "Ambiguous Identity in an Unambiguous Sex/Gender Structure: The Case of Bisexual Women (1996)." Storr, pp. 167–85.

Azuela, Mariano. *Los de abajo*. 1915. Madrid, Cátedra, 1980.

Babuscio, Jack. "The Cinema of Camp (aka Camp and the Gay Sensibility)." Cleto, pp. 117–35.

Balderston, Daniel and José Maristany. "The lesbian and gay novel in Latin America." *The Cambridge Companion to the Latin American Novel*, edited by Efraín Kristal, Cambridge UP, 2005, pp. 200–216.

Barajas Durán, Rafael. *Sólo me río cuando me duele: La cultura del humor en México*. Mexico City, Editorial Planeta Mexicana, 2009.

Barbachano Ponce, Miguel. *El diario de José Toledo*. Mexico City, 1964.

Barker, Nicola. *Not the Marrying Kind: A Feminist Critique of Same-Sex Marriage*. Palgrave Macmillan, 2012.

Barreda Solórzano, Luis de la. *La sociedad mexicana y los derechos humanos. Encuesta Nacional de Derechos Humanos, Discriminación y Grupos Vulnerables*. Mexico City, UNAM, 2015.

Bartlett, Neil. "Forgery." Cleto, pp. 179–84.

Bartra, Roger. *La jaula de la melancolía: Identidad y metamorfosis del mexicano*. Mexico City, Juan Grijalbo, 1996.

Bary, Leslie. "Oswald de Andrade's 'Cannibalist Manifesto.'" *Latin American Literary Review*, vol. 19, no. 38, July 1991, pp. 35–47.

Bautista, Juan Carlos, director. Amor Chacal. Producciones Pili y Mili, 2001.

Bejel, Emilio. *Gay Cuban Nation*. University of Chicago Press, 2001.

Bell, David and Jon Binnie. *The Sexual Citizen: Queer Politics and Beyond*. Cambridge, Polity, 2000.

Beltrán Felix, Geney. "La destrucción del norte." Review of *La marrana negra de la literatura rosa* by Carlos Velázquez. *Letras Libres*, no. 144, Dec. 2010, pp. 88–90.

Bencomo, Anadeli. "*La hermana secreta de Angélica María*: La parodia del 'género' en Luis Zapata." *Revista de Literatura Mexicana Contemporánea*, vol. 9, no. 18, Jan. 2003, pp. 71–82.

———. "La imaginadora: el arte narrativo de Ana García Bergua." *Explicación de Textos Literarios*, vols. 1-2, no. 36, 2008, pp. 78–90.

Bergmann, Emilie. "Abjection and Ambiguity: Lesbian Desire in Bemberg's *Yo, La Peor De Todas*." *Hispanisms and Homosexualities*, edited by Sylvia Molloy and Robert McKee Irwin, Duke UP, 1998, pp. 229–47.

Bersani, Leo. *Is the Rectum a Grave? and Other Essays*. U of Chicago P, 2009.

Beverley, John, Michael Aronna and José Oviedo, editors. *The Postmodernism Debate in Latin America*. Duke UP, 1995.

Blanco, José Joaquín. "Ojos que da pánico soñar." *Función de medianoche*, by José Joaquín Blanco, Mexico City, Ediciones Era, 1981, pp. 181–90.

———. *Las púberes canéforas*. Mexico City, Océano, 1983.

———. *Mátame y verás*. Mexico City, Ediciones Era, 1994.

———. *Crónica literaria: Un siglo de escritores mexicanos*. Mexico City, Cal y Arena, 1996.

Botellita de Jerez. "Guaca Rock de la Malinche." *Naco es chido*, Polygram, 1987.

Bretón de los Herreros, Manuel. *¡Muérete y verás!*, Biblioteca Virtual Miguel de Cervantes, 2001, www.cervantesvirtual.com/obra/muerete-y-veras/. Accessed 7 Jun. 2016.

Britton, Andrew. "For Interpretation: Notes against Camp." Cleto, pp. 136–42.

Brokeback Mountain. Directed by Ang Lee, Focus Features/River Road Entertainment/Alberta Film Entertainment/Good Machine, 2005.

Bryant, Wayne M. *Bisexual Characters in Film: From Anaïs to Zee*. Haworth, 1997.

Buffington, Robert. "Homophobia and the Mexican Working Class, 1900–1910." *The Famous 41: Sexuality and Social Control in Mexico, 1901*, edited by Robert McKee Irwin, Edward J. McCaughan and Michelle Rocío Nasser, Palgrave Macmillan, 2003, pp. 193–225.

Bustamante Bermúdez, Gerardo. "Que no somos iguales . . . dice la gente. La construcción autobiográfica masculina en Las verdades de Chavela." *Un juego que cabe entre nosotras: Acercamientos a la crítica y a la creación de la literatura sáfica*, edited by Elena Madrigal and Leticia Romero, Mexico City, vocesentinta, 2014, pp. 201–22.

Butler, Judith. *Gender Trouble: Feminism and the Subversion of Identity*. 1990. Routledge, 1999.

Cagle, Chris. "Rough Trade: Sexual Taxonomy in Postwar America." *RePresenting Bisexualities: Subjects and Cultures of Fluid Desire*, edited by Donald E. Hall and Maria Pramaggiore, NYU Press, 1996, pp. 234–52.

Calva Pratt, José Rafael. *Utopía gay*. Mexico City, Editorial Oasis, 1983.

Capadocia: un lugar sin perdón. HBO, 2008–2012.

Cárdenas, Noé. "Fruta verde, de Enrique Serna." *Letras Libres*, no. 98, Feb. 2007, pp. 83–84.

Carmín tropical. Directed by Rigoberto Perezcano, IMCINE, 2014.

Carrier, Joseph. *De los otros: Intimacy and Homosexuality among Mexican Men*. Columbia UP, 1995.

Carrillo, Héctor. *The Night is Young: Sexuality in Mexico in the Time of AIDS*. U of Chicago P, 2002.

———. "How Latin Culture Got More Gay." *New York Times*, 17 May 2013, p. A21.

Casas de Faunce, María. *La novela picaresca latinoamericana*. Madrid, Planeta/Universidad de Puerto Rico, 1977.

Case, Sue Ellen. "Towards a Butch-Femme Aesthetic." *Discourse*, no. 11, 1988, pp. 55–73.

Casique Rodríguez, Irene. "Fuentes y datos sobre la violencia contra las mujeres en México. Aprendizajes, dificultades y retos acumulados." *Realidad, datos y espacio. Revista internacional de estadística y geografía*, vol. 8, no. 1, 2017, pp. 6–16.

Castrejón, Eduardo A. *Los cuarenta y uno: novela crítico-social*. 1906. Mexico City, UNAM, 2010.

Castro Ricalde, María de la Cruz. "Lesbians Made in Mexico: Sexual Diversity and Transnational Fluxes." *Despite All Adversities: Spanish-American Queer Cinema*, edited by Andrés Lema-Hincapié and Debra A. Castillo, SUNY Press, 2015, pp. 203–20.

Casullo, Nicolás, ed. *El debate modernidad-posmodernidad*. 2nd ed., Buenos Aires, Retórica, 2004.

Cázares H., Laura. "Del rancho a la capital: *Púrpura* de Ana García Bergua." *Territorio de leonas: Cartografía de narradoras mexicanas en los noventa*, edited by Ana Rosa Domenella, Mexico City, Universidad Autónoma Metropolitana/Casa Juan Pablos, 2001, pp. 339–53.

Chavela. Directed by Catherine Gund and Daresha Kyi, Aubin Pictures, 2017.

Clausen, Jan. "Extract from *My Interesting Condition* (1990)." Storr, pp. 107–111.

Cleto, Fabio, editor. *Camp: Queer Aesthetics and the Performing Subject. A Reader*. U of Michigan P, 1999.

Cohen, Cathy J. "Punks, Bulldaggers, and Welfare Queens: The Radical Potential of Queer Politics?" *The Routledge Queer Studies Reader*, edited by Donald E. Hall and Annamarie Jagose with Andrea Bebell and Susan Potter, Routledge, 2013, pp. 74–95.

Connell, Raewyn. *Masculinities*. 3rd ed., U of California P, 2005.

Core, Philip. "From *Camp: The Lie that Tells the Truth*." Cleto, pp. 66–79.

Cornejo Polar, Antonio. "Mestizaje, transculturación, heterogeneidad." *Revista de Crítica Literaria Latinoamericana*, vol. 20, no. 40, 1994, pp. 368–71.

———. "Mestizaje e hibridez: Los riesgos de las metáforas. Apuntes." *Revista Iberoamericana*, vol. 68, no. 200, 2002, pp. 867–70.

———. *Writing in the Air: Heterogeneity and the Persistence of Oral Tradition in Andean Literatures*. Translated by Lynda J. Jentsch. Duke UP, 2013.

Covarrubias, Alicia. "*El vampiro de la colonia Roma*, de Luis Zapata: La nueva picaresca y el reportaje ficticio." *Revista de Crítica Literaria Latinoamericana*, vol. 20, no. 39, 1994, pp. 183–97.

"cursi." WordReference.com, 2016, http://www.wordreference.com/es/en/translation.asp?spen=cursi. Accessed 3 Jun. 2016.

Danielson, Marivel T. *Homecoming Queers: Desire and Difference in Chicana Latina Cultural Production*. Rutgers UP, 2009.

Däumer, Elisabeth D. "Extract from 'Queer Ethics; or the Challenge of Bisexuality to Lesbian Ethics' (1992)." Storr, pp. 152–61.

Davidson, Cathy N. "The Picaresque and the Margins of Political Discourse." *Revolution and the Word: The Rise of the Novel in America*, by Cathy N. Davidson, Oxford UP, 2004, pp. 233–305.
de Alba, Luis, creator. *El mundo de Luis de Alba*. Televisa, S.A. de C.V. 1978–1981.
de la Mora, Sergio. *Cinemachismo: Masculinities and Sexuality in Mexican Film*. U of Texas P, 2006.
"Debate derivado de PINK." *YouTube*, uploaded by mecias02031987, 28 March, 2016, https://www.youtube.com/watch?v=7fcqmLcaIss.
Denizet-Lewis, Benoit. "The Scientific Quest to Prove—Once and For All—That Someone Can Be Truly Attracted to Both a Man and a Woman." *The New York Times Magazine*, 23 Mar. 2014, pp. 24–29; 44.
Dimayuga, José. *¿Y qué fue de Bonita Malacon?* Mexico City, Jus, 2013.
Dollimore, Jonathan. "Authenticity." Cleto, pp. 221–36.
Domínguez Michael, Christopher. "De Sodoma a Gomorra." Review of *Púrpura* by Ana García Bergua. *Letras Libres*, no. 8, Aug. 1999, pp. 91–92.
Domínguez-Ruvalcaba, Héctor. *Modernity and the Nation in Mexican Representations of Masculinity: From Sensuality to Bloodshed*. Palgrave Macmillan, 2007.
———. "Atisbos a la subjetividad de los victimarios en el cine y el ciberespacio en México." *Iztapalapa*, vol. 79, no. 36, 2015, pp. 93–110.
———. "Los mecanismos cómicos de la homofobia en algunos programas de Televisa." *La cuestión del odio: Acercamientos interdisciplinarios a la homofobia en México*, edited by Héctor Domínguez-Ruvalcaba, Xalapa, Veracruz, Mexico, Universidad Veracruzana, 2015, pp. 117–37.
———. *Translating the Queer: Body Politics and Transnational Conversations*. London, Zed Books, 2016.
Doña Herlinda y su hijo. Directed by Jaime Humberto Hermosillo, Clasa Films Mundiales, 1985.
Dussel, Enrique. *The Invention of the Americas: Eclipse of the Other and the Myth of Modernity*. Continuum, 1995.
Dyer, Richard. "It's Being so Camp as Keeps Us Going." Cleto, pp. 110–16.
Eadie, Jo. "Extracts from Activating Bisexuality: Towards a Bi/Sexual Politics (1993)." Storr, pp. 119–137.
Eco, Umberto. "Lo posmoderno, la ironía, lo ameno." *Apostillas a* El nombre de la rosa, by Umberto Eco. Translated by Ricardo Pochtar, Barcelona, Lumen, 1988, pp. 658–64.
Egan, Linda. *Carlos Monsiváis: Culture and Chronicle in Contemporary Mexico*. U of Arizona P, 2001.
El lugar sin límites. Directed by Arturo Ripstein, Conacite Dos, 1978.
El portero, directed by Miguel Delgado, performance by Mario Moreno "Cantinflas," Posa Films, 1950.
El sexo débil. Argos Comunicación, Cadena Tres, Sony Pictures Television, 2011.

"El Verguillas." YouTube, uploaded by FAScomedy, 29 Sept. 2009, https://www.youtube.com/watch?v=zhm6qstdn6M.

Enrigue, Álvaro. "Notas para una historia de lo cursi." *Letras Libres*, no. 33, sept. 2001, pp. 44–48.

Enríquez, Victoria. *Con fugitivo paso* . . . Mexico City, 1997.

Fabre, Luis Felipe. *Escribir con caca*. Mexico City, Sexto Piso, 2017.

Fagan, Allison. "Negotiating Language." *The Routledge Companion to Latino/a Literature*, edited by Suzanne Bost and Frances R. Aparicio, Routledge, 2015, pp. 207–15.

Figari, Carlos. "Queer Articulations." *Critical Terms in Caribbean and Latin American Thought: Historical and Institutional Trajectories*, edited by Yolanda Martínez-San Miguel, Ben. Sifuentes-Jáuregui, and Marisa Belausteguigoitia, Palgrave Macmillan, 2016, pp. 231–38.

Fiol-Matta, Licia. "Queer/Sexualities." *Critical Terms in Caribbean and Latin American Thought: Historical and Institutional Trajectories*, edited by Yolanda Martínez-San Miguel, Ben. Sifuentes-Jáuregui, and Marisa Belausteguigoitia, Palgrave Macmillan, 2016, pp. 217–30.

Flinn, Caryl. "The Deaths of Camp." Cleto, pp. 433–57.

Foster, David William. *Sexual Textualities: Essays on Queer/ing Latin American Writing*. U of Texas P, 1997.

———. *Ensayos Sobre Culturas Homoeróticas Latinoamericanas*. Ciudad Juárez, Chihuahua, Mexico, Universidad Autónoma De Ciudad Juárez, 2009.

Foucault, Michel. *The History of Sexuality*. Vol. I. Translated by Robert Hurley. Vintage, 1985.

Franco, Jean. *The Decline and Fall of the Lettered City*: Latin America in the Cold War. Harvard UP, 2002.

Freud, Sigmund. *Jokes and Their Relation to the Unconscious*. 1905. Translated by James Strachey. Norton, 1960.

———. "Humour." 1927. Translated by Joan Riviere. *Art and Literature: Jensen's 'Gradiva,' Leonardo da Vinci and Other Works*, edited by Albert Dickson, Penguin, 1990, pp. 425–433.

Frida. Directed by Julie Taymor, with performance by Salma Hayek, Miramax, 2003.

Frida, naturaleza viva. Directed by Paul Leduc, Clasa Films Mundiales, 1983.

Fuentes, Carlos. *La región más transparente*. Mexico City, Fondo de Cultura Económica, 1958.

Game of Thrones. HBO, 2011–2019.

Garber, Marjorie. *Bisexuality and the Eroticism of Everyday Life*. 1995. Routledge, 2000.

García Bergua, Ana. *Púrpura*. Mexico City, Ediciones Era, 1998.

García Hernández, Arturo. "*Fruta verde*, novela de aprendizaje sobre amor cínico: Enrique Serna." jornada.unam.mx, La Jornada, 11 Dec. 2006, http://www.jornada.unam.mx/2006/12/11/index.php?section=cultura&article=a10n1cul.

García Ponce, Juan. *Figura de paja*. Mexico City, Joaquín Mortiz, 1964.
Garza, Elisa A. "Chicana Lesbianism and the Multi-Genre Text." *Tortilleras: Hispanic and U.S. Latina Lesbian Expression*, edited by Lourdes Torres and Inmaculada Pertusa, Temple UP, 2003, pp. 196–210.
Gil, Eve. *Réquiem por una muñeca rota (cuentos para asustar al lobo)*. Mexico City, Fondo Editorial Tierra Adentro/Conaculta, 2000.
Gómez de la Serna, Ramón. "Lo cursi." *Lo cursi y otros ensayos*, by Ramón Gómez de la Serna, Buenos Aires, Editorial Sudamericana, 1943, pp. 7–54.
González-Block, Miguel Ángel and Ana Luisa Liguori. "El SIDA en los de abajo." *Nexos*, May 1993, pp. 15–20.
González Echevarría, Roberto. "A Clearing in the Jungle." *Myth and Archive: A Theory of Latin American Narrative*, by Roberto González-Echevarría, Cambridge UP, 1990, pp. 1–42.
González Pérez, César O. *Travestidos al desnudo. Homosexualidad, identidades y luchas territoriales en Colima*. Mexico City, Miguel Ángel Porrúa, 2003.
Gordus, Andrew. "Transgrediendo fronteras: Género, sexualidad y espacio en *Brenda Berenice o el diario de una loca*." *Memoria: XVI Coloquio de las literaturas mexicanas*, Hermosillo, Sonora, Mexico, Universidad de Sonora, 1999, pp. 285–91.
Güemes, César. "Llegué tarde a las letras, porque escribía en secreto: García Bergua." Interview of Ana García Bergua. *La Jornada*, 1 Sept. 1999, p. 31.
Guillén, Claudio. "Toward a Definition of the Picaresque." *Literature as System*, by Claudio Guillén, Princeton UP, 1971, pp. 71–106.
———. "Genre and Countergenre: The Discovery of the Picaresque." *Literature as System*, by Claudio Guillén, Princeton UP, 1971, pp. 135–58.
Gundermann, Christian. "Todos gozamos como locos: los medios de comunicación masiva y la sexualidad como módulos de filiación entre Manuel Puig y Alberto Fuguet." *Chasqui*, vol. 30, no. 1, 2000, pp. 29–42.
Gutiérrez, León Guillermo. "El vampiro de la colonia Roma. Función del espacio y el cuerpo en el discurso homoerótico." *Revista de Humanidades: Tecnológico de Monterrey*, nos. 27–28, 2009, pp. 235–47.
Hazlo como hombre, directed by Nicolás López, Sobras International Pictures/A Toda Madre Entertainment/Bh5, 2017.
"'Hazlo como hombre,' quinta película mexicana más vista en la historia." *punto. mx*, Punto MX, 14 Sept. 2017, punto.mx/publicacion/hazlo-como-hombre-quinta-pelicula-mexicana-mas-vista-en-la-historia-31825.
Hemmings, Clare. "Extracts from Locating Bisexual Identities: Discourses of Bisexuality and Contemporary Feminist Theory (1995)." Storr, pp. 193–200.
———. "Rescuing Lesbian Camp." *Journal of Lesbian Studies*, vol. 11, nos. 1–2, 2007, pp. 159–66.
Hirsch, Marianne. "The Novel of Formation as Genre: Between Great Expectations and Lost Illusions." *Genre*, no. 12, 1979, pp. 293–311.

House of Cards. Netflix, 2013–2018.
"Humor." *Oxford English Dictionary*, 2013.
Hutchins, Loraine, and Lani Kaahumanu, eds. *Bi Any Other Name: Bisexual People Speak Out.* Boston, Alyson Publications, 1991.
"Informe Crímenes de Odio Por Homofobia." letraese.org.mx, Letra S, http://www.letraese.org.mx/proyectos/proyecto-1-2/. Accessed 3 June 2016.
Irwin, Robert McKee. "La Pedo Embotellado: Sexual Roles and Play in Salvador Novo's La Estatua de Sal." *Studies in the Literary Imagination*, vol. 33, no. 1, 2000, pp. 125–32.
———. *Mexican Masculinities.* U of Minnesota P, 2003.
Irwin, Robert McKee, Edward J. McCaughan, and Michelle Rocío Nasser, eds. *The Famous 41: Sexuality and Social Control in Mexico, c. 1901.* Palgrave Macmillan, 2003.
Isherwood, Christopher. *The World in the Evening.* Random House, 1954.
Jiménez, Armando. *Picardía mexicana.* 1958. Mexico City, Editores Mexicanos Unidos, 1978.
Johnson, E. Patrick. " 'Quare' Studies, or '(Almost) Everything I Know about Queer Studies I Learned from my Grandmother." *The Routledge Queer Studies Reader*, edited by Donald E. Hall and Annamarie Jagose with Andrea Bebell and Susan Potter, Routledge, 2013, pp. 96–118.
King, Thomas A. "Performing 'Akimbo': Queer Pride and Epistemological Prejudice." *The Politics and Poetics of Camp*, edited by Moe Meyer, Routledge, 1994, pp. 20–43.
Kinsey, Alfred C., Wardell B. Pomeroy, and Clyde E. Martin. "Extracts from *Sexual Behavior in the Human Male* (1948)." Storr, pp. 31–37.
Klein, Fritz. "Extracts from *The Bisexual Option: A Concept of One Hundred Percent Intimacy* (1978)." Storr, pp. 38–48.
Kuipers, Giselinde. "The Sociology of Humor." *The Primer of Humor Research*, edited by Victor Raskin, Mouton de Gruyter, 2008, pp. 365–402.
Kulick, Don. *Travesti: Sex, Gender, and Culture among Brazilian Transgendered Prostitutes.* U of Chicago P, 1998.
La casa de las flores. Netflix, 2018–2020.
La casa del ogro, directed by Fernando de Fuentes, Compañía Mexicana de Películas, 1939.
La otra familia. Directed by Gustavo Loza, Río Negro, 2011.
Las Aparicio. Directed by Moisés Ortiz Urquidi, Argos Cine, 2015.
Lassen, Christian. *Camp Comforts: Reparative Gay Literature in Times of AIDS.* Bielefeld, Transcript Verlag, 2011.
Leonard, Irving A. *Baroque Times in Old Mexico.* U of Michigan P, 1966.
Lewis, Vek. *Crossing Sex and Gender in Latin America.* Palgrave Macmillan, 2010.
Liguori, Ana Luisa. "Las investigaciones sobre bisexualidad en México." *Debate Feminista*, vol. 6, no. 11, 1995, pp. 132–56.

López, Oscar. "*El vampiro de la colonia Roma*: O del travestismo posmoderno." *Revista de Literatura Mexicana Contemporánea*, vol. 4, no. 10, Apr. 1999, pp. 72–78.

Love, Heather. "Truth and Consequences: On Paranoid Reading and Reparative Reading." *Criticism*, vol. 52, no. 2, 2010, pp. 235–41.

Lugones, María. "Colonialidad y género." *Tabula Rasa*, no. 9, 2008, pp. 73–101.

Lyotard, Jean François. *The Postmodern Condition: A Report on Knowledge*. Translated by Geoff Bennington and Brian Massumi, U of Minnesota P, 1984.

Madame Satã. Directed by Karim Aïnouz, VideoFilmes/Dominant 7/Lumière/Wild Bunch, 2002.

Made in Bangkok. Directed by Flavio Florencio, Me Río de Janeiro Producciones/Cacerola Films/FOPROCINE, 2015.

Madrigal, Elena. *Contarte en lésbico*. Montreal/Mexico City, Éditions Alondras/Monarca Impresoras, 2010.

———. "Un carnaval para el yo lésbico: los cuentos de Gilda Salinas." *Lectora*, vol. 17, 2011, pp. 93–103.

Mancera Lara, Bertha. "Género y homofobia en los medios de comunicación." *Homofobia: laberinto de la ignorancia*, edited by Julio Muñoz Rubio, Mexico City, UNAM, 2012, pp. 185–92.

Marquet, Antonio. *¡Que se quede el infinito sin estrellas! La cultura gay al final del milenio*. Mexico City, Universidad Autónoma Metropolitana, 2001.

Medina, Alberto. "De nómadas y ambulantes: *El vampiro de la colonia Roma* o la utopía suplantada." *Revista Canadiense de Estudios Hispánicos*, vol. 32, no. 3, 2008, pp. 507–21.

Meyer, Moe, "Introduction: Reclaiming the Discourse of Camp." *The Politics and Poetics of Camp*, edited by Moe Meyer, Routledge, 1994, pp. 1–19.

Michel, Frann. "Do Bats Eat Cats? Reading What Bisexuality Does." *RePresenting Bisexualities: Subjects and Cultures of Fluid Desire*, edited by Donald E. Hall and Maria Pramaggiore, NYU P, 1996, pp. 55–69.

Mignolo, Walter. *The Darker Side of the Renaissance: Literacy Territoriality, and Colonization*. U of Michigan P, 1995.

Modisto de señoras. Directed by René Cardona, Jr., performance by Mauricio Garcés, Productora Fílmica Real, 1969.

Molloy, Sylvia. "Too Wilde for Comfort: Desire and Ideology in *Fin-de-Siècle* Spanish America." *Social Text*, nos. 31–32, 1992, pp. 187–201.

Monsiváis, Carlos. "El hastío es pavo real que se aburre de luz en la tarde (Notas del camp en México)." *Días de guardar*, by Carlos Monsiváis, Mexico City, Ediciones Era, 1970, pp. 171–92.

———. "Agustín Lara: El harem ilusorio (Notas a partir de la memorización de la letra de 'Farolito')." *Amor perdido*, by Carlos Monsiváis, Mexico City, Ediciones Era, 1977, pp. 61–86.

———. *Escenas de pudor y liviandad*. Mexico City, Juan Grijalbo, 1988.

———. "Mexicanerías: el albur." *Escenas de pudor y liviandad*, by Carlos Monsiváis, Juan Grijalbo, 1988, pp. 301–308.

———."Léperos y catrines, nacos y yupis." *Mitos Mexicanos*, edited by Enrique Florescano, Mexico City, Aguilar, 1995, pp. 165–72.

———. "Ortodoxia y heterodoxia en las alcobas." *Debate Feminista*, vol. 6, no. 11, 1995, pp. 183–210.

———. "Los que tenemos una manos que no nos pertenecen (A propósito de lo 'Queer' y lo 'Rarito'). *Debate Feminista*, vol. 8, no. 16, 1997, pp. 11–33.

———. *Salvador Novo: Lo marginal en el centro*. 2nd ed., Mexico City, Ediciones Era, 2004.

———. "El mundo soslayado." 1998. Prologue to *La estatua de sal*, by Salvador Novo, Mexico City, Fondo de Cultura Económica, 2008, pp. 13–72.

———. "La cursilería." *Los ídolos a nado: Una antología global*, by Carlos Monsiváis, Barcelona, Debate, 2011, pp. 13–33.

Montaldo, Graciela. "Modernity and Modernization: The Geopolitical Relocation of Latin America." *Critical Terms in Caribbean and Latin American Thought: Historical and Institutional Trajectories*, edited by Yolanda Martínez-San Miguel, Ben. Sifuentes-Jáuregui, and Marisa Belausteguigoitia, Palgrave Macmillan, 2016, pp. 163–64.

Montaño, Luis. *Brenda Berenice o el diario de una loca*. Mexico City, Domés, 1985.

Moraga, Cherríe. *Loving in the War Years: Lo que nunca pasó por sus labios*. Boston, South End Press, 1983.

Moraga, Cherríe, and Gloria Anzaldúa, editors. *This Bridge Called My Back: Writings by Radical Women of Color*. Watertown, MA, Persephone Press, 1981.

Moreno Figueroa, Mónica G. "Distributed Intensities: Whiteness, Mestizaje and the Logics of Mexican Racism." *Ethnicities*, vol. 10, no. 3, 2010, pp. 387–401.

Morir de pie. Directed by Jacaranda Correa, Martfilms, 2011.

Morreall, John. *The Philosophy of Laughter and Humor*. SUNY P, 1987.

Mulkay, Michael. *On Humor: Its Nature and Its place in Modern Society*. Blackwell, 1988.

Munt, Sally R. *Heroic Desire: Lesbian Identity and Cultural Space*. London, Cassell, 1998.

Muñecas de medianoche. Directed by Rafael Portillo, Cinematográfica Calderón S.A., 1979.

Muñoz, José Esteban. *Disidentifications: Queers of Color and the Performance of Politics*. U of Minnesota P, 1999.

Muñoz Rubio, Julio. "La ciencia hegemónica contemporánea y la homofobia." *Homofobia: laberinto de la ignorancia*, edited by Julio Muñoz Rubio, Mexico City, UNAM, 2012, pp. 47–64.

mymachinedomination. Comment on *Pink*. Internet Movie Database (IMDB), 5 Apr. 2016, www.imdb.com/title/tt5525360/reviews?ref_=tt_urv.

"naco." *Diccionario de mexicanismos*, 2nd ed., 2010.
"naco." *Diccionario de la Lengua Española*, 2016.
"Naco y Fresa—Episodio 1: El i-Pos." YouTube, uploaded by nacoyfresa, 1 July 2006, https://www.youtube.com/watch?v=w0Tt7Nr8NXM.
Nájar, Alberto. "El albur, el 'código secreto' de México." bbc.com/mundo, BBC, 11 Mar. 2011, http://www.bbc.com/mundo/noticias/2011/03/110311_mexico_albur_lenguaje_secreto_pea.shtml.
Navarrete, Federico. *Alfabeto del racismo mexicano*. Barcelona, Malpaso, 2016.
———. *México racista: Una denuncia*. Mexico City, Grijalbo, 2016.
Nestle, Joan, ed. *The Persistent Desire: A Femme-Butch Reader*. Los Angeles and NY, Alyson Books, 1992.
Newton, Esther. "Role Models." Cleto, pp. 96–109.
Noches de cabaret. Directed by Rafael Portillo, Cinematográfica Calderón S.A., 1978.
Novo, Salvador. *Sátira: El libro ca . . .* Mexico City, Editorial Diana, 1978.
———. *La estatua de sal*. 1998. Mexico City, Fondo de Cultura Económica, 2008.
Núñez Noriega, Guillermo. *Sexo entre varones. Poder y resistencia en el campo sexual*. 2nd ed., Mexico City, Miguel Ángel Porrúa, 1999.
Olivera Córdova, María Elena. *Entre amoras: Lesbianismo en la narrativa mexicana*. Mexico City, UNAM, 2009.
———. "¿Hay homofobia en la literatura?" *Homofobia: Laberinto de la ignorancia*, edited by Julio Muñoz Rubio, Mexico City, UNAM, 2012, pp. 161–72.
Oropesa, Salvador. "La representación del yo y del tú en la poesía satírica de Salvador Novo: La influencia del albur." *Chasqui*, vol. 24, no. 1, 1995, pp. 38–52.
Oz. HBO, 1997–2003.
"Pablo Cheng se arrepiente de hacer la película 'Pink.'" *sdpnoticias.com*, SDP Noticias, 13 Apr. 2017, www.sdpnoticias.com/enelshow/famosos/2017/04/13/pablo-cheng-se-arrepiente-de-hacer-la-pelicula-pink.
Palaversich, Diana. "El femenino monstruoso y la crisis del género en *La hermana secreta de Angélica María*." *Antípodas*, nos. 11–12, 1999–2000, pp. 233–48.
Palma Castro, Alejandro. "Espacios en *El vampiro de la colonia Roma*. Hacia una estética camp." *Revista de Literatura Mexicana Contemporánea*, vol. 14, no. 36, Jan. 2008, pp. 23–29.
Paz, Octavio. *El laberinto de la soledad*. 2nd ed. Mexico City, Fondo de Cultura Económica, 1959.
"Película Pink, un fracaso en taquilla." *vanguardia.com.mx*, VanguardiaMX, 16 March 2016, https://vanguardia.com.mx/articulo/pelicula-pink-un-fracaso-en-taquilla.
Pérez, Francisco R. "El Infierno Social y Personal Del Marginado: El Homosexual En La Ciudad de México." *CLA Journal*, vol. 41, no. 2, Dec. 1997, pp. 204–21.
Pérez Gay, Rafael. "Mátame y verás," review of novel by José Joaquín Blanco. *Nexos*, Oct. 1994, pp. 95–97.

Pink. Directed by Francisco del Toro, performances by Pablo Cheng and Charly López, Armagedon Films, 2016.

Portilla, Jorge. "Fenomenología del relajo." *Fenomenología del relajo y otros ensayos*, by Jorge Portilla, Mexico City, Fondo de Cultura Económica, 1984, pp. 13-95.

Prieur, Annick. *Mema's House, Mexico City: On Transvestites, Queens and Machos*. U of Chicago P, 1998.

Quebranto. Directed by Roberto Fiesco, Mil Nubes-Cine, FOPROCINE, Ruta 66, CUEC, FONCA, 2013.

Quijano, Aníbal. "Coloniality of Power, Eurocentrism, and Latin America." Translated by Michael Ennis. *Nepantla*, vol. 1, no. 3, 2000, pp. 533-80.

Quiroga, José. *Tropics of Desire: Interventions from Queer Latino America*. NYU P, 2000.

Rama, Ángel. *Transculturación narrativa en América Latina*. Mexico City, Siglo XXI Editores, 1982.

———. *La ciudad letrada*. Hanover, New Hampshire, Ediciones del Norte, 1984.

Ramos, Samuel. *Perfil del hombre y la cultura en México*. 1934. Mexico City, Secretaría de Educación Pública, 1987.

Reséndiz Oikión, Ernesto. "Las lesbianas en trienta y cuatro obras de autores mexicanos." *Un juego que cabe entre nosotras: Acercamientos a la crítica y a la creación de la literatura sáfica*, edited by Elena Madrigal and Leticia Romero, Mexico City, vocesentinta, 2014, pp. 139-72.

Reyes Ávila, Carlos. *Travesti*, Mexico City, Conaculta, 2009.

Revueltas, José. *Los muros de agua*. 1941. Mexico City, Ediciones Era, 1973.

Rich, Adrienne. "Compulsory Heterosexuality and Lesbian Existence." *Signs*, vol. 5, no. 4, 1980, pp. 631-60.

Rico, Francisco. "La novela picaresca y el punto de vista." *La novela picaresca y el punto de vista*, by Francisco Rico, Barcelona, Seix Barral, 1973, pp. 93-141.

Rivera Garza, Cristina. *Nadie me verá llorar*. Mexico City, Tusquets, 1999.

Rivera-Valdés, Sonia. *The Forbidden Stories of Marta Veneranda*. Translated by Dick Cluster, et al. New York, Seven Stories Press, 2001.

Robertson, Pamela. "What Makes the Feminist Camp." *Cleto*, pp. 266-82.

Roffiel, Rosamaría. *Amora*. Mexico City, Planeta, 1989.

Rudo y cursi. Directed by Carlos Cuarón, performances by Gael García Bernal and Diego Luna. FFI/UI/Canana Films, 2008.

Rueda Esquibel, Catrióna. *With Her Machete in Her Hand: Reading Chicana Lesbians*. U of Texas P, 2006.

Ruiz, Bladimir. "Prostitución y homosexualidad: Interpelaciones desde el margen en *El vampiro de la colonia Roma* de Luis Zapata." *Revista Iberoamericana*, vol. 65, no. 187, 1999, pp. 327-39.

———. "*Utopia gay*, de Jose Rafael Calva, y las contradicciones dentro del discurso narrativo de la diferencia." *Revista Canadiense de Estudios Hispánicos*, vol. 30, no. 2, 2006, pp. 291-309.

Ruiz, Eduardo. "'El reverso del 'Milagro Mexicano'": La crítica de la nación en *Las batallas en el desierto* y *El vampiro de la colonia Roma*." *Ciberletras*, no. 26, Dec. 2011, n.p.

Ruiz-Alfaro, Sofia. "A Threat to the Nation: México Marimacho and Female Masculinities in Postrevolutionary Mexico." *Hispanic Review*, vol. 81, no. 1, 2013, pp. 41–62.

Russo Garrido, Anahi. "'El Ambiente' According to Her: Gender, Class, "Mexicanidad," and the Cosmopolitan in Queer Mexico City." *NWSA Journal*, vol. 21, no. 3, 2009, pp. 24–45.

———. "The Emergence of Lesbian Safe Places in Mexico City (1970–2010)." *Journal of Postcolonial Cultures and Societies*, vol. 4, no. 2, 2013, pp. 47–98.

Salas, Elizabeth. *Soldaderas in the Mexican Military: Myth and History*. U of Texas P, 1990.

Salinas, Gilda. *Del destete al desempance: Cuentos lésbicos y un colado*. Mexico City, Trópico de Escorpio, 2008.

Salinas Hernández, Héctor Miguel. *Políticas de disidencia sexual en América Latina. Sujetos sociales, gobierno y mercado en México Bogotá y Buenos Aires*. Mexico City, Ediciones Eón, 2010.

———. *Matrimonio igualitario en la Ciudad de México. ¿Por qué quieren casarse los gays?* Mexico City, Vocesentinta, 2013.

Salmerón Tellechea, Cecilia. "La Generación Beat como correlato de *El vampiro de la colonia Roma*." *Revista de Literatura Mexicana Contemporánea*, vol. 10, no. 24, 2004, pp. 73–84.

Salón México, directed by Emilio Fernández, performance by Marga López, Clasa Films Mundiales, 1949.

Sánchez Prado, Ignacio M. "Carlos Monsiváis: crónica, nación y liberalismo." *El arte de la ironía: Carlos Monsiváis ante la crítica*, edited by Mabel Moraña and Ignacio M. Sánchez Prado, Mexico City, Era/UNAM, 2007, pp. 300–36.

Santos, Lidia. *Tropical Kitsch*. Translated by Elisabeth Enenbach, Princeton/Madrid, Marcus Wiener/Iberoamericana, 2006.

Schaefer, Claudia. *Danger Zones: Homosexuality, National Identity, and Mexican Culture*. U of Arizona P, 1996.

Schneider, Luis Mario. "El tema homosexual en la nueva narrativa mexicana." *La novela mexicana entre el petróleo, la homosexualidad y la política*. Mexico City, Nueva Imagen, 1997.

Scholes, Robert. "Toward a Structuralist Poetics of Fiction." *Structuralism in Literature: An Introduction*, by Robert Scholes, Yale University Press, 1971, pp. 59–142.

Schroeder-Rodríguez, Paul A. *Latin American Cinema: A Comparative History*. U of California P, 2016.

Schuessler, Michael. "Vestidas, Locas, Mayates and Machos: History and Homosexuality in Mexican Cinema." *Chasqui*, vol. 34, no. 2, 2005, pp. 132–44.

Schulenburg, Chris T. "*El vampiro de la colonia Roma*: Mexico City's Maps and Gaps." *Chasqui: Revista de Literatura Latinoamericana*, vol. 39, no. 2, Nov. 2010, pp. 85-98.

Sedgwick, Eve Kosofsky. "Paranoid Reading and Reparative Reading, or, You're So Paranoid, You Probably Think This Essay Is about You." *Touching Feeling: Affect, Pedagogy, Performativity*, by Eve Kosofsky Sedgwick, Duke UP, 2003, pp. 123-51.

Serna, Enrique. *El miedo a los animales*. Mexico City, Joaquín Mortiz, 1995.

———. "El naco en el país de las castas." *Las caricaturas me hacen llorar*, by Enrique Serna, Mexico City, Joaquín Mortiz/UNAM/Conaculta, 2002, 97-104.

———. "Machismo torcido." *Las caricaturas me hacen llorar*, by Enrique Serna, Mexico City, Joaquín Mortiz/UNAM/Conaculta, 2002, pp. 25-27.

———. *Fruta verde*. Mexico City, Planeta, 2006.

———. *La doble vida de Jesús*. Barcelona, Penguin Random House Grupo Editorial, 2015.

Sifuentes Jáuregui, Ben. "The Swishing of Gender: Homographic Markings in Lazarillo de Tormes." *Hispanisms and Homosexualities*, edited by Silvia Molloy and Robert McKee Irwin, Duke UP, 1998, pp. 123-40.

———. *Transvestism, Masculinity, and Latin American Literature: Genders Share Flesh*. Palgrave Macmillan, 2002.

———. *The Avowal of Difference: Queer Latino American Narratives*. SUNY P, 2014.

———. "¡ . . . es tu madre!: Pedro Infante and Melodramatic Masculinity." *Letras Hispanas*, no. 11, 2015, pp. 134-46.

Sinfield, Alan. *The Wilde Century: Effeminacy, Oscar Wilde and the Queer Moment*. London, Cassell, 1994.

Smith, Paul Julian. *Queer Mexico: Cinema and Television Since 2000*. Wayne State UP, 2017.

Sommer, Doris. *Foundational Fictions: The National Romances of Latin America*. 1984. U of California P, 1991.

Sontag, Susan. "Notes on 'Camp.'" Cleto, pp. 53-65.

Soto, Sandra K. *Reading Chican@ Like a Queer: The De-Mastery of Desire*. U of Texas P, 2010.

Storr, Merl. *Bisexuality: A Critical Reader*. Routledge, 1999.

sugarfreepeppermint. Comment on *Pink*, Internet Movie Database (IMDB), 23 Apr. 2017, www.imdb.com/title/tt5525360/reviews?ref_=tt_urv.

Tate, Julee. "From Girly Men to Manly Men: The Evolving Representation of Male Homosexuality in Twenty-First Century Telenovelas." *Studies in Latin American Popular Culture*, no. 29, 2011, pp. 102-14.

Téllez, Artemisa. "'A Chloe le gustaba Olivia.' Implicaciones de una literatura que quisiera llamarse lésbica." *Homofobia: laberinto de la ignorancia*, edited by Julio Muñoz Rubio, Mexico City, UNAM, 2012, pp. 173-84.

Thornton, Niamh. "Ana García Bergua's *Púrpura*: Gay Narrative and the Boom Femenino in Mexico." *The Boom Femenino in Mexico: Reading Contemporary Women's Writing*, edited by Nuala Finnegan and Jane E. Lavery, Newcastle upon Tyne, Cambridge Scholars, 2010, pp. 217–40.

———. "Being Fruity in the Big City: Re-membering the Past in Enrique Serna's *Fruta verde*." *(Re)Collecting the Past: History and Collective Memory in Latin American Narrative. Hispanic Studies: Culture and Ideas*, edited by Victoria Carpenter, Peter Lang, 2010, pp. 145–65.

Todo el mundo tiene a alguien menos yo. Directed by Raúl Fuentes, Centro Universitario de Estudios Cinematográficos, 2012.

Todo incluido. Directed by Rodrigo Ortúzar, Jazz Films Producciones, 2008.

Torres, Lourdes. Introduction. *Tortilleras: Hispanic and U.S. Latina Lesbian Expression*, edited by Lourdes Torres and Inmaculada Pertusa, Temple UP, 2003, pp. 1–15.

Triezenberg, Katrina. "Humor Enhancers in the Study of Humorous Literature." *Humor*, vol. 17, no. 4, 2004, pp. 411–18.

Tyler, Carole-Ann. "Boys Will Be Girls: Drag and Transvestic Fetishism." Cleto, pp. 369–92.

Udis-Kessler, Amanda. "Notes on the Kinsey Scale and Other Measures of Sexuality (1992)." Storr, pp. 49–56.

Valis, Nöel. *The Culture of Cursilería: Bad Taste, Kitsch and Class in Modern Spain*. Duke UP, 2002.

Vargas Cervantes, Susana. *Mujercitos*. Granollers, Spain, RM Verlag, 2014.

———. "Travestis y vestidas en México: una identidad política." horizontal.mx, Horizontal, 21 Apr. 2016, http://horizontal.mx/travestis-y-vestidas-en-mexico-una-identidad-politica/. Accessed 19 Jan. 2017.

———. "Defendamos ¿el matrimonio?" horizontal.mx, Horizontal, 11 Oct. 2016, http://horizontal.mx/defendamos-el-matrimonio/. Accessed 19 Jan. 2017.

———. "Queer, cuir y las sexualidades periféricas en México." horizontal.mx, Horizontal, 15 Dec. 2016, http://horizontal.mx/queer-cuir-y-las-sexualidades-perifericas-en-mexico. Accessed 19 Jan. 2017.

Velázquez, Carlos. *La marrana negra de la literatura rosa*. Mexico City, Sexto Piso, 2010.

Venkatesh, Vinodh. *The Body as Capital: Masculinities in Contemporary Latin American Fiction*. U of Arizona P, 2015.

———. *New Maricón Cinema: Outing Latin American Film*. U of Texas P, 2016.

———. "*La doble vida de Jesús*: Genealogías internas en la obra de Enrique Serna." *La sonrisa afilada: Enrique Serna ante la crítica*, edited by Martín Camps, Mexico City, UNAM, 2017, pp. 261–77.

Villarejo, Amy. *Lesbian Rule: Cultural Criticism and the Value of Desire*. Duke UP, 2003.

Walker, Ja'nina J., Sarit A. Golub, David S. Bimbi and Jeffrey T. Parsons. "Butch Bottom-Femme Top? An Exploration of Lesbian Stereotypes." *Journal of Lesbian Studies*, vol. 16, no. 1, 2012, pp. 90–107.

Westmoreland, Maurice. "Camp in the Works of Luis Zapata." *Modern Language Studies*, vol. 25, no. 2, 1995, pp. 45–59.

Wicks, Ulrich. *Picaresque Narrative, Picaresque Fictions*: A Theory and Research Guide. New York, Greenwood, 1989.

Wind, Ariel. "Mexico City and Its Monsters: Queer Identity and Cultural Capitalism in Luis Zapata's *El vampiro de la colonia Roma*." *Revista Canadiense de Estudios Hispánicos*, vol. 38, no. 3, 2014, pp. 579–604.

Zapata, Luis. *Las aventuras, desventuras y sueños de Adonis García, el vampiro de la colonia Roma*. Mexico City, Juan Grijalbo, 1979.

———. *Adonis García: A Picaresque Novel*. Translated by E. A. Lacey. San Francisco, Gay Sunshine Press, 1981.

Index

acampando, 16–18
AIDS crisis, 3, 15–16, 203n4
Alba, Luis de, 194–95n12
albures, 36–38, 144–45
Alessio Robles, Ricardo, 42
allegory, 10–11, 24, 83, 94, 96, 103, 110, 114, 183, 187
   Bildungsromane and, 125
   bisexuality and, 122, 124–25, 137
   in Calva's *Utopía gay*, 65–77
   Mexican culture and, 119
   Mexican national identity and, 109
   nation-building allegories, 5
   social conflicts and, 134–35, 136, 137
Alonso, Odette, 192n6
   Con la boca abierta, 158, 165
Alvarado, Veracruz, 123–24
Amícola, José, 17
Amor chacal, 123–24
Amor libre, 67, 159
Andrade, Oswaldo de, 194n10
androcentrism, 157–58, 164
Angelides, Steven, 120
Anglo-American sexualities, 7
anxiety, modernity and, 101
Anzaldúa, Gloria, 160–61, 164, 173
Las Aparicio, 159
Argentina, same-sex marriages in, 2
Así del precipicio, 159, 187

Attardo, Salvatore, 195n14
Ault, Amber, 120
Azuela, Mariano, *Los de abajo*, 40
azul, 163, 166, 171, 172, 182

"bad taste," 8, 17, 20, 21, 25, 28, 112, 182
El baile de los 41, 3
   Pablos, David, 190
Barajas, Rafael "El Fisgón," 37–38, 39
Barbachano Ponce, Miguel, *El diario de José Toledo*, 52, 53
Barker, Nicola, 68–69
Bartra, Roger, 20, 22–23, 36, 98–99, 108, 110, 121, 124, 138, 195n16, 201n15
Bautista, Juan Carlos, 192n6
Bejel, Emilio, 5, 108–9
Bell, Monna, 178
Bemberg, María Luisa, *Yo, la peor de todas*, 159
Bencomo, Anadeli, 94
Bersani, Leo, 122
Bhabha, Homi, 20
Bildungsromane, 11, 117–46, 154–55
biphobia, 118–19, 120, 202n1
bisexuality, 9, 11, 82, 117–55
   allegory and, 124–25, 137
   ambiguous nature of, 118–19, 137–39, 144–45

223

bisexuality *(continued)*
   Bildungsromane and, 125–27
   in cinema, 202–3n3, 202n2
   definitions of, 117–18
   destabilizing effect of, 118–19
   female, 202–3n3
   humor and, 123–25
   male, 123, 202–3n3
   as metaphor, 118–19
   Mexican national culture and, 120–21
   Mexican national identity and, 123
   in Mexico, 119–25, 202–3n3, 203n4
   portrayal of, 202–3n3, 202n2
   repression of, 126
   social conflicts and, 125–27, 137
   on television, 202n2
   in the US, 202–3n3
Blanco, José Joaquín, 16–17, 47, 52, 53, 55, 65, 187, 192n6, 197n2
   Mátame y verás, 11, 126, 127–36, 155, 175, 189, 203n5
   "Ojos que da pánico soñar," 54–55, 131
   Las púberes canéforas, 53
the body
   centrality of, 6
   colonialism and, 7
   coloniality and, 83
   gender and, 6–7, 121, 163–64
   gender construction and, 163–64
   gender crossing and, 6–7
   identity and, 83
   intersex, 83–94
   national identity and, 83
   performance of gender and, 163
   race and, 163–64
   racialized, 6
   resistance and, 83
   sensualization of, 5
bohemianism, 24–25

Bonelli, Coral, 80
Botellita de Jerez, 28
bourgeois consumerism, 88–89, 91, 136. *See also* consumer culture
Brazil, same-sex marriages in, 2
Bretón de Herreros, Manuel, *Muérete y verás*, 127
butch identities, 162, 171
Butler, Judith, 14, 121, 162

cafonas, 25
Calva, José Rafael, 55, 65, 68
   Utopía gay, 9, 10, 53, 54, 65–77, 79, 83, 171, 188, 197n3
camp, 7–11, 13–38, 54, 72–73, 79, 137, 162–63, 186–88. *See also* camp humor
   ambivalence and, 179
   camp aesthetics, 15–16
   camp culture, 65
   camp performance, 4
   criticism as apolitical and conservative, 14
   definition of, 9, 13
   disidentification and, 8, 9, 162
   gender nonconformity and, 13, 33, 95–96, 157
   homosexuality and, 16
   Latin America and, 16–18
   lesbian camp, 162
   as liberating discourse, 162
   machorra camp, 157–83
   in Novo, 13–50, 40, 47, 50
   queerness and, 13–16, 162
   queer recovery of, 162
   queer theory and, 14
   sexual dissidence and, 187
   social functions of, 38–39
   subversive potential of, 14, 17–18
   translation of concept to Mexican context, 7, 16–18

transvestism and, 13
unintentional, 187–88
women's camp, 162, 165–66
camp humor, 17–18, 33, 66, 77, 93–98, 101–5, 110, 114–15, 126–31, 139–40, 149, 154–55, 165–66, 171, 183
  AIDS crisis and, 15–16
  cursi humor and, 35
  function of, 137–38
  gender nonconformity and, 161
  gender parody and, 14, 56–65, 71–73, 75, 83–88, 175
  reparative uses of, 102–3, 147
  subversive potential of, 23–24
Campo, Rafael, 16
Capadocia, 159, 202n2
capitalism, 11, 74, 166, 194n7
caricature, 108, 109–15, 129, 133, 173
Carmelita Tropicana, 8, 17, 161, 162
Carmín tropical, 80
Carrier, Joseph, 120
Carrillo, Héctor, 120
Cartesian dualism, 98
La casa de las flores, 68, 81, 202n2
Case, Sue Ellen, 162
Castrejón, Eduardo, 191–92n3
Castro Ricalde, María, 159
Catholicism, 3, 69, 74, 76, 91. See also Virgin of Guadalupe
caudillismo, 166
Ceballos Maldonado, José, *Después de todo*, 52
chacales, 124, 203n6
Chavela, 189
Cheng, Pablo, 186, 187–88
Chicana lesbian feminist writers, 160, 164, 173. See also *specific writers*
Chicano family culture, patriarchal, 161
"Chingadalupe," 108, 110, 201n15

the *chingón*, 121, 123
chotear, 36, 203n8
choteo, 8, 17, 162
chotos, 124, 203n8
cinema, 2–3, 86–88, 91–92, 93, 103–7, 109, 124, 185–89, 190. See also *specific films*
  bisexuality in, 202–3n3, 202n2
  cinematic melodrama, 10–11
  documentaries, 80
  effeminacy in, 191–92n3
  lesbian humor in, 189
  lesbian sexuality in, 159
  "maricón cinema," 193n10
  Mexican national identity and, 109
  "semi-Sapphic," 159
civilization vs. barbarism debate, 19
civil unions, 2, 107–8. See also marriage
class, 8–11, 25, 28, 35, 108, 113, 121, 161, 171, 173, 189, 194–95n12
  in Blanco's *Mátame y verás*, 126–36
  bourgeois consumerism, 88–89, 91, 136
  classism, 9, 11
  cursilería and, 21
  dissidence and, 55, 80–81
  in García Bergua's *Púrpura*, 140–41
  gender and, 68–69
  Marxism and, 55, 71, 73, 77
  in Montaño's *Brenda Berenice*, 96, 99–100
  in Serna's *Fruta verde*, 149–50, 152–53, 155
  working-class masculinity, 182
Clavel, Ana, *Cuerpo náufrago*, 124
the "closet," 6, 7, 160
collectives, 192n7
  constitution of, 10
  feminist collectives, 176

collectives *(continued)*
   lesbian collectives, 162, 170, 171, 175
   of sexual dissidence, 192n4
Colombia, same-sex marriages in, 2
coloniality, 5, 6, 12, 28, 65, 155, 161
   the body and, 7, 83
   cursilería and, 161
   gender and, 19, 23–24, 56, 64, 69, 75, 83, 122, 154, 188, 193n6
   homosexuality and, 122
   modernity and, 19
   persistence of, 136
   of power, 47, 48, 56, 64, 154, 188, 193n6
   of race, 154
   sexuality and, 19, 23–24, 56, 64, 69, 75, 83, 188, 193n6
   subject formation and, 5
   subjectivities and, 23
coming out of the closet, trope of, 6, 7, 160
Conaculta (Consejo Nacional para la Cultura y las Artes), 41
Connell, Raewyn, 2, 5
conservative groups, 3
consumer culture, 10, 54–56, 77, 88–89, 91, 94, 103, 136. *See also* bourgeois consumerism
Contemporáneos literary group, 39, 40
copy, culture as, 94
Cornejo Polar, Antonio, 22, 194n11
Cortés, Hernán, 122, 201n15
cosmopolitanism, 19, 49–50
"creative kitsch," 28
criollos, 28
crónicas, 39, 170, 171
cross-gender identification, 80–81. *See also* gender-crossing; transgender
Cuarón, Alfonso, 124
Cuban identity, 5, 161–62

Cuéllar, José Tomás de, *Baile y cochino*, 158
Cuesta, Jorge, 39, 41, 42
cultural anachronism, 41, 76, 88–90, 149
cultural nationalism, 50, 140–41
   parody of, 48–49
culture as copy, 94
cursi humor, 36, 56, 66, 73, 77
   bisexuality and, 126–29, 139–40, 155
   camp humor and, 35
   gender-crossing and, 83–86, 94, 96, 101–5, 110, 114–15
   gender nonconformity and, 161
   lesbian *cursilería* and, 162–66, 171, 175, 183
   reparative uses of, 102–3, 147
   subversive potential of, 23–25
cursilería, 7–12, 54, 57–58, 63–65, 79, 186–88, 201n14. *See also cursi* humor
   as aesthetic strategy, 4
   ambivalence and, 46, 179
   appropriation of, 47
   belatedness and, 18
   bisexuality and, 123, 132–33, 137–40, 145, 149–55
   class and, 21
   coloniality and, 161
   as cultural anachronism, 74–75, 88–90
   cursi bueno, 47
   cursi malo, 47
   definition of, 13, 18, 22–23
   dismodernity and, 176
   effeminacy and, 73
   femininity and, 10, 61–62, 101–2
   gender and, 74, 95
   gender-crossing and, 95
   humor and, 23–25, 35, 98–105
   lesbianism and, 157–83

melodrama and, 91–92
modernity and, 18–20, 33
lo naco and, 33
in Novo, 13–50
paranoid reading practices and, 24–25
parody and, 92–93
race and, 21, 176
recycling of, 176–77
reparative reading practices and, 24–25
sentimentalism and, 75
sentimentality and, 28
sexual dissidence and, 187
social functions of, 39
subject formation and, 22–23
cynicism, 176–78

D'Alessio, Lupita, 107, 177, 201n14
Dallal, Alberto, *Mocambo*, 52
Danielson, Marivel T., 164
Darío, Rubén, 19, 48
Däumer, Elisabeth D., 120
de la Torre y Mier, Ignacio, 205n1
del Toro, Francisco, 185–86
Descartes, René, 98–99
Desde Gayola, 3, 33, 35
Díaz, Porfirio, 33, 82, 194n8, 205n1
Díaz Ordaz, Gustavo, 39
Dickens, Charles, 125
didacticism, 164–65
Dimayuga, José, 161, 204n5
  ¿Y qué fue de Bonita Malacón? 11, 158–59, 160, 165–70, 183, 189, 202–3n3
Dios Peza, Juan de, 25, 46–47
disavowal, 6
discrimination, 41, 44, 50, 57, 65, 80–81, 96, 114, 158, 173
dismodernity, 12, 20, 35, 41, 50, 75, 98–99, 117–55, 176

dissidence, 24, 47, 50, 57, 71, 95, 96, 104, 113, 166, 176. *See also* sexual dissidence
  class and, 55
dissident identities, 5, 163–64, 175–76
dissident sexualities, 182
dissident subjectivities, 104, 166, 183
  effeminacy and, 163
  homosexuality and, 39–40
  politics of, 55
documentaries, 80
Dollimore, Jonathan, 7, 14
Domínguez-Ruvalcaba, Héctor, 5–6, 76–77, 81, 124, 191–92n3, 200n2, 203n4, 203n6, 203n8
Doña Herlinda y su hijo, 67–68, 124
Douglas, Alfred, 67, 199n15
drag, 95. *See also* cross-dressing
drag kings, 162
Dussell, Enrique, 18–19

Ediciones Quimera, 192n6
effeminacy, 1, 40–41, 48, 71–73, 95, 111, 112, 120, 124, 127, 130, 149, 157, 162, 186–87
  cursilería and, 73
  dissidence and, 163
  homosexuality and, 33, 34–35, 63, 79
  male homosexuality and, 79
  in Mexican literature, 191–92n3
  stereotypes of, 191–92n3
  in Zapata's *Vampiro*, 56–65
"effeminate literature," vs. "virile" literature, 40
Egan, Linda, 24
Enríquez, Victoria, *Con fugitivo paso*, 158, 165
entertainment industry, 86–90

essay (genre), 63
essentialism, 121, 160
Etcétera, 127–28
expectations, reversal of, 181–82

Fabre, Luis Felipe, 41
female identities, 10
female masculinities, 162
female queer sexualities, 157–83. *See also* lesbian sexuality
female sexuality, 111–12, 158
the feminine
  ambivalence toward, 41
  cursilería and, 61–62
  negative evaluation of, 46
  rejection of, 4, 37, 79, 123 (*see also* misogyny)
  re-valuation of, 102
feminine masculinity, 158, 183
femininities, 50, 113, 124, 132, 138–39, 163, 167–69, 183
  contradictory notions of, 86
  cross-dressing and, 91–109
  cursilería and, 10, 101–2
  devalued, 62
  disidentification with, 162
  hypersexualized, 87
  mass media and, 10, 104–9
  Mexican myth of, 108, 110
  parody and, 87–88
  performance of, 79–80, 87–88, 104–6, 111, 147–48, 157, 162, 169, 172–73, 175, 181
  rejection of, 76
  stereotypes of, 171, 172, 179, 181–82
feminism, 3
  feminist collectives, 176
  lesbian feminism, 158, 159, 160, 164, 165, 182
  women of color feminism, 160–61

feminization, 36, 37, 75, 121–22, 126
femme identities, 171
Fiesco, Roberto, 3
  Quebranto, 80
film. *See* cinema; *specific films*
El Fisgón, 37–38. *See also* Barajas, Rafael
Florencio, Flavio, *Made in Bangkok*, 80
Fontanarrosa, Roberto, 203n9
the 41, 1–3, *30–31*, 33–35, 52, 79, 157, 191n1
Foster, David William, 8
Foucault, Michel, 122
fresas, 194–95n12
Freud, Sigmund, 38
Fuentes, Carlos, *La región más transparente*, 52
Fuentes, Fernando de, 191–92n3

Gabriel, Juan, 3
Gamboa, Federico, 60–61
  Santa, 63–64, 158
García Bergua, Ana, *Púrpura*, 11, 126, 136–45, 155, 187, 189
García Ponce, Juan, *Figura de paja*, 158, 164
gay rights discourses, 71, 187
gender, 8–11, 50, 54, 77, 80, 96, 121, 123, 130–32, 150, 155, 189. *See also* gender nonconformity
  the body and, 121, 163–64
  class and, 68–69
  coloniality and, 19, 23–24, 56, 64, 69, 75, 83, 122, 154, 188, 193n6
  construction of, 4, 85–86, 121, 163–64
  cursilería and, 74, 157–83
  gender binaries, 157, 172
  humor and, 57
  inequality and, 38

lesbian *cursilería* and, 157–83
marriage equality and, 192n4
modernity and, 94
parody and, 11, 50, 84
performance of, 57, 105–6, 138, 157–83 (*see also* gender roles)
performativity of, 121
power and, 119
stereotypes of, 23–24, 33
gender-crossing, 10, 66, 70–72, 79–116, 80, 95, 114. See also *jotas*; *locas*; *travestis*; *vestidas*
  the body and, 6–7
  gender nonconformity and, 167
  marginalization of, 82–83
  stereotypes of, 81
gender nonconformity, 1, 5, 7, 9–12, 35–36, 54, 72, 96, 113, 192n7. See *also* sexual dissidence
  camp and, 13, 33, 95–96, 157, 161
  cross-dressing and, 167
  female, 2, 157–83
  homosexuality and, 77, 168
  humor and, 161, 163
  lesbians and, 164, 168
  Mexican Revolution and, 158
  Novo and, 47
  portrayal of, 188
  women and, 2, 157–83
gender norms, 6, 11, 57, 63, 82–84, 103
  disidentification with, 94, 171
  rejection of (*see* gender nonconformity)
  same-sex marriages and, 68
  traditional, 74–75
gender parody, 10–11, 14, 17–18, 56–65, 71–72, 75, 83, 85–88, 95, 101–2, 162, 175, 182
gender roles
  binary, 166, 171

  changing, 35
  conditional, 62
  fluid, 175
  indeterminacy and, 147–49
  inversion of, 182
  performance of, 56–65
  reiteration of, 182
  traditional, 68–69, 91, 104–8, 109, 110, 113, 145, 151, 162, 182
gender tropes, recycling of, 102–3
General Theory of Verbal Humor (GTVH), 195n14
genres, parody of, 10
Gide, André, 48
Gil, Eve, *Réquiem por una muñeca rota*, 158, 202–3n3
Global North, 5–6, 17, 20, 23, 94, 101, 121–22, 160
Global South, 38, 121, 150
Goblot, Edmond, 28
Goethe, Johann Wolfgang von, 125
Gómez de la Serna, Ramón, 21, 47
Guau, 3
Gutiérrez Nájera, Manuel, 33

Hartman, Angélica María, 200n6
Hazlo como hombre, 185, 186–87, 189
HBO Latin America, 159
Hemmings, Clare, 120, 162
Henríquez Ureña, Pedro, 42
hermaphroditism, 117
Hermosillo, Jaime Humberto, 67–68
  Amor libre, 159
Hernández, Julián, 3
heteronormativity, 5–9, 19, 44, 50, 65, 68–69, 81, 154, 159, 192n4
  bisexuality and, 119
  deprivileging of, 77
  disidentification and, 55, 76, 170, 177, 183, 188
  marriage and, 75, 77

heteronormativity *(continued)*
    reinforced through humor, 3–4
    same-sex marriages and, 77
heteropatriarchy, 159. *See also*
    patriarchy
heterosexuality, 124
    ambiguous nature of, 118–19
    compulsory, 160 (*see also*
       heteronormativity)
    marriage and, 68–69
HIV/AIDS, 118. *See also* AIDS crisis
homoeroticism, 51, 55, 103, 123, 124
homonormativity, 6, 9, 56, 65, 154
    bisexuality and, 119
    disidentification with, 76, 170, 183,
       188
    privilege and, 187
    same-sex marriages and, 77
homophobia, 3–6, 35, 38, 79, 121,
       135–36, 186–89
    humor and, 51–78
    internalization of, 63, 97
    misogyny and, 2
    violence and, 9, 188
homosexuality, 1, 10, 40, 48, 56, 95,
       113, 124, 191n1
    ambiguous nature of, 118–19
    camp and, 16
    coloniality and, 122
    dissidence and, 39–40
    effeminacy and, 33, 34–35, 63, 79
    gender nonconformity and, 77
    humor and, 51–78
    in the mass media, 2–3
    narrative and, 52
    positive portrayals of, 197n1, 197n2
    rejection of, 5
    stereotypes of, 1–2, 43, 56–65, 71,
       187
    as theme in Mexican literature,
       51–53
    tolerance of, 185
homosociality, 5, 37, 124, 158

honor, 105
huachafo, 25
humor, 8–12, 17, 50, 124, 194–95n12.
    See also specific kinds of humor
    ambiguity and, 165, 188, 190
    bisexuality and, 123–25
    camp and, 17–18
    as coping mechanism, 101
    cursilería and, 98–99, 157–83
    definition of, 29–35
    disidentification and, 171
    function of, 172
    gender and, 57, 163, 172
    heteronormativity reinforced
       through, 3–4
    homophobia and, 51–78
    incongruity and, 29–31, 35
    Latin Americanist literary criticism
       and, 9
    lesbian *cursilería* and, 157–83
    machismo and, 38
    male homosexuality and, 37, 51–78
    melodramatic language and, 93
    Mexicanist literary criticism and, 9
    Mexican national identity and, 36–
       37
    in Mexico, 36–39
    paranoid reading practices and, 39
    as positive mode of self-expression,
       63
    queerness and, 4, 10
    reparative uses of, 39, 56, 72–73,
       96, 126, 127, 131–32, 137, 155,
       171, 175–76
    as rhetorical device, 115
    ritual insult humor, 162
    self-deprecating, 41, 44, 46–47, 50,
       55, 60–61, 131, 148, 172, 173
    self-referential, 53
    social functions of, 38–39, 76, 77,
       172
    subversion and, 35, 38
hybridity, 194n11

identity, 4
  the body and, 83
  identity politics, 165
incongruity, humor and, 29–31, 35
indeterminacy, 144, 147–48, 149
indigeneity, 123
Indigenous ancestry, 169
Indigenous culture, 5–6, 195n6
Indigenous iconography, appropriation of, 153
Indigenous sexual practices, European discourse and, 5–6
intersexuality, 10, 82–94, 117
intertextuality, 83, 95
irony, 94–96, 114, 124, 128, 137, 145–48, 152–55, 161–62, 166, 170–73, 177–78, 182–83
Irwin, Robert, 5, 8, 43–44
Isherwood, Christopher, 13–14

Jiménez, Armando, *Picardía mexicana*, 36–37
Jiménez, José Alfredo, 176
jotas, 10, 79–81, 83–84, 95, 102, 103, 104–9, 114, 188
jotos, 41, 57, 124, 203n8
Juana Inés de la Cruz, Sor, 159
Jurado, Rocío, 99

Kahlo, Frida, 202–3n3
Kinsey, Alfred, 117–18
kitsch, 7–8, 17, 20, 23, 50
  Mexican nationalism and, 48–49
  subversive potential of, 28
Klein, Fritz, 118
Klein, Melanie, 193n3
Klein Sexual Orientation Grid (KSOG), 118
Krauze, Ethel, *Infinita*, 158

labeling practices, 171
Lara, Agustín, 21, 24–25
Lassen, Christopher, 15–16

Latina lesbian feminist/queer tradition, 164
Latin America. *See also specific countries*
  camp and, 16–18
  Latin American identities, 4
  Latin Americanist literary criticism, 9
  Latin American literature, 4
  Latin American positionality, 11, 50
  Latin American sexualities, 7
  Latin American subject formation, 5
  national romances in, 5
  perspectives from, 4
  popular music in, 175–77
  queerness in, 5–6
  same-sex marriages in, 2
  sexual dissidence in, 6
Layevaska, Irina, 80
Leduc, Paul, 202–3n3
lesbian camp, 162
lesbian characters, portrayal of, 164–65, 197n1
lesbian collectives, 162, 170, 171, 175
lesbian cultures, 160–61, 170–71
lesbian feminism, 159, 160
  disidentification with, 182
  lesbian feminist novels, 158, 164
  lesbian feminist writers, 165
lesbian identity
  mass media and, 179–80
  reparative expressions of, 163
lesbian identity politics, 165
lesbianism. *See also* homosexuality; lesbian sexualities
  Cuban identity and, 161–62
  cursilería and, 157–83
  heteropatriarchy portrayal of, 159
lesbians
  gender nonconformity and, 164
  rights of, 164
  stereotypes of, 162–64

lesbian sexualities, 2, 9, 157–83
  cursilería and, 157–83
  gender nonconformity and, 157–83
  humor and, 163
  masculinities and, 163–64
  reduction to traditional gender models, 162
  as symptom of social degeneration, 158
lesbian subjectivities, 11–12, 166, 170, 171, 175–76
lesbian visibility, 159–60
lesbophobia, 11–12, 170
Levi Calderón, Sara, *Dos mujeres*, 158, 197n1, 204n3
Lewis, Vek, 10, 82–83, 94, 114
Lezama Lima, José, 194n10
LGBT+ identities, 6
LGBTQ people, 1–2
LGBT studies, 17
LGBTTTI, 186
liberalism, 194n7, 194n8
Liguori, Ana Luisa, 123, 203n5
literary tradition, parody and, 63–64
literatura rosa, 110, 113
Lizardi, José Joaquín Fernández de, *El periquillo sarniento*, 64
locas, 6, 58, 61, 63, 70, 72–73, 79–80, 84, 95, 104–9, 114, 176, 188. See also *loquera*
logic, 70
López, Marga, 201n13
López, Nicolás, 186–87
  Hazlo como hombre, 3
loquera, 73
Love, Morganna, 80
Loza, Gustavo, 186
lucha libre, 182
El lugar sin límites, 81

El Machete, 40

machismo, 4, 6, 50, 63, 76, 82, 135, 172–75, 179–80
  humor and, 38
  internalization of, 97
  inversion of, 44
  satirization of, 189
machorras, 2, 163, 165–66, 183
  machorra camp, 157–83
  stereotypes of, 165
macho sentimentality, myth of, 138
Made in Bangkok, 80
Madrigal, Elena, 8, 160, 161, 170–71
  "Arielle," 202–3n3
  Contarte en lésbico, 11–12, 159, 165, 166, 180–83, 189
  "A dos, de tres caídas," 182
  "Pensión de viudez," 180–81
male homosexuality, 1–2, 93. See also homosexuality
  camp and, 162
  definition of, 122
  effeminacy and, 79
  gay male culture, 14
  gay male identity, 14
  humor and, 6, 37
  neoliberalism and, 159
  "penetration paradigm" and, 122
  stereotypes of, 79, 111, 187, 191–92n3
la Malinche, 122, 201n15
"Manifesto Antropófago," 194n10
la Manigüis, 33, 35
marginality, 63, 169
marginalization, 64, 65, 108, 114, 123, 126, 136
"maricón cinema," 193n10
marimachos, 165–66, 183
  marimacho camp, 162
  stereotypes of, 165
Marín, Guadalupe, 41
Mariposas en el adamio, 108–9
Marquet, Antonio, 8, 16–17

marriage, 105, 107–8, 113, 134, 169. *See also* marriage equality; monogamy; same-sex unions
  conventions of, 11
  heteronormativity and, 75, 77
  heterosexuality and, 68–69
  ideology of, 69
marriage equality, 2, 68, 192n4. *See also* same-sex unions
Mars-Jones, Adam, 16
Martí, José, 19, 48
Marxism, 55, 71, 73, 77
masculine privilege, 70, 128, 130, 151
masculinities, 2, 5, 11, 50, 51–78, 82, 95–99, 124, 129, 130–32, 136–39, 163, 167, 169
  bourgeois, 185
  construction of, 138
  disidentification with, 162
  female, 11
  feminine, 158, 183
  hegemonic, 5, 10, 37, 40, 77, 81, 126, 149, 155, 163
  hegemonic vs. nonhegemonic, 58
  lesbian sexuality and, 163–64
  Mexican national identity and, 158
  nonhegemonic, 5
  performance of, 147–48, 164, 172–74, 175, 181, 183
  stereotypes of, 171, 172, 180–82
  threatened, 63
  women and, 162
  working-class, 182
mass culture, 22, 24, 179. *See also* mass media
  parody of, 9
  recycling of, 9, 20–21, 176–77
mass media, 10, 17, 37, 47, 79, 85–86, 94–95, 99, 113, 192n5. *See also specific media*
  femininity and, 104–6, 108–9
  homosexuality in, 2–3, 83–84, 179–80

lesbian identity and, 179–80
  modernity and, 169
  queer identity and, 2–3, 83–84
  recycling of tropes, 102–3
  tropes of, 2–3, 10, 83–84, 102–3, 108–9
mayates, 124, 167, 203n6
melodrama, 88–89, 104–5, 107–8, 112, 140, 152–53, 169, 175–77
  cinematic melodrama, 10–11
  cursilería and, 91–92
  humor and, 92–93
  melodramatic language, 46–47, 92–93
mestizaje, 25–26, 28, 48–50, 122–23, 135, 144, 194n11
metanarrative, 65
Mexicanist literary criticism, humor and, 9
Mexican literary tradition, 94, 160
  allegorical, 183, 187, 189
  effeminacy in, 191–92n3
  homosexuality as theme in, 51–53
  queering of, 10, 102–3
  sexuality in, 53
Mexican national culture
  allegory and, 119
  androcentrism of, 164
  bisexuality and, 120–21
Mexican national identity, 40, 50, 58, 64, 114
  allegory and, 109
  bisexuality and, 123
  cinema and, 109
  humor and, 36–37
  kitsch and, 48–49
  masculinities and, 158
  race and, 25–29
Mexican popular culture, 86–91
  LGBTQ people in, 1–2
  "penetration paradigm" and, 123–24

Mexican Revolution, 2, 3, 33–34, 39, 40, 101–2, 158
Mexican Supreme Court, 2
Mexico City
    1901 police raid in, 1 (*see also* the 41)
    queer subculture of, 40, 41
México marimacho, 164
mimicry, 7
    postmodern, 20
misogyny, 2, 36–37, 38, 46, 79
modernismo, 19, 22, 23–24, 48
modernity, 8–12, 123, 140–41, 143, 151–54, 166, 169–70, 176–77, 181, 183, 187, 189, 194n10
    anxieties about, 64
    anxiety and, 101
    bisexual *Bildungsromane* and, 126, 128, 130, 132–36
    colonialism and, 19
    cursilería and, 18–24, 33, 46–50
    gender and, 85–86, 88–91, 94–105
    hegemonic notions of, 145
    humor and, 54, 56, 58, 62–65, 71–74, 77
    mass media and, 169
    Mexico and, 63
    neoliberal, 159
    northern discourses of, 10
    race and, 64, 134–35
    rejection of, 19
    subjectivities and, 18–19, 23–24
    vs. tradition, 19
Molloy, Sylvia, 48
monogamy, 62, 65, 69, 101, 192n4
monolingualism, 161
Monsiváis, Carlos, 1, 3–4, 8–10, 16–18, 21–29, 37, 39–50, 63, 79, 97, 179, 194–95n12
Montaño, Luis, *Brenda Berenice o el diario de una loca*, 10, 83–84, 108–9, 114, 136, 171, 188
Moraga, Cherríe, 160–61, 164
Moreno Figueroa, Mónica, 26
Morir de pie, 80
mujires, 95
Mulkay, Michael, 35
multilingualism, 161
Muñoz, José Esteban, 4, 8, 9, 17, 161
muxe', 80, 200n2

NaCo of Tijuana, 28
nacos, 25–29, 33, 163, 182, 194–95n12, 195n13. See also *naquez*
NAFTA, 127
naquez, 11, 24–29, 33–34, 98–99, 101, 123, 126, 127, 132, 133, 134, 135, 169–70
narrative
    homosexuality and, 52
    sexuality and, 53
the nation, 5
national identity, 4, 5, 25–29, 83, 114, 191–92n3. See also Mexican national identity
national romances, 5, 110, 113
nation-building allegories, 5. See also allegory
naturalism, 63, 64–65, 158
Navarrete, Federico, 122
negative affect, transcendence of, 10
neoliberalism, 5, 11, 68, 127, 135, 136, 159, 187, 192n4
Nervo, Amado, 21
Netflix, 81, 186
"new maricón cinema," 193n10
New Maricón Cinema, 6
nonnormative sexualities, 68
northern theoretical paradigms, 5
nostalgia, 151, 155
"novel of the Revolution," 40
Novo, Salvador, 3, 13, 33, 55, 62, 63, 76, 79, 97
    "La Diegada," 41, 97

La estatua de sal, 9, 13, 34–35, 39–50, 51, 62, 83, 131, 171, 175, 189, 191–92n3
Nuevo amor, 51

objectification, 81
Olivera, María Elena, 8, 158, 164–65, 167, 170
Olmos, Carlos, 204n15
oppression, 8, 10, 83, 161
Orozco, José Clemente, "Los anales," 40
La otra familia, 68, 159, 186, 187

Pablos, David, 3
El baile de los 41, 190
Pacto Civil de Solidaridad, 107–8
Palancares, Jesusa, 163
Palaversich, Diana, 17
paranoid reading practices, 4, 8–11, 187–88, 193n3
parodies, 7, 9, 47, 66–67, 69, 95, 103–4, 109–15. *See also* gender parody
  of *Bildungsroman*, 117–55
  of Catholicism, 76
  of cultural nationalism, 48–49
  cursilería and, 92–93
  dismodern, 126
  gender and, 11, 50, 84
  of genres, 10
  literary tradition and, 63–64
  melodramatic language and, 92–93
  "national romances" and, 113
  of naturalism, 64–65
patriarchy, 2, 19, 37, 159–60, 161
Paz, Octavio, 37, 138, 202–3n3
  El laberinto de la soledad, 11, 119, 121–23
pelado, 36
Peña Nieto, Enrique, 3
penetration, 36–37

"penetration paradigm," 119–24
peninsulares, 28
Perezcano, Rigoberto, *Carmín tropical*, 80
Pérez Gay, Rafael, 135
persecution, 55
the picaresque, 63, 64, 198n7, 199n12
Pickford, Mary, 91
Pink: El rosa no es como lo pintan, 68, 185–89
pinkwashing, 3
Po, Paolo, *41 o el muchacho que soñaba en fantasmas*, 52
political action, 4, 192n4
politics, 160, 161
popular culture, 4, 28, 37, 84, 86–91, 109–15, 175–76, 182. *See also* Mexican popular culture
popular music, 175–77, 183
Porfiriato, 82, 140–41
Portilla, Jorge, 36
Portillo, Rafael
  Muñecas de medianoche, 81
  Noches de cabaret, 81
Posada, José Guadalupe, 1, 30–31, 30–31, 33–34, 35
positionality, 161
postcolonialism, 5, 8, 9, 11, 38, 188
"postfeminist" writers, 165
postmodernity, 7, 11, 20, 126
power, 23–24, 28
  coloniality of, 47, 48, 56, 64, 154, 188, 193n6
  gender and, 119
  sexuality and, 119
prejudice, 11
Prieur, Annick, 120, 203n6, 203n8
privilege, 7–8, 55, 64, 70, 99–100, 150, 182
  homonormativity and, 187
  masculine, 70, 128, 130, 151
  whiteness and, 176

promiscuity, 48
publishing, 51, 52, 192n6
Puenzo, Lucía, XXY, 93
Puig, Manuel, 17, 20, 47, 113
  El beso de la mujer araña, 109
putos, 124

queer dissidence, 6. See also sexual dissidence
queer identity
  construction of, 103
  mass-media tropes and, 83–84
  reparative expressions of, 163
queerness, 4, 8–12, 17, 40, 50, 86, 105, 113, 115, 157
  camp and, 13–16
  dismodernity and, 35
  humor and, 10
  Latin American, 5–6, 160
  normalization of, 77
  portrayal of, 185
  stereotypes of, 188
queer politics, anti-essentialist view of, 55
queer reading practices, 5
queer resistance, 83
queer sexualities, naquez and, 169–70
queers of color, 4
queer subjectivities, 10, 62–63, 77, 86, 109–15, 145, 188
queer subjectivity, 10
queer themes, 2–3, 4, 5
queer theory, 14, 17, 119, 192n4
"queerying," 6
Quevedo y Zubieta, Salvador, México marimacho, 158
Quijano, Aníbal, 19, 51, 193n6
Quiroga, José, 158

race, 8–11, 50, 55, 64, 81, 96, 123, 166, 189. See also mestizaje
  bisexuality and, 127, 129–30, 132–34, 144–45, 150–55
  the body and, 163–64
  coloniality of, 154
  cursilería and, 21, 169–82
  Mexican national identity and, 25–29
  modernity and, 64, 134–35
  national identity and, 25–29
  racial consciousness, 50
  racial identity, 47–48
  racialization, 11, 25–26, 126
  racial privilege, 152–53
  racism, 9, 11, 47–48, 127, 135, 141–42, 161–62, 169 (see also discrimination)
radionovelas, 92
Ramos, Samuel, 37
Raskin, Victor, 195n14
  Semantic Script Theory of Humor (SSTH), 30–31, 32, 34
rationality, 95
reading
  bourgeois practices of, 46–47
  reading internationally, 187
realism, 93, 114, 125
regional aesthetics, 48
regional identities, 4, 5, 113, 194n11
relajo, 36, 37–38, 65, 84, 105, 114, 131–32, 145
religion, 69
reparative reading practices, 8–11, 187–88, 193n3
Reséndiz, Ernesto, 167
resistance, 6, 8, 44, 83, 161
Revueltas, José, Los muros de agua, 158
Reyes Ávila, Carlos, Travesti, 82
Reynoso, David, 200n8
Rich, Adrienne, 160
Ricoeur, Paul, 193n3
Ripstein, Arturo, El lugar sin límites, 81
ritual insult humor, 162
Rivera, Diego, 41, 97

Rivera Garza, Cristina, *Nadie me verá llorar*, 49–50, 82, 202–3n3
Rivera Valdés, Sonia, "Five Windows on the Same Side," 160
Robertson, Pamela, 162
Roffiel, Rosamaría, 165
  Amora, 158, 160, 164–65, 197n1
romance literature, 22, 103, 110, 113, 125
  parody of, 109–15
romantic clichés, 181
romantic discourse, 175–76
rosa, 163, 166, 171, 172, 175, 182
Rueda Esquibel, Catrióna, 164
Rulfo, Juan, 166
Russo, Anahi, 163, 171

Salinas, Gilda, 9, 47, 160, 161, 182
  "Achiote de golondrinas," 177–78
  "Alaska tropical," 173
  "Los años verdes," 173
  "El cofre el tesoro, 173–75
  "Entre copas ...34B," 173, 177
  "El desempance," 178–79
  Del destete al desempance: Cuentos lésbicos y un colado, 11, 159, 165, 166, 170–80, 183, 189
  "El destete," 172–73, 176–77
  "Roles bimbo," 175
Salón México, 109
same-sex unions, 2–3, 9, 55, 67–69, 77, 107–8, 185–86, 205n8
Sánchez, Luis Rafael, 20
Santos, Lidia, 4, 7–8, 9, 17, 20–21, 23, 47
sarcasm, 70, 129, 132
Sarduy, Severo, 7–8, 20, 47
Sarmiento, Domingo F., 19
satire, 41–42, 55, 61, 69–73, 76, 103, 130, 135, 155, 161–62, 186
Schaefer, Claudia, 8, 54
Schneider, Luis Mario, 8, 52, 53, 54
Schwarz, Roberto, 20

scopophilia, 159
Sedgwick, Eve, 4, 8, 9, 15, 25, 193n3
Semantic Script Theory of Humor (SSTH), 30–31, 32, 34, 195n14
sentimental education, 46–47, 112, 151, 154, 169
sentimentality, 22–23, 28, 44–45, 48, 58, 62, 75, 85–86, 90–91, 95–96, 101, 133, 140, 153, 176–77
Serna, Enrique, 9, 27–28, 37, 204n15
  La doble vida de Jesús, 82, 124–25
  Fruta verde, 11, 126, 145–55, 189
  El miedo a los animales, 82
Serrano, Irma, 60
sex, 130, 155
  coloniality of, 56, 64, 69, 75, 83, 188, 193n6
sex binaries, evasion of, 157
sexism, 65, 162
sex norms, 11, 103, 105
El sexo débil, 3, 68
sexual dissidence, 6–12, 41, 47, 49–50, 65, 164, 166, 183–86, 192n7
  camp and, 187
  collectives of, 192n4
  consumer culture and, 54–56
  cursi and, 187
  marriage equality and, 192n4
  portrayal of, 187, 188
sexual diversity, 119, 192n7. *See also* sexual dissidence
  tolerance of, 189
sexual identity, 51–52, 63
  expression of, 56–65
  gender-based categories of, 198n9
sexuality, 8–11, 77, 80, 121, 123, 129, 157–83, 189
  ambiguous nature of, 118–19
  coloniality and, 19, 23–24
  female, 158
  narrative and, 53
  new discourses on, 35
  norms of, 6

sexuality *(continued)*
  power and, 119
  stereotypes of, 23–24
sexual repression, 37
"sexual revolution," 3
sex work, 9, 63–64, 81, 82
Sifuentes-Jáuregui, Ben., 5, 6, 7, 17, 121–22, 160, 163
silences, 6
sin, language of, 6
Smith, Paul Julian, 80, 191–92n3, 192n5
social acceptance, search for, 95
social conflicts, 10, 130, 146–47, 155, 170, 189, 194n11
  allegory and, 137
  bisexuality and, 125–27, 137
  embodiment of, 166
  portrayal of, 185
social control, 91, 158
social degeneration, 158
social forces, 166
social movements, 3
social norms, 135, 175
  disidentification with, 95–96, 165
  transgression of, 179
social order
  challenged through humor, 124–25
  reinforced through humor, 124, 162
soldaderas, 158
Solomonoff, Julia, *El último verano de la Boyita*, 93
Sommer, Doris, 5, 110
Sontag, Susan, 7, 14, 16
Soto, Sandra K., 164
Southern Cone, 17
Stendahl (Marie-Henri Beyle), 125, 144
stereotypes, 11–12, 41, 115, 188
  biphobia and, 120
  of cross-dressing, 81
  of effeminacy, 191–92n3
  of femininity, 171, 172, 179
  of gender, 23–24, 33
  of homosexuality, 1–2, 56–65, 71, 79, 111, 187, 188, 191–92n3
  of Indigenous culture, 195n6
  of *jotos*, 57
  of lesbians, 162–64
  of *machorras*, 165, 183
  of *marimachos*, 165
  of masculinities, 171, 172
  reproduction of, 14
  of sexuality, 23–24
  subversive recycling of, 17–18
  of *travestis*, 108
  of women, 75
subculture, 41
subject formation, 6
  colonialism and, 5
  cursilería and, 22–23
  Latin American, 5, 6
subjectivities, 10, 65–77, 82–83, 94, 96, 103, 114, 145, 162. *See also specific subjectivities*
  coloniality and, 23
  construction of, 94, 114–15, 125
  homosexual, 56
  of *jotas*, 83–84
  modernity and, 18–19, 23–24
  portrayal of, 187
  queer, 86
  racialized, 25–26
  vestida, 103
subversion, 23–24, 28, 37, 38, 96, 102, 108, 115, 121, 187–88

taste, 7–8, 17, 20–21, 28, 182
Tate, Julee, 191–92n3
Taymore, Julie, 202–3n3
Telehit, 3
telenovelas, 3, 68, 81, 98, 99, 159, 191–92n3, 201–2n18
Televisa, 191–92n3, 194–95n12

television, 159, 190, 191–92n3, 194–95n12, 202n2. *See also* telenovelas
Téllez, Artemisa, 165, 183
Thornton, Niamh, 137–38
Todo el mundo tiene a alguien menos yo, 159
Todo incluido, 159, 187
Torres Bodet, Jaime, 41–42
totonaco, 25
Tovar, Rigo, 28
Tovar, Serio, *Cuatro lunas*, 2–3
Tovar Ávalos, Enrique, 45–46
"trade" men, 124
tradition, 74
  vs. modernity, 19
traileras, 162
transcendence, 69
transculturation, 194n11
transgender, 80, 83–94
transphobia, 188
transphobic violence, 9, 188
transvestism, 7, 9, 13, 17, 80
travestis, 10, 66, 70–72, 79–116, 121, 157, 176, 199n14, 200n1, 200n10
  marginalization of, 81–82
  stereotypes of, 108
  subjectivities of, 108–9, 114
travestizaje, 82–83. *See also* travestis
tropicalistas, 20
Troyano, Alina, 161. *See also* Carmelita Tropicana
TV Azteca, 191–92n3

uniculturalism, 161
United States
  lesbian visibility in, 160
  perspectives from, 4
  US Latina/o/x LGBT visibility in, 160–61
Uruguay, same-sex marriages in, 2
US literature, AIDS crisis and, 15–16
US popular culture, 87, 90, 91

utopian literature, parody of, 76

Valdemar, Carlos, *Cielo tormentoso*, 52
Vargas, Chavela, 3, 163, 176–77, 192n4
Vargas, Susana, *Mujercitos*, 81
Vecinos, 191–92n3
Velázquez, Carlos, 201n12
  "La jota de Bergerac," 10–11, 84, 103, 104–9, 188
  "La marrana negra de la literatura rosa," 11, 84, 103, 109–15, 189
  La marrana negra de la literatura rosa, 103–15
Venkatesh, Vinodh, 4, 5, 6, 68, 159, 193n10
vestidas, 10, 79–116, 80–81, 84, 103, 104–9, 114, 157, 176, 188, 200n10
victimization, 108
La vida en el espejo, 3, 191–92n3
vignettes, 170. *See also* crónicas
Villa, Gustavo, 43
Villarejo, Amy, 160
Villarrutia, Xavier, 39, 41, 43, 196–97n19
  Nocturnos, 51
Villoro, Juan, *Materia dispuesta*, 125
violence, 80–81, 108, 114, 122–23, 188
  homophobia and, 9
  transphobia and, 9
  against women, 3
Virgin of Guadalupe, 122, 201n15
virgin/whore dichotomy, 91–92, 108, 110
"virile" literature, vs. "effeminate literature," 40
Voces en Tinta, 192n6

whiteness, 26, 49–50, 141–42, 145, 182
white privilege, 64, 176
white supremacy, 123

Wilde, Oscar, 13, 41, 48, 67, 199n15
Williams, Tamara, 125
women, 11, 157–84. *See also* lesbianism; lesbians
  discrimination and, 158
  gender nonconformity and, 157–83
  masculine, 162
  rights of, 164
  stereotypes of, 75
women of color feminism, 160–61
women's camp, 162, 165–66
Woolf, Virginia, *Orlando*, 124

XXY, 93

Yo, la peor de todas, 159
Y tu mamá también, 124

Zapata, Luis, 47, 55, 68, 192n6, 197n2, 201n11
  Las aventuras, desventuras y sueños de Adonis García, el vampiro de la colonia Roma, 9, 10, 52–54, 56–65, 74–79, 83, 94–95, 101, 136, 164, 171, 175, 189, 204n5
  La hermana secreta de Angélica María, 10, 82–83, 83–94, 114
  La historia de siempre, 68
Zapotec Indigenous people, 80, 200n2

www.ingramcontent.com/pod-product-compliance
Lightning Source LLC
Chambersburg PA
CBHW020648230426
43665CB00008B/350